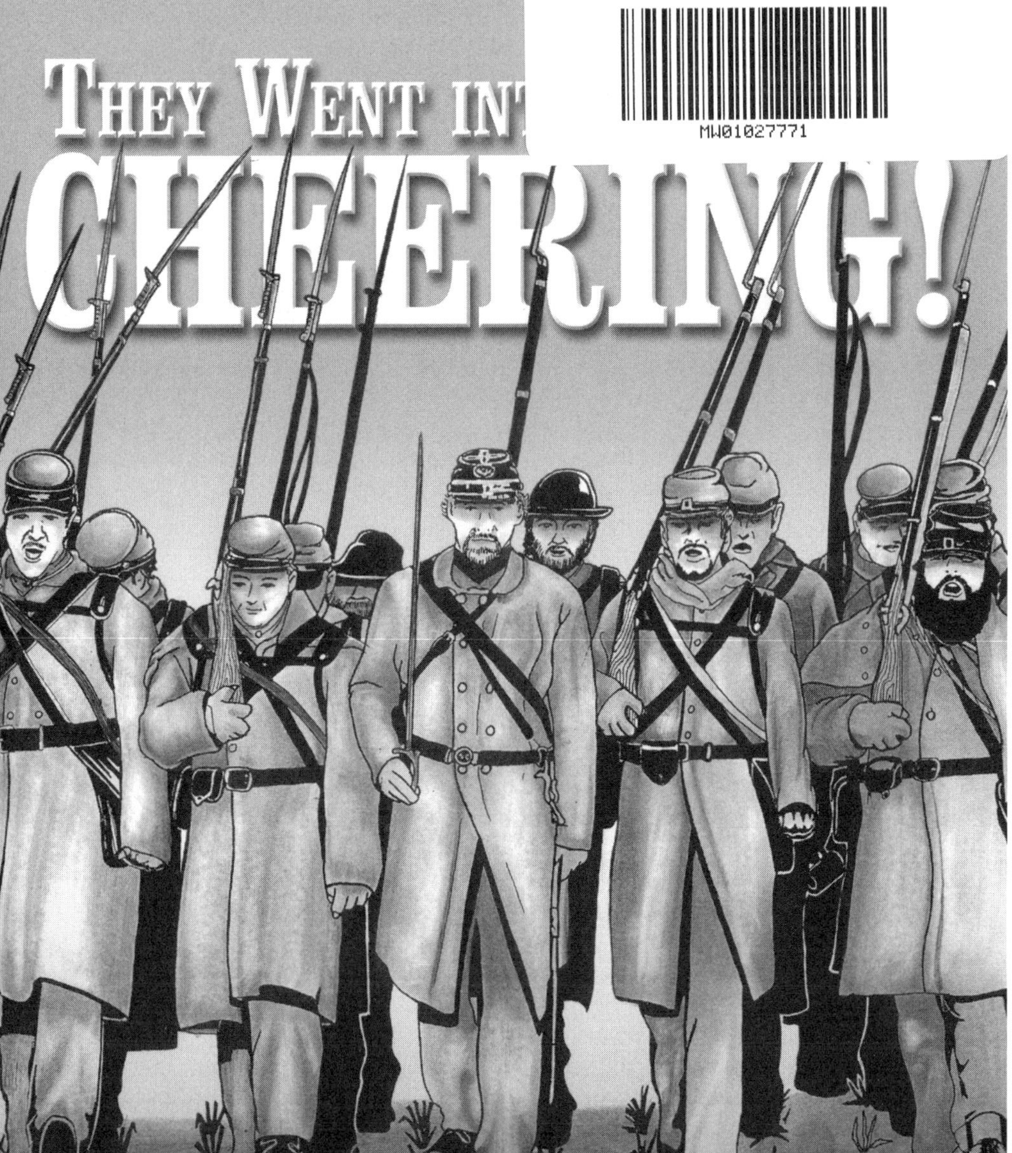

Confederate Conscription

IN NORTH CAROLINA

Walter C. Hilderman III

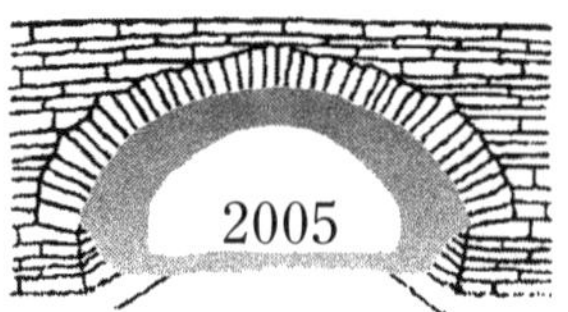

Parkway Publishers, Inc.
Boone, North Carolina

available from:
Parkway Publishers, Inc.
Post Office Box 3678
Boone, North Carolina 28607
www.parkwaypublishers.com
Tel/Fax: (828) 265-3993

Library of Congress Cataloging-in-Publication Data

Hilderman, Walter Carrington.
They went into the fight cheering! : Confederate conscription in North Carolina / by Walter Carrington Hilderman, III.
p. cm.
Summary: "This book discusses the day-to-day operation of the Confederate conscription process in North Carolina during the Civil War"--Provided by publisher.
Includes bibliographical references (p.) and index.
ISBN 1-933251-25-5
1. Confederate States of America. Army--Recruiting, enlistment, etc. 2. Draft--Confederate States of America--History. 3. Draft--North Carolina--History--19th century. 4. North Carolina--History--Civil War, 1861-1865--Manpower. 5. United States--History--Civil War, 1861-1865--Manpower. I. Title.
E545.H55 2005
973.7'42--dc22

2005027863

Book Design by Aaron Burleson, spokesmedia
Cover illustration by Roger Foster
Author photograph by Leonard R. "Deacon" Jones

Dedication

To

Private Alfred C. Cowen

Table of Contents

Illustrations

Maps

Preface

Despite the immense impact of compulsory military service on the American Civil War, little has been written about Confederate conscription. Only two book-length works have been published on the topic: Albert Moore's *Conscription and Conflict in the Confederacy*, in 1924, and Memory Mitchell's *Legal Aspects of Conscription and Exemption in North Carolina, 1861-1865*, in 1965. These are excellent works and were indispensable in the writing of this volume. However, they reveal little about the day-to-day operation of the conscription process, the activities of those charged with its enforcement, or its impact on the Southern population.

In his five volume work entitled *Histories of the Several Regiments and Battalions from the State of North Carolina in the Great War, 1861-'65,* Walter Clark ended a two page discussion of North Carolina Confederate conscription with, "The Conscript Bureau was an indispensable agency and in the main an efficient one, though of course never a popular one." In fact, conscription was the most hated law in the Confederacy.

Clark's *Histories* was the fundamental source of information on North Carolina Confederate military units until the North Carolina Department of Archives and History began publishing *North Carolina Troops, 1861-1865: A Roster,* in 1966; a project that is ongoing. The North Carolina Archives *Roster* is perhaps the finest publication of its kind. The *Roster* and Clark's *Histories* have in common a paucity of information on Confederate conscription law and its enforcement. In the case of Clark's *Histories*, this shortcoming maintained the misconception that most Southern men rushed to volunteer for the Confederate army in 1861. As to the North Carolina Archives *Roster* project, the decision was made in the 1960s to follow a numerical progression in publishing regimental histories, as opposed to a chronological arrangement. That decision, while made for good reasons, has delayed research on conscription and appreciation of its impact for more than a decade.

While North Carolina is the focal point of this work, a great deal of information is presented on conscription in other parts of the Confederacy. The process was by no means consistent from one region to another and was subject to endless revision and conflict. Conscription, as applied in North Carolina, stands as the best example of how the process was supposed to work.

In *Numbers & Losses in the Civil War,* Thomas L. Livermore described the difference between Confederate and Union systems of compulsory military service: "This law and the proceedings under it placed every man in the Confederacy who came within the definition of the law at once in the service, unlike the draft laws of the United States, which placed no one in service until selected by draft." In other words, once the first conscript law was passed, every male citizen of the Confederacy between the ages of eighteen and thirty-five was in the army (whether or not he ever presented himself for enrollment) unless or until he was released by the government. On the other hand, no male citizen of the United States was in the Union army until he was inducted. This distinction probably mattered little to men on either side who were forced into the army. Thus, the terms "conscription" and "draft" are used interchangeably in this volume. "Enrolling officer" and "conscript officer," likewise, are used interchangeably. Confederate government documents most often use the term "enrolling," but the public usually spoke of "conscript" officers and offices.

An issue closely related to compulsory military service is that of desertion. While Confederate desertion and the government's efforts to control it are discussed in this work, it should be noted that the United States also struggled with this problem. A report compiled by the Deserters Branch of the Provost Marshal General's Office stated that there were 278,644 Union desertions during the war. That number was later revised to an estimation of 200,000. The number of Confederate deserters has been estimated at 104,000. These figures must be appreciated in terms of the total number of men who served on each side. It is likely that over 2,200,000 men served in the armed forces of the United States. On the Confederate side, between 750,000 and 1,000,000 men served in the military. Numbers tell only part of the story.

In an effort to allow the people who experienced this tragic era to tell their stories in their own words, direct quotations have been used extensively in this volume. Spelling and word usage have been left unaltered when quoting from original sources unless doing so would be confusing to the reader. Brackets are used to indicate the changes in those instances.

When discussing military activities in the three main theaters of the Civil War, this work employs the terms "eastern Confederacy" to describe the Confederate Atlantic coast states, "central Confederacy" or "Department No. 2" to designate the operational area of the Army of

Tennessee prior to the Atlanta campaign, and "western Confederacy" or, more often, "Trans-Mississippi" to describe the area west of the Mississippi River.

The footnotes contain some source citations but usually provide information that is immediately useful to the reader. The endnotes contain additional source citations and supplemental information.

Acknowledgments

In the early 1960s, my aunts, Nancy Long and Helen Hilderman, gave me a notebook containing family letters that had been written during the Civil War. Like many Southern youngsters in those days, I was particularly interested in that part of American history. It still amazes me that my aunts were so trusting with the last physical evidence of our family's connection to the great American tragedy.

Naturally, I assumed that my great-great-grandfather had eagerly volunteered for the Confederate army when the first shots were fired. Such was not the case. Through his letters, I found that he and most of his army companions were known as "conscripts." When I first came across the word, I had to look it up in the dictionary. The words "eager" and "volunteer" were *not* part of the definition.

What started as youthful curiosity grew into a life-long hobby of research and reenacting and now, forty-five years later, has resulted in this book. During that time, I have been helped by many people, some of whom I would like to mention here.

Well before I was old enough to drive, I met Mr. Ralph W. Donnelly at the central library in Charlotte, North Carolina. He introduced me to the library's history room and put me in contact with the National Archives; two resources that I use to this day.

At North Carolina's Department of Archives and History, Louis H. Manarin, W. T. (Hank) Jordan, and, more recently, Donna Kelly, George Stevenson, Kenny Simpson, Joe Mobley, Chris Meekins, Dick Lankford, and Matthew Brown have all assisted me on more occasions than I can recall. Donny Taylor, Larry Walker, Greg Mast, "Skip" Smith, Tim Greene, Charles W. Clark III, Bob Tolar, and dozens of other reenactors have answered my questions and offered advice over the years.

Page Gebsen of Wilmington, North Carolina, and Rachel Canada and Keith Longiotti at the University of North Carolina at Chapel Hill were generous with their help and support. Linda McCurdy and Janie C. Morris at Duke University, Ruth Ann Coski and Heather Milne at the Museum of the Confederacy, and Teresa Roane of the Valentine Museum assisted me many times. Judson Crow helped with Cowen family history, and Richard Melvin provided information on the 39th North Carolina Troops. Thanks also to Aimee Russell and Lee Goodan at the Gaston County Museum of Art and History.

Willie Ray Johnson at Kennesaw Mountain National Battlefield

Park helped me with research on that battle, and John Durham at Guilford Courthouse National Military Park assisted with North Carolina Militia and Home Guard information.

Proofreading and encouragement have been provided by Reverend George Thompson, Pat Hilderman, Nora Brooks, Roslie McCrory, Christy Carper, Tex O'Neill, Allison Matlack, and Hugh Harkey.

Bob Krick of the National Park Service, Lewis Wyman at the Library of Congress, Mike Musick at National Archives, and Randy Slaff at the Naval Heritage Museum and Enterprise have each provided me with valuable information.

Many thanks to Matt Bumgarner, Joe Danner, Gene Woodard, O. C. Stonestreet, and Louis Alexander for helping me find conscript camp locations, and to Lyle Holland, Mark Collier, and Lonnie Blizzard for help on the 1862 battle of Kinston.

Shelly Dooley, who passed away during the course of this project, gave me information on Franz Hahr and allowed me to use his self-portrait in this volume.

Most of all, I am grateful to the two fine Southern ladies, Nancy Long and Helen Hilderman, who knew that their twelve-year-old nephew would be interested in a stack of old letters.

Introduction

Confederate conscription laws were a radical departure from the philosophy that led the South toward secession. Southern states left the Union individually, not to form a powerful central government, but to rid themselves of one. Each of the seceding states wanted sovereignty. They formed the Confederacy only to protect the interests they held in common: state's rights, agriculture, slavery, and defense.

Under the Confederate constitution, the states provided governmental regulation and services to the population. Individuals were citizens of and answerable to their local and state governments, not to the national government. This was how most Southerners (and many Northerners) felt the United States was supposed to function but did not.

The most significant result of the American Civil War was the creation of a national citizenry with the ratification of the Fourteenth Amendment to the United States Constitution on July 9, 1868. Previously, individuals were citizens of their respective states, not of the United States. By virtue of national citizenship, individuals came under the primary control and protection of the federal government. State governments lost influence and authority over their populations.

This reassignment of power was not a new concept and was precisely what the South had feared. For decades before the war, Southerners watched as the North tried to extend its influence, through the national government, to issues that Southerners regarded as matters for the individual states: slavery and the tariff being primary concerns. Much smaller in voting population, the South could only resist this effort in the United States Senate. The fragile balance of power in the Senate would last only as long as the South pushed its philosophies westward. Slave states had to be admitted to the Union at the same rate as free states.

The election of Abraham Lincoln, with his non-expansion of slavery doctrine and high tariffs policy, convinced many Southerners that the interests of the Northern states would soon ride roughshod over those of the South. Many Southerners regarded secession as the only solution. What they did not foresee was the amount of centralized governmental control that warfare with the United States would bring to their lives.

During the course of the war, the Confederacy's progression of conscription laws, taxes, and impressment regulations demonstrated that the Southern states were willing to abandon most of their fundamental goals, including sovereignty and the preservation of slavery, in order to gain independence. Win, lose, or draw, the Southern way of life would change forever. The South reached much more deeply into its population in order to maintain its military than the North. The resulting social and political upheaval, combined with the casualties and destruction generated by four years of war, crippled much of the South for generations.

In pre-war North Carolina, the economy was based on small, subsistence-level family farms with few or no slaves. Much of the state's slave population lived on middle-class family farms. There were comparatively few big plantations with large slave labor forces. Slave-holding aristocrats did not have the same political influence in North Carolina that they did in the Deep South. What little manufacturing there was in the state depended on agriculture: textiles, the wine industry, and the production of tar, pitch, and turpentine from the state's vast pine forests. These industries usually employed whites and some free African-Americans instead of slaves.

Politically, most white North Carolinians identified with their state government and supported state's rights but were opposed to secession. While they agreed with the Southern perspective on most social, political, and economic issues, North Carolinians wanted neither secession nor war.

During the war, North Carolina's geographic location provided protection from the large battles that ravaged much of the rest of the Confederacy. That same geographic feature also made the state crucial to Southern war efforts relating to manpower, importation, and distribution.

Less than a year after the war started, the Confederate Congress enacted a program of national compulsory military service. Implementation of the conscription acts and related laws required large networks of enrolling offices, examining boards, new taxes, property impressment, and, ultimately, Confederate governmental control of agriculture, industry, and transportation. Large military bases were constructed in each state, complete with guards and supporting forces. Local enrolling officers gathered men for the army while civilian officials gathered taxes to pay for the war. Thus, the Confederate government reached into every corner of the South. Ironically, their aversion to this kind of national governmental intrusion was the very issue that caused Southerners to support secession in the first place.

This vast bureaucracy came to be responsible not only for supplying and monitoring the Confederate war effort, but also for apprehending those fleeing from wartime service.

By the end of the war, almost 134,000 North Carolinians had participated in the Confederate military effort. This number includes 54,000 volunteers, 21,000 conscripts, 45,000 men who "volunteered" under the threat of conscription, 9,000 Junior and Senior Reserves, and 5,000 Militia and Home Guardsmen.[a]

---

[a] McCaslin, *Portraits of Conflict*, p. 42. The number of men who were coerced into military service under the threat of conscription is based on estimates provided by Confederate authorities *(O.R.*, Series IV, v. 3, p. 358) and on the dates of organization for North Carolina regiments (*North Carolina Troops, 1861-1865: A Roster*).

THE CONSCRIPTS

There should be no odium attach[ed] to this name. Those who have remained at home are mainly such as were so affectingly situated as to their family or so importantly engaged as to their business as to render it not only inexpedient but absolutely unreasonable for them to go until it became really necessary. They are as good, as true as others and it is earnestly hoped that there will be no ungenerous word spoken about them. I am sure no such word will be spoken by a true patriot a real southern lady or gentleman.
BY ONE NOT A CONSCRIPT.

The Carolina Watchman
Salisbury, North Carolina
July 7, 1862

Chapter One

Hard Places

Kennesaw Mountain, Georgia.
Saturday, June 25, 1864.

Privates A. S. Gaddy, Alfred C. Cowen, and Albert G. Thompson had been with the 39th North Carolina Troops for less than two weeks. In that brief time, they had been given ample opportunity to show the hardened veterans of the army that they would make passable soldiers. They were not the sickly, ill-prepared conscripts who were usually sent to the Confederate armies from camps of instruction. Thompson and his friends were veterans of many months of service in Colonel Peter Mallett's North Carolina conscript battalion. They were no strangers to the artillery fire that now surrounded them. Today, on picket duty, they held their ground and tried not to become part of the steady stream of casualties that the bombardment was producing.

Gaddy, Cowen, Thompson and approximately twenty other soldiers from Camp of Instruction No. 1 (Camp Holmes at Raleigh, North Carolina) had chosen to join the 39th North Carolina Troops when Colonel Mallett's battalion was disbanded by the Confederate War Department. They left Raleigh by train and arrived at Marietta, Georgia, on June 11, 1864. Since early May, General William Tecumseh Sherman's Union army had been pushing and outflanking General Joseph Johnston's Confederates through northwest Georgia toward Marietta and the ultimate prize of Atlanta.

The new arrivals joined Brigadier General Matthew Ector's brigade near Lattimer's Mills. Ector's brigade, in General Samuel G. French's division, consisted of four regiments from Texas and two from North Carolina, the 29th and 39th North Carolina Troops. This brigade was the object of a Union flanking movement on June 18 and withdrew to a strong position between the adjacent peaks of Kennesaw and Little Kennesaw mountains. There, with the rest of Johnston's army, Ector's men waited and dared Sherman to attack.

Upon reporting for duty in the 39th regiment, the soldiers were assigned to Captain Arthur Dyche's Company A. At Kennesaw Mountain, they became part of the endless picket rotation. Each regiment took its turn for twenty-four hours at a time in no man's land between the two armies. Approximately seven hundred yards out in front of the rest of the brigade, the picket positions were under sporadic fire from Union artillery and pickets. The soldiers concealed themselves as well as they could and waited for the inevitable full-scale Union attack. The pickets' job was to warn the rest of the army of the advance of any large body of enemy infantry.

On June 25, the sun rose to promise another humid and miserable summer day. From atop Little Kennesaw Mountain, General French could see columns of Union supply wagons moving in front of his part of the Confederate line. He believed that a major Union attack was being prepared. At ten a.m., French ordered his artillery batteries to open fire on the enemy targets arrayed below them. In response to the Confederate shelling, Union artillery positions increased their rate of fire as well. Batteries of the 1st Illinois Light Artillery and the Iowa Light Artillery fired round after round toward the nearest Confederate positions: those occupied by Ector's brigade. The men of the 39th North Carolina Troops had no choice but to stay put and hope for the best.

Around noon, one of the many shells that landed among the Confederate pickets struck both Gaddy and Thompson. Thompson's left foot was badly mangled. Gaddy was also struck on the foot, but he was not as seriously injured. Both men were taken to a nearby field hospital where the rest of Thompson's foot was amputated. Alfred Cowen was also injured during the same bombardment. Albert Thompson wrote to his wife, Cate, the next day:

> Medical College Hospital
> Atlanta Ga.
> June 26th 1864
>
> Dear Wife
> I am at the above named place with my left leg amputated just above the ankle it was done on the 25th about 12 oclock while on picket Mr Cowen was struck with a bum [artillery shell] on the side of the head & shoulder but was not hurt bad enough to leave his post I left him there when I left [1]

Another of the North Carolinians, Andrew Price from Union County, was much more graphic when he wrote to his wife the same day and related what he and his friends had experienced since their arrival in Georgia:

> We got to Our Regiment yesterday was a week ago They ware fighting when we got their they have bein fighting more or less ever day Since We fell back to this mountain las night was a week ago and have helt our position ever since We are on top of the mountain and the yankees are at the foot of it we can see them ever day.... We have not had a regerly engagement in our Brigade since we have got on this mountain We have been under heavy cannonading all the time Several of the men killed and wounded by bum shells They have been fighting hard on our left but I do not know how the fight went We Ware on Pickett yesterday Our Regment was on Pickett one day & night we ware in a pretty hard place.... we had four men wounded in our company yesterday while we ware on pickett and I am sorry to Say that two of the men was men that come with us from Camp Holmes One was that Mr. Thompson that you saw at the Hospital at Raleigh his foot was struck by a Shell and tore all to pieces his leg had to be amputated the other one was A. S. Gaddy from union county he was struck by the Same Shell on the foot but I think that his foot Can be Saved. The ballance of the union [county] boys is all well but Rone and Mars they are Sick at the Hospital. I am very well Pleased with our officers our Captain Cant be beet in the Confederacy I feel thankful to my God that I have escaped the Balls [bullets] So far. Nothing more at present write soon I remain your Husband A J Price Direct to Atlanta. Ga Ectors Brigade 39 Reg NC Troops in care of Capt Dyche [2]

Charleston Harbor, South Carolina.
Thursday, July 28, 1864

Like the new arrivals at Kennesaw Mountain, Burgess Gaither and his cousins, Sid and Perry M. ("Mel") Summers, had served in Colonel Mallett's North Carolina conscript battalion. Instead of choosing an infantry regiment when faced with the break-up of the battalion, they decided to join the Confederate navy. Mel Summers had been corresponding with Burgess's sister, Mollie. Now stationed at Charleston, Burgess was sick. He was so sick that Mel needed to inform the family of the situation:

> C.S.N. Ship genel hosp
> Charleston SC
> July 28 1864
>
> Miss Mollie gaither
> Dear Cousin as your Brother request me to write you a few Lines to Let you know how he is getting a long I am sorry to inform you that he is very sick he has been getting worse ever since I wrote he is Suffering a great deal at this time.... it is a very bad place for a sick person the Weather is so warm Burgess is Lying Close to one of the Windows and we are nursing him the best we know how and will Continue to. Burgess says for you not to be uneasy about him I cannot tell you positively what Burgess diseas is he complains of his back and head I expect it will terminate.... Mollie I want you to all rest Satisfyed that we will do all for Burgess that we Can toward his relief and welfair in this world.... I must close my remarks your Brother says for you to write soon without delay Excuse bad writing & spelling for I am so Confused that I Canot hardly write As Ever your True Cosin
> P M Summers [3]

The North Carolinians at Kennesaw Mountain and Charleston had spent the previous two years enforcing the most hated law in the Confederacy: conscription. Ironically, they too were conscripts.

Approximately half of the 134,000 North Carolinians that served in the Confederate military did so unwillingly. This statistic reflects more on the efficiency of conscription enforcement in North Carolina rather than on any unique reluctance on the part of North Carolinians to serve.[a] All over the South, the volunteer spirit that created the Confederate army in the summer of 1861 had evaporated by early 1862. The Confederate Congress was forced to enact the first national compulsory military service law in America in order to keep early-war volunteers in the army and to provide additional manpower for a long war.

[a] Of the more than eighty-one thousand men who were formally conscripted into the Confederate army, over twenty-one thousand came from North Carolina. (Clark's *Histories*, v. V, p. 1.)

In North Carolina, responsibility for conscription enforcement was given to a former New York City businessman named Peter Mallett. In the summer of 1862, he drafted several hundred men who had already avoided military service for more than a year, put them under the command of officers who had lost reelection bids in their volunteer regiments, and built around them the most efficient conscription system in the Confederacy.

But before any of that could happen, the South had to learn that the "first modern war" could not be won with volunteers.[4]

Chapter Two

You Can Get No Troops From North Carolina

April 1861 - February 1862

Fearing the use of Fort Sumter as a base for an invasion of their state, South Carolinians fired on and occupied the Charleston harbor fortress on April 12, 13, and 14, 1861. When the United States flag was lowered by Union troops in the garrison, the Confederacy was at war. North Carolina, however, was still in the Union.

Though several states had already left the Union and joined the Confederacy, North Carolina secessionists had been defeated the previous February when a state-wide referendum determined that there would be no convention to consider secession. Pro-Confederate sentiment was considerable in the state, but the sharp polarization on economics and slavery that existed in the Deep South had not developed in North Carolina. The two-party system in the state worked well, rendering extremism unattractive. The state's small farm orientation tended to neutralize the market economy issues over which North and South disagreed. Most North Carolinians lived on farms that just managed to keep their families fed. They did not see the question of tariffs as a significant issue in their lives.

One-third of the state's 992,600 people were African-Americans. Ten percent of those, about thirty thousand, were free. A significant portion of the slave population lived on small farms, working side-by-side with the white family. Almost three-fourths of white families in the state did not own slaves.

While most North Carolinians believed that secession was legal, they were not inclined to leave the Union; nor were they eager to fight a war for the right of another state to do so. The March 4, 1861, inaugural speech by Abraham Lincoln did not change these attitudes. Until Fort Sumter, most North Carolinians saw no reason to collide with the Lincoln government.

In response to the fall of Fort Sumter, President Lincoln called for the states remaining in the Union to supply a total of seventy-five thousand troops for immediate service. North Carolina was now at war. The state was expected to provide her fair share of the effort needed to defeat the Confederacy. The preliminary call for troops was telegraphed from the United States Secretary of War to Governor John Ellis on April 15. North Carolina was required to supply two regiments totaling fifteen hundred soldiers.[5] Governor Ellis's response was defiant:

> Your dispatch is received, and if genuine, which its extraordinary character leads me to doubt, I have to say in reply that I regard the levy of troops made by the administration for the purpose of subjugating the States of the South as in violation of the Constitution and a gross usurpation of power. I can be no party to this wicked violation of the laws of the country and to this war upon the liberties of a free people. You can get no troops from North Carolina.... [6]

Governor Ellis knew that Lincoln's attempt to force his state into a war against other Southern states would instantly radicalize the population. The state's rush toward secession was accelerated on April 27 when President Lincoln extended the naval blockade of Confederate ports to include North Carolina.

Ellis called the North Carolina legislature into special session to authorize a secession convention. On May 20, the convention unanimously declared the state's independence:

> We the people of the State of North Carolina do... declare and ordain that the Union now subsisting between the State of North-Carolina and the other States, under the title of the United States of America, is hereby dissolved, and that the State of North-Carolina is in full possession and exercise of all those rights of sovereignty which belong and appertain to a free and independent State.[7]

Military organizations in the state had been making preparations for weeks. Everyone had known since the fall of Fort Sumter that an army would be needed. The North Carolina Militia had existed since colonial times, but in early 1861, it suffered from public apathy and governmental neglect. State law required every eighteen through forty-five-year-old white male, from governor to private citizen, to enroll in the militia unless exempted for religious or health reasons. Militia regiments were organized geographically by counties.[8]

There were also local para-military groups that existed in many communities. These volunteer companies had been increasing in popularity since the 1850s. They were comprised of the more highly motivated community men, but they were not connected with state government. These men wanted to participate in military service on a more professional level than their concurrent militia membership afforded. Volunteer companies met and drilled more often than the militia, occasionally bought their own uniforms and equipment (militiamen usually had no state supplied uniforms or weapons), and were generally capable of responding more rapidly than the militia. As a result of John Brown's attempt to start a nationwide slave revolt at Harpers Ferry in 1859, men all over the South joined existing volunteer companies or started new ones.

After North Carolina seceded, many of these companies enlisted, en masse, and were assigned to the first regiments organized by the state. One such regiment was the 1st North Carolina Volunteers commanded by Colonel Daniel H. Hill. Three companies of this regiment went to aid in the defense of Virginia several days before North Carolina seceded.

North Carolina's military responsibilities increased with her admission to the Confederacy. State resources were needed not only to defend her own borders, but also to protect Richmond, the Confederacy's capitol and the expected point of initial Union attacks. State military authorities began raising volunteer regiments to send to the North Carolina coast and for service in Virginia.

The first few weeks of war with the United States went reasonably well for the Confederacy. At the battle of Big Bethel in June, the 1st North Carolina Volunteers and several Virginia regiments soundly defeated Union forces. In July, Confederates routed a Union army at Manassas Junction, Virginia. The 6th North Carolina State Troops played a central role in that battle. The defeated Union army fled to nearby Washington. The city's population feared that the capitol might have to be evacuated until everyone realized that the Confederate army was too disorganized to seize the moment. Southerners rejoiced at the prospect of a quick and victorious end to the war.

Throughout the summer and early fall of 1861, men across the South rushed to join volunteer companies that were being organized. It seemed that no one wanted to miss the adventure and glory of winning a short war. North Carolinians were no different. Local prominent men, few with prior military experience outside the militia, began recruiting among their families and friends. They advertised from church pulpits, with printed circulars, and in newspapers:

One Hundred Men Wanted
For the First Regiment of State Troops

> The undersigned are now raising a company of State troops to complete the first regiment of which Col. Stokes is in command. It is desirable that this company should be formed as speedily as practicable, that it may secure a position under so efficient and experienced an officer as Col. Stokes and the more speedily it is formed the more speedily it will be led to meet an enemy now ready to commence its long threatened attempt to invade our homes and subjugate a free people. Recruits will be enlisted at Greenville, Pitt County, by the undersigned until the company is formed.
>
> E. C. Yellowly. Capt.
>
> Greenville, July 10, 1861 A. J. Hines, 1st Lieut. [9]

Dozens of these companies gathered at their county seats or local militia "rendezvous" camps, elected officers, chose colorful company names, and sent word to Raleigh of their readiness to be trained and equipped. When advised to do so, they traveled to Raleigh, usually by train, and reported for duty at one of the half-dozen camps that the state hurriedly established around the city.

North Carolina Adjutant General John F. Hoke and the General of the State Troops James G. Martin coordinated the arrival of the companies. The volunteers were grouped together in the standard ten company, one thousand man regiments. The regiments were given numerical designations in the order of their formation. Companies within the regiments were given letter designations, A through K (usually omitting the letter J), in order of their assignment to the regiment.[a] Cavalry and artillery regiments were organized by a similar process. Within seven months, twelve North Carolina regiments enlisted for three years or for "the war" (whichever was shorter), twenty-eight regiments signed up for twelve months, and one signed for six months. There were also several independent battalions and companies.[10]

[a] As an example, Dr. James T. Kell of southeast Mecklenburg County organized the Mecklenburg Beauregards in the late summer of 1861. The recruits elected their officers at the county seat of Charlotte on September 13. They then reported to Camp Mangum near Raleigh and were processed through the system with other recently arrived companies from various parts of the state. By September 26, the Mecklenburg Beauregards had become Company K of the 30th North Carolina Troops and Dr. Kell was the company's captain (*North Carolina Troops 1861-1865: A Roster*, v. VIII, p. 412). When handwritten, the letters I and J were easily mistaken for one another; thus, J was not often used.

After several weeks at Raleigh, new regiments were usually sent to the coast for further training and to discourage Union designs in that area. During this time, the soldiers contracted the usual camp diseases commonly experienced by large groups of men living in close quarters for the first time: mumps, measles, chicken pox, etc. Officers had the opportunity to harden their men to army discipline, camp life, and marching long distances with heavy loads. Knowledgeable officers changed their regiment's camp location several times each month to teach the men to discard anything that was not essential. Regiments of volunteers that were trained in this manner generally developed excellent esprit de corps. By February 1862, North Carolina had contributed forty-one regiments, nearly forty thousand men, to the Provisional Army of the Confederate States (P.A.C.S.).[11]

Gathering men was the easy part; there were plenty of eager volunteers. However, providing uniforms, equipment, and healthcare for thousands of men was an almost insurmountable task. Tons of food and firewood had to be sent to Raleigh each day. Thousands of tents were needed at Raleigh and on the coast.

As expected, the crowded conditions led to sickness among the troops. In May, Governor Ellis appointed Dr. Charles E. Johnson as surgeon general. By the end of July, Dr. Johnson had established two general hospitals at Raleigh. He organized a network of smaller "wayside" hospitals along the state's rail lines at Weldon, Raleigh, Salisbury, Charlotte, Tarboro, and Goldsboro.[a] He also established three additional hospitals for North Carolina soldiers in Virginia.

North Carolina provided many of her volunteers with weapons taken from the United States Arsenal at Fayetteville. When seized on orders from Governor Ellis, the arsenal yielded enough ordnance equipment to arm thirty-seven thousand men with the usual stand-of-arms: musket, bayonet and scabbard, percussion cap box, cartridge box and shoulder strap, and waist belt. The vast majority of the weapons were old muskets that had been given to the state by the Federal government under the provisions of the Militia Act of 1808. Thus, most of North Carolina's early volunteers were issued standard, though dated, military arms and equipment. North Carolina sent ten thousand stand-of-arms to Virginia. By late 1861, the arsenal

[a] The Confederate government assumed overall management of the hospital system in August 1862. By the end of the war, there were thirteen general hospitals and seven wayside hospitals in North Carolina (Murray, *Wake: Capital County of North Carolina*, p. 462-65; and, *War Between the States, Nursing in North Carolina* by Phoebe Pollitt and Camille N. Reese, Confederate Veteran magazine, v. 2, 2002, p. 22-31).

supply was exhausted. At that time, some North Carolina regiments left Raleigh armed with spear-like weapons called "pikes" or with no weapons at all. To help relieve the shortage, the Confederate government adopted regulations that provided for the donation, purchase, and/or seizure of privately owned muskets, rifles, and double-barrel shotguns. Richmond set the prices to be paid and authorized county sheriffs to collect the weapons.

Cloth for uniforms was produced at the forty-eight textile mills located in North Carolina. State contracts were awarded for this purpose, and a factory was established in Raleigh where the cloth was cut according to specified patterns. The pieces were then sewn into completed uniforms. The sewing was often done by local women who were paid a set price for each garment they assembled.[12] Still, there were so many volunteers that many soldiers began their military service in homemade uniforms or in uniforms provided through retail suppliers. North Carolina Army Quartermaster Major John Devereux operated a program to collect blankets and clothing for needy soldiers. He advertised in newspapers during the winter of 1861-62 for donations of these items. Again, county sheriff offices became the collection centers.

There was a shortage of leather. Leather was the preferred material for belts and cartridge boxes in all branches of military service, not to mention the thousands of saddles and harnesses that were needed. Providing shoes and boots for soldiers would require additional tons of leather. On the average, each infantryman would need shoe repair or replacement every thirty days during active campaigning. The state used "prepared cloth" (canvas covered with black waterproof paint) for waist belts, cartridge box straps, and shoes to help relieve the leather shortage.

While North Carolina and the rest of the Confederacy mobilized, United States War Department planners were not idle. They gathered ships for the blockade and began developing plans to attack the Confederate coast. Richmond was the ultimate target. Union strategists wanted to cut railroad supply lines leading toward that city from Southern ports while simultaneously keeping Confederate forces occupied far from Virginia. New Bern, Wilmington, Charleston, and Savannah were the most obvious targets. Union transport vessels could land troops on the coast and keep them supplied while being protected by gunboats from the blockading fleet.

The Confederacy's preoccupation with the tactical defense of Richmond prevented the military from taking decisive steps to protect the more distant, strategic approaches to the capitol. North Carolina and Confederate authorities argued over who was responsible for the defense of northeastern North Carolina and how much effort should be expended in that region. Still, some construction projects began, and the recently organized North Carolina regiments in the area were thought to provide some deterrence.

Earthen fortifications armed with heavy coastal artillery were constructed along the northern Outer Banks and Roanoke Island. The plan was to deny Federal access to the interior of Albemarle Sound (one of the approaches to Richmond) at a narrow and readily defendable point. Troops that were sent to occupy these forts had to build them first, often working side-by-side with slave laborers contracted from nearby plantation owners.

Additional construction was needed to defend Pamlico Sound to the south of Albemarle Sound. The results were Forts Hatteras and Clark, located at Hatteras Inlet, and other smaller fortifications at Oregon and Ocracoke inlets.

Even with these efforts, the Confederacy did not sufficiently fortify and support the area. The early-war focus on Richmond by North and South would work to the detriment of both sides. The Confederacy was slow to realize the strategic importance of the North Carolina coast, and early Union successes in the area would not be exploited in a timely manner.[13]

In late summer 1861, after the battle at Manassas, the attention of Union authorities was drawn specifically to Hatteras Inlet. Not only was the town of Hatteras an active port, but privateers and makeshift Confederate naval vessels were operating from there. Merchant ships en route to Northern ports were being seized in the area. Union planners, not yet realizing the strategic importance of North Carolina's sounds, developed a plan to attack Hatteras Inlet, destroy the two forts, obstruct the inlet, and then withdraw.[14]

On August 27, 1861, a Union fleet of nine warships and two troop transports arrived off Hatteras Inlet. The commander, General Benjamin F. Butler, planned a straightforward assault against the Confederate defenses. He would first bombard the forts with the fleet's big guns, then land his infantry on shore. Artillery in the two forts totaled seventeen large guns. Butler's fleet carried more than eight times that number.[15]

The shelling of Fort Clark, the smaller of the two forts, began at ten a.m. on August 28. Under cover of the artillery fire, a three-hundred man Union force came ashore in the wind-driven surf.

Meanwhile, Confederate defenders in the fort quickly expended what little artillery ammunition they had. Realizing that they would soon be overrun, the garrison abandoned Fort Clark and withdrew to nearby Fort Hatteras.

Nightfall and worsening weather conditions halted the day's fighting. The Union landing party occupied Fort Clark. The artillery crews from Fort Clark, several companies of the 17th North Carolina Troops, and the Fort Hatteras garrison huddled together and hoped for reinforcements from the mainland. None came.

The shelling of Fort Hatteras began at seven-thirty the next morning and continued for almost three hours. With no sign of reinforcements and a room near the main powder magazine on fire, the Confederates raised the white flag. The Union force inside Fort Clark never had to make a move against the second fort. Their presence kept the Southerners crowded in Fort Hatteras while the naval bombardment convinced them to surrender. The victory was shared by both branches of service, but intense naval gunfire was the key.[16]

Forts Hatteras and Clark had been the first line of defense for the Outer Banks. As a result of their loss, the Confederates were forced to abandon other smaller forts in the area rather than see them surrounded and captured. Roanoke Island was the next logical place to make a stand.

The expedition's success was hailed as a major victory in the North and was a useful public relations boost for the Lincoln government on the heels of the humiliating defeat at Manassas. In the South, the Hatteras defeat was regarded as an embarrassment to North Carolina whose troops had performed well at Big Bethel and Manassas. The capture of two forts and the abandonment of several others without a fight caused friction between the state and Confederate governments. Each blamed the other for inattention and lack of support.

During the fall, Federal strategists finally realized that control of Pamlico and Albemarle Sounds would be a great advantage. General Butler had seen the potential of the region shortly after his victory at Hatteras Inlet and left a small occupying force when he withdrew. As the war department struggled to develop a comprehensive strategy to take Richmond, the importance of Roanoke Island became apparent. If the war could be ended quickly with a more or less direct strike at Richmond, Albemarle Sound was a likely approach. In a longer war, requiring the starvation of Confederate forces operating in Virginia, control of Pamlico Sound was desirable. Either way, Roanoke Island at the juncture of the two sounds would need to be secured. Once this was done, Union forces could occupy coastal towns to use as bases for inland raids. By advancing along the Roanoke and Neuse rivers, they could attack North Carolina's railroad system.

Goldsboro, on the Neuse River, was an important rail junction that connected with Weldon, North Carolina. Major rail lines from the eastern Confederacy converged near Weldon, crossed the Roanoke River, and continued on to Petersburg and Richmond. If the Union army could capture Weldon or Goldsboro just long enough to destroy the railroad tracks, bridges, and depots, Confederate forces around Petersburg and Richmond would be cut off from their best source of supply. In order to begin implementing this strategy, Union Army General-in-Chief George McClellan ordered General Ambrose Burnside to assemble a force large enough to launch an amphibious attack against Roanoke Island.

During the closing weeks of 1861, Burnside gathered his forces at Annapolis, Maryland, and arranged for naval vessels commanded by Commodore Louis M. Goldsborough to meet him there. McClellan's written orders to Burnside, finally delivered in early January, contained the plan for the invasion of North Carolina:

> In accordance with verbal instructions heretofore given you, you will, after uniting with Flag-officer Goldsborough at Fort Monroe, proceed under his convoy to Hatteras inlet, where you will, in connection with him, take the most prompt measure for crossing the fleet over the Bulkhead into the waters of the sound.... you will assume command of the garrison at Hatteras inlet.... Your first point of attack will be Roanoke Island.... Having occupied the island and its dependencies, you will at once proceed to the erection of the batteries and defenses necessary to hold the position with a small force.[17]

Union plans for attacking Roanoke Island materialized before the Confederate government was convinced of the necessity of holding the place. Repeated requests for more troops, artillery, and fort construction in the area fell on deaf ears in Richmond.

When the new year dawned, Roanoke Island's defenses were under-manned, under-gunned, and pathetically under-supported by the "mosquito fleet." This was an odd assortment of non-military vessels, armed with light-weight field artillery that was manned by cross-trained Georgia infantrymen. Confederate forces on the island were under the immediate command of Colonel Henry Shaw and included his 8th North Carolina State Troops, the 31st North Carolina Troops, and part of the 17th North Carolina Troops.[a] These soldiers were suffering from a combination of camp diseases, bureaucratic neglect, and low morale. On the unlikely shoulders of this force rested the fate of North Carolina's coast from near the Virginia border southward to Morehead City.

General Burnside's combined army and naval force of thirteen thousand men attacked Roanoke Island on February 7, 1862. After shelling the island's defenses and pounding the Confederate navy into retreat, Burnside directed the landing of ten thousand Federal soldiers. A small Confederate force near the beach retreated without firing a shot, thus assuring a Union foothold. The landing force spent the night on the island with no Confederate attempts to dislodge them. In the meantime, two Virginia regiments arrived to reinforce the North Carolinians.

The next morning, Union forces attacked Confederate positions near the center of the island. The Southerners relied too heavily on their field position. They blocked the main road leading toward their earthworks, but failed to adequately defend the supposedly impassable swamps on their flanks. When Union soldiers emerged from the swamp on the Confederates' right, the defenders retreated. Colonel Shaw decided that he had lost the only defendable position on the island and surrendered his entire force. The remaining Confederate ships were destroyed at Elizabeth City several days later.

In the course of seven months, North Carolina's natural defensive barrier, the Outer Banks, had been squandered. Union forces were now free to roam the inland waterways of the state, land troops, and attack at will. Union infantry supported by gunboats would soon advance inland along North Carolina's rivers.[b]

[a] Most of the soldiers in the 17th North Carolina Troops had been captured at Hatteras but were later exchanged (*Roster*, v. VI, p. 118).

[b] In 1862, the Confederacy built Fort Branch near Hamilton, North Carolina, thus blocking Union efforts to approach Weldon using the Roanoke River (Shiman, *Fort Branch And The Defense Of The Roanoke Valley 1862-1865).*

For the remainder of the war, increasing Union pressure in the eastern part of the state would cause concern in both Richmond and Raleigh. The early lack of Confederate government support that resulted in the loss of this region embittered North Carolinians and their leaders toward the new national government.[a] Union movement along the coast and raids deep into the state from occupied territory would come to divert a significant portion of state and national resources. An early wartime lesson for North Carolina was that fixed fortifications were only as strong as the support they received. For the North, plans to exploit this success had already been made.

The full extent of Union designs on North Carolina was revealed in General McClellan's original orders to Burnside in January. After instructing General Burnside on the seizure of Roanoke Island, McClellan had also ordered him to:

> ... make a descent on New Bern, having gained possession of which and the railroad passing through it, you will at once throw a sufficient force upon Beaufort and take the steps necessary to reduce Ft. Macon and open that port. When you seize New Bern you will endeavor to seize the railroad as far west as Goldsboro.... Should circumstances render it advisable to seize and hold Raleigh, the main north and south line of railroad passing through Goldsboro should be so effectually destroyed for considerable distances north and south of that point as to render it impossible for the rebels to use it to your disadvantage. A great point would be gained, in any event, by the effectual destruction of the Wilmington and Weldon Railroad....[18]

[a] In finding that troops on the island should have been better reinforced, a congressional investigating committee ultimately blamed the loss of Roanoke Island on Secretary of War Judah P. Benjamin and the local Confederate army department commander, General Benjamin Huger (*The Tri-Weekly Mercury*, Charleston, South Carolina, April 22, 1862, p. 1, reproduced in *Civil War Extra*, v. 1, p. 234).

Chapter Three

The Absolute Necessity

March - November 1862

In building the Provisional Army of the Confederate States during the first year of the war, the Confederate government remained loyal to the concept of state's rights.[a] Each state was required to provide six percent of its white population as soldiers. In North Carolina's case, that requirement meant nearly thirty-eight thousand men. Congress did not interfere with the states as they supplied the required manpower by whatever means they chose.

After the war's first large battle at Manassas with its shocking casualty lists, military planners on both sides realized that the conflict would be neither short-lived nor settled with only a few battles. Initial calls for volunteers had been eagerly answered, especially in the South where the war was seen as an invasion and a struggle against Union tyranny. After Manassas, the fighting seemed to wind down. For the next several months, there were no large or decisive battles. As the conflict appeared to lose momentum, volunteering slowed.

The North, defeated in its attempt to take Richmond quickly, began thinking in terms of a longer war. The Lincoln government would have to develop plans for an aggressive war that would subjugate and occupy the Confederacy. Formulating a war of movement and deciding when and where to strike would take time. The South chose a strategy that was designed to defend its borders east of the Mississippi River and wait for the North to tire of the struggle. The area west of the Mississippi River was so large that a more fluid approach would have to be utilized.[b] In order to implement this plan, Confederate President Jefferson Davis divided the Confederacy into geographic military departments, which were subdivided into districts.

---

[a] The Provisional Army of the Confederate States was created by an act of congress on February 28, 1861. The law authorized President Davis to accept "from the several States" troops who had enlisted for not less that twelve months (*O.R.*, Series III, v. 5, p. 690).

[b] Throughout the war, the Confederate military drew and redrew the department's boundaries and shuffled its commanders (Boatner, *The Civil War Dictionary*, p. 845-46).

Soldiers on both sides quickly became bored with army life. Most of the Southern troops were farmers whose families were beginning to suffer in their absence. These men had volunteered for the six or twelve months that the war was expected to last and now felt that they had done their part. They expected to leave the army and go home when their enlistment time was up.

As the summer of 1861 gave way to fall, Union armies began to move and apply steady pressure at vulnerable points. Small battles were fought in Virginia, Missouri, and Kentucky. Union forces were active along the Atlantic coast. The United States, though faced with initial defeats, did not sue for peace. No additional states joined the Confederacy. Northwestern Virginia was openly pro-Union.

Adding to Richmond's worries, Southern military forces began to suffer a series of reversals in early 1862. In January, Confederates were defeated at the battle of Mill Springs, Kentucky. Forts Henry and Donelson fell to Union forces in February ending Confederate control of western Tennessee and access to the upper Mississippi River. The Union army occupied Nashville without a fight. Northwest Virginia was slipping away and steady progress was made by Union forces in North Carolina after the capture of Roanoke Island. The war was going to demand more soldiers from both sides. While the North appeared ready to fight a protracted war, the Southern army began to weaken.

The South's six-month volunteers, like D. H. Hill's 1st North Carolina regiment, began to leave the army in October 1861 when their enlistments expired. The Confederate Congress passed a series of short-term measures and incentives to keep the twelve-month regiments in the army and to induce additional volunteering. In December, cash bounties, furloughs, and free transportation to and from home were offered to soldiers who reenlisted. Soon after, reenlisting troops were allowed to reorganize their regiments by electing new officers. In February, regiments already received into Confederate service were authorized to send recruiting parties to their home counties to enlist their friends and relatives.[19] The Confederate government pressured the states to provide even more troops than the original quotas had required. The governors of North Carolina, South Carolina, Georgia, and Texas ordered drafts of men from their respective militias.[20] These efforts met with only limited success.

While defeats elsewhere in the Confederacy were serious, they paled in comparison to the threat that was approaching Richmond from the east. Over one hundred thousand Union soldiers landed on the Virginia peninsula in March 1862. Their commander, General George McClellan, arrived in April and laid siege to Yorktown. This was the North's long awaited second attempt to take Richmond.

McClellan was cautious and methodical, but the size of his army and the inevitability of its move toward the Southern capitol added to the sense of desperation felt by Confederate congressmen. They saw that their states' reliance on volunteerism, even with Confederate incentives, could not possibly supply the military force needed to save Richmond, much less win a long war. The Southern army was shrinking as the North became more aggressive. Congress realized that the Confederacy would most likely lose the war during the summer of 1862.

President Davis, a former United States Secretary of War, appreciated the gravity of the situation. He had spoken against continuing to build an army on short term enlistments.[21] While Davis regarded national compulsory military service as an evil that should be considered only in times of extreme crisis, he realized that this was such a time.

Secretary of War George W. Randolph possessed an even more complete grasp of the Confederacy's predicament. He not only supported conscripting additional men, but also advocated forcing the twelve-month volunteers to stay in the army beyond their period of enlistment. President Davis felt that keeping volunteers beyond their original enlistment time constituted a broken promise.

Confederate congressmen knew that passing a *national* compulsory military service law in order to fight a war against the principle of strong central government was an absurd contradiction. Thousands of Southerners were bound to regard national conscription as a serious encroachment on state's rights. A large portion of the Southern population, consistent with the principles of state's rights, was opposed to *any* national government, much less mandatory military service in defense of one.

In the end, most Confederate leaders and congressmen saw not only the need to maintain the army, but to enlarge it. Congress had seen the six-month volunteers leave the army in spite of incentives to stay. One hundred and forty-eight regiments of the Confederate army were twelve-month volunteers. They would be free to leave the army beginning in April, in time for spring planting on their farms. There was no reason to believe that the majority of them would stay beyond their time. Even if they did reenlist, under the provisions of the incentives, most of the army would have to be reorganized and set in motion *before* the Union army reached Richmond: a task that was considered to be impossible.[22]

The bloodbath at Shiloh, Tennessee, during the first week of April and the looming fall of Yorktown only heightened the urgency of the situation. The Confederacy needed soldiers to stay in the army in order to save Richmond and required additional men to fight a long and bloody war. On April 16, 1862, Jefferson Davis signed America's first national compulsory military service law. The Confederate Congress had passed the measure by a majority of almost two to one. Mindful of the controversy that would ensue, congress introduced the legislation with an explanation as to why such an extraordinary step was being taken:

> In view of the exigencies of the country, and the absolute necessity of keeping in the service our gallant Army, and of placing in the field a large additional force to meet the advancing columns of enemy now invading our soil: Therefore... The Congress of the Confederate States of America do enact....[23]

This law, the first in a series of laws collectively referred to as the "conscript acts," allowed President Davis to put into military service:

> ... all white men who are residents of the Confederate States, between the ages of eighteen and thirty-five years at the time the call or calls may be made, who are not legally exempted from military service. All of the persons aforesaid who are now in the Armies of the Confederacy, and whose term of service will expire before the end of the war, shall be continued in the service for three years from the date of their original enlistment, unless the war shall have been sooner ended... [24]

The new law prevented the one-year volunteers from leaving the army for two more years and provided for the conscription of additional three-year soldiers as they were needed. Responsibility for the administration of the law was assigned to the adjutant and inspector general, under the supervision of the secretary of war.

The law authorized President Davis, with the governors' consent, to use state (militia) officers to enforce the conscript law. If a governor should refuse to cooperate, Confederate army officers were to be used.

In passing the conscription law, the Confederate Congress set upon a course that it would follow throughout the war. In order to achieve sovereignty, the individual Southern states would first have to relinquish their sovereignty to the Confederate government.

Immediately after passage of the conscription act, Confederate officers began using the inevitability of conscription to shame men into volunteering. Only two weeks after the law was enacted, Colonel Zebulon Baird Vance of the 26th North Carolina regiment sent the following item to be printed in a Raleigh newspaper:

> Near Kinston, (N.C.)
> April 29, 1862
> THE RECENT ACT OF CONGRESS REQUIRES each Company to be raised to 125 rank and file. Company E, of my regiment requires 28 men, (from Chatham county) Company G, from Chatham, 20 men; Company B; from Union county, 28 men; Company C, from Wilkes, 50 men; Company D, from Wake, wants 70 men; Company K, from Anson, wants 51 men; Company H from Moore County, wants 16 men; Company A, from Ashe county, wants 23 men. Men liable to draft in those counties had better come along at once and fill up their companies like white men, and not wait for the sheriff to bring them to me. [25]

Similar notices appeared in newspapers throughout the South. Men wishing to avoid the stigma of having to be forced to the defense of their homeland responded to this tactic. The threat of conscription began supplying soldiers to the Confederacy many weeks before the law could be enforced. Hundreds of North Carolina men joined existing regiments. By late summer, twenty-three additional regiments of these "volunteers" had been organized.[a]

The conversion from a recruitment and training system for volunteers to one geared toward mandatory service would take time. Under the provisions of the conscription law, each state had to recommend to the war department an "officer not below the rank of Major" to manage the enrolling, equipping, training, and initial

[a] See dates of organization in *North Carolina Troops 1861-1865: A Roster.* A typical regiment organized during this period was the 57th North Carolina Troops. The unit was assembled at Salisbury on July 31, 1862, and consisted of "nearly all conscripts" according to Lieutenant Colonel Hamilton C. Jones (Clark's *Histories*, v. 3, p. 409). Although they would not pass through the formal conscription process, North Carolina regiments organized after April 1862 were, nonetheless, products of the coercive atmosphere created by the conscript law.

deployment of the conscripts.[26] Each of these officers would also have to develop an administrative system to classify and account for all men who were exempted or deferred from military service.

For this daunting task, General Theophilus Hunter Holmes,[a] commander of Confederate forces in North Carolina, recommended Captain Peter Mallett. Holmes was the fifty-eight-year-old son of a former North Carolina governor, a career military man, and most importantly, a close friend of President Jefferson Davis. Holmes knew the Mallett family and considered Captain Mallett to be a fine drill master and disciplinarian.

Mallett had been born to an influential Fayetteville family on May 25, 1825, and received his formal education in North Carolina. His father, Charles Peter Mallett, was a textile manufacturer, operated a stagecoach company, and held interests in banking and shipping. By 1845, young Mallett had shown enough interest and ability that his father sent him to represent family business interests in New York City. He worked for his father for two years and then became a wholesaler. In 1848, he married Annabella Gibbs, daughter of a successful North Carolina rice planter. The couple returned to New York, where they prospered until the financial panic of 1857.

Mallett then became involved in the shipping trade between New York, Wilmington, Charleston, and Savannah. While a resident of New York, he served in the 7th Regiment New York State Militia rising to the rank of lieutenant. By 1861, his shipping firm owned a fleet of twelve schooners and six other vessels. When the war started, rather than report to Washington, D.C. with his militia regiment, Mallett packed up his family, abandoned his business holdings and returned to his native state.[27] Several of Mallett's brothers and cousins had already joined the Confederate army.

Upon his arrival at Fayetteville, Mallett immediately began raising a company of volunteers. When organized and accepted into the service, this company was designated as Company C, 3rd North Carolina State Troops. He served as the captain of this unit in North Carolina and Virginia until the spring of 1862.[28] When recommended to command the North Carolina Conscript Bureau, Peter Mallett possessed the perfect combination of military experience, business expertise, and state connections for the job. Two days before his

---

[a] Holmes graduated from West Point in 1829, served in the Seminole War in Florida, and had distinguished himself during the war with Mexico. In March 1862, his West Point friend, Jefferson Davis, promoted him to major general and placed him in command of the Department of North Carolina (Johnston, *Vance Papers*, v. 1, p. 136).

thirty-seventh birthday, he was promoted to major, assigned to the Confederate army's adjutant and inspector general, and ordered to report to the state capitol.

Major Mallett arrived in Raleigh and began organizing his bureau. The conscript law required North Carolina to close most of the volunteer recruit camps. The closings were to be accomplished by May 17.[29] A maximum of two camps in each state were to be designated as "camps of instruction" under the new law.

Mallett divided the state into two sections, east and west, and established a camp of instruction in each area. The camps would require facilities sufficient to process thousands of conscripts over the next several months. Predictably, there would be a rush of activity in the summer and fall as men who were inclined to voluntarily comply with the law did so. Mallett was faced with having to assemble his bureau as quickly as possible in order to receive the first and perhaps largest group of conscripts. President Davis's first call was for the entire age group covered by the law. All Southern men age eighteen to thirty-five had to be enrolled and examined in preparation for the induction of those who were not exempted.

Congressional districts in each state were designated as the primary administrative subdivisions for conscription. Mallett needed to select surgeons to conduct the initial medical examinations of enrollees in the districts. Additional medical staffs would be required at the camps of instruction. He also began to search for qualified military personnel. He needed drill masters, camp guard officers, and officers for a supporting force that would be responsible for bringing in conscripts who refused to be enrolled.

Mallett's drill masters could not be afforded the luxury of on-the-job training. They had to be proven experts in the manual-of-arms as well as company and battalion maneuvers. They would have to arrive at the camps prepared to teach these skills to recruits in a short period of time.

The camp guard and supporting force officers needed to be effective leaders, men who could instill loyalty and obedience in their subordinates. The business of guarding conscripts, arresting deserters, and enforcing conscript laws in the face of negative public sentiment would require great resolve. Supporting force officers, in particular, would need these traits. They would soon be called upon to manage independent company operations far from the camps of instruction on some occasions and to function within a battalion or regimental structure at other times.

Fortunately, the same conscription law that made this large military bureaucracy necessary indirectly provided for its staffing. The law allowed the enlisted men of regiments already in the field to elect new officers. These elections took place in April and May 1862. Most officers kept their positions, but the process resulted in a substantial number of men being voted out as company and regiment officers. They were now subject to conscription. They had either to report to the camps of instruction as privates or seek appointment as officers elsewhere.

The reason for this predicament varied from man to man. Some of them were poor officer material from the beginning having attained their rank by virtue of hometown status or by having originally organized their volunteer companies. Some officers had decided that service in a front-line military unit was too demanding. Others simply lost the popularity contests that the election process occasionally became. The result was that in the summer of 1862, a number of former officers were seeking assignments. Many of these men had a year or more of experience in the army. Mallett had to be careful; there were certainly unsuitable candidates, but he could choose the best from among those available. He often selected men whose families he knew or those he had met while in the 3rd North Carolina State Troops.

Mallett knew that the most efficient way to gather North Carolina's men for enrollment was to utilize the existing militia organization that contained all of the men covered by the conscript act. Fortunately, the state's new governor, Henry T. Clark, agreed.[a] The governor also felt that the state's population would be more likely to tolerate conscription if it was enforced by local militia officers, as opposed to officers supplied by the Confederate government. While the governor would assist in the conscription effort, he did not care to give Mallett complete control of his state officers.

On June 11, Governor Clark authorized his militia officers to assemble their regiments at any time that Mallett might choose. Although there would later be some disagreement between Clark and Mallett on the extent to which militia officers were to assist, Mallett began building a positive working relationship with them from the start.[30]

---

[a] Henry T. Clark had assumed the governorship in July, 1861, when Governor Ellis died in office (Boatner, *Civil War Dictionary*, p. 156).

Mallett chose the state capitol for the location of his headquarters and primary camp of instruction. Raleigh featured a central location, rail lines, efficient communications with the rest of the state, and close proximity to the executive, legislative, and judicial branches of government. From Raleigh, he could more easily maintain contact with agricultural, manufacturing, and transportation interests. He would need to coordinate the activities of all of these entities to accomplish his work.

The adjutant and inspector general provided procedures for establishing the camps:

> II.-Enrollment and Disposition of Recruits
> 3. The enrolled men in each State will be collected in camps of instruction by the officers in command of the recruits, the said camps to be selected with reference to health and the facilities for obtaining subsistence and transportation. The number of theses camps shall not exceed two in each State, without authority from the Department; and to each will be allowed a quartermaster and a commissary.[31]

Mallett selected thirty-two acres of land on a hilltop two miles northeast of the capitol building. The Raleigh and Weldon Railroad tracks crossed Pigeon House Creek nearby, providing the required water and transportation. The land was level enough for parade grounds and buildings and high enough above the creek to stay dry. Mallett named the camp after his friend and mentor, General Theophilus Holmes. Thus, Camp Holmes became Camp of Instruction No.1 for the state of North Carolina.[a]

Mallett designated Camp Hill near Statesville as his second conscription camp. This site had been used as a militia camp and drill field since before the war with Mexico, and, like Camp Holmes, was near the railroad.[b] Conscripts from the western part of the state could be gathered, equipped, trained, and then sent directly to Virginia.[32] Those contesting their conscription on legal or medical grounds would be sent to Camp Holmes to await disposition of their cases.

[a] Camp Holmes was located in the area that is now immediately west of the intersection of Whitaker Mill Road and Old Wake Forest Road in Raleigh.

[b] The site of Camp Hill in Statesville is near the intersection of Garner Bagnal Boulevard and Buffalo Shoals Road.

In order to provide for the transformation from civilian to soldier of thousands of North Carolinians, Mallett's two camps would need barracks, medical facilities, quartermaster and ordnance depots, administrative offices, and guardhouses. Mallett had to staff these functions and make arrangements for the necessary construction.

Because the camps were intended to handle large numbers of conscripts as opposed to willing volunteers, a guard force would be needed at each location. While the guards remained at the camps, a separate supporting force would operate throughout the state, gathering recusant conscripts, escorting new soldiers to their assigned units, and returning deserters to their regiments. Several hundred soldiers would be needed for these duties.

Again, the conscript law could provide the required manpower. Military authorities felt that the camp guard and supporting force could be staffed with older, less fit conscripts. The process of enrolling all men between the ages of eighteen and thirty-five would automatically identify likely candidates for this kind of assignment, especially men in the upper end of the age group who were capable of doing acceptable service from a relatively permanent base. Militia officers assigned to enrolling duty could watch for men who were somewhat less capable and recommend them for diversion from assignment to regiments in the field to duty in the conscript bureau. Men selected for this duty could be assured that they were likely to remain within the state for the foreseeable future and be less likely to face combat with the enemy. Men who were offered this opportunity usually chose to serve in Major Mallett's bureau.

This assurance was the unique feature of service in Mallett's battalion. The soldiers assigned to this duty were themselves conscripts. They were now charged with enforcing the very same law that had forced *them* into the army. They would have to enforce unpopular conscript laws on their fellow citizens. Yet as volunteers in Mallett's bureau, they could be expected to render faithful service in return for the relative safety of their assignment. Soon, thousands of unwilling men would have to be pushed through the conscription system and into the army. Mallett's soldiers would have to make that process work.[a]

[a] While the term "Mallett's battalion" was most often used to identify the unit, no official designation was ever given. Wartime documents and post-war reminisces have referred to the battalion as the Camp Holmes Guard, Raleigh Guards, State Guards, the North Carolina Conscript battalion, etc. In December 1862, Mallett apparently identified himself to Union authorities as the colonel of the 68th North Carolina Troops. At that time, no such unit existed.

In June, Mallett notified his immediate superior in Richmond, Confederate Adjutant and Inspector General Samuel Cooper,[a] of his selection of the Raleigh camp site. He also outlined his initial plan for enrolling the state's manpower:

> Raleigh, N.C., June 10, 1862
> General S. Cooper
>
> Adjutant and Inspector General:
> Sir: I have the honor to report that I have selected a desirable location in this vicinity for a camp of instruction.... I propose, with your approval, sending a commissioned officer and an assistant surgeon to each county (with the [militia] muster roll furnished by the State as a check) to enroll, accept substitutes, examine and give certificates to all persons who may be exempt from disability. This will save transportation for many exempts who would otherwise be obliged to go to camp at great inconvenience to themselves and unnecessary expense to the Government. By dividing the State into sections the work can be accomplished with comparatively few officers. After enrollment, substitutes accepted, and certificates given to exempts at each precinct or muster ground, the conscripts will be sent immediately to camp for instruction and distribution.... This plan of operation which I take the liberty of proposing was suggested by General Holmes.[33]

Mallett's plan for the North Carolina Bureau of Conscription was influenced by several factors. First, Mallett's prior experience in the New York Militia and 3rd North Carolina State Troops had taught him the fundamentals of military administration and command. Second, his experience as a businessman prompted an appreciation for efficiency and fiscal restraint. Third, although the conscription law provided a general framework for the task ahead, it left significant implementation details up to the conscript commanders' discretion. Here, Mallett relied on General Holmes's experience and influence. Mallett's job would require him to interact with high-level army officers and government officials. While traveling in these circles, he

[a] Cooper, a sixty-three-year-old New Jersey native, was the Confederacy's highest ranking soldier (Boatner, *Civil War Dictionary*, p. 175). As A. & I.G. his office was responsible for all of the war department's army orders, personnel records, and inspections (Current, *Encyclopedia of the Confederacy*, p. 1685).

would need seasoned political advice. Mallett was smart enough to seek and follow the old general's counsel.

Mallett had Camp Holmes ready by mid-June when Adjutant and Inspector General Cooper submitted a progress report to the secretary of war. Mallett had not officially opened the camp, but Cooper was satisfied enough with the activities there and at the camps of instruction in Virginia and South Carolina that he reported them to "have been established" on June 14. The other Confederate states had not made such progress.[34] Mallett had accomplished a great deal in a short period of time, but serious problems were developing.

National compulsory military service, as opposed to state militia service, which was also mandatory, was proving to be unpopular all over the South. The conscript law's substitution provision plainly favored the well-to-do. A rich man could afford to hire a surrogate to take his place in the army; the average Southerner could not. To thousands of poor farmers, substitution and the few exemptions and deferments that were initially allowed seemed to be a way for men with money or connections to avoid military service. The mountain populations of North Carolina, South Carolina, Tennessee, and Virginia in particular took this view. Early-war enthusiasm for military service had run its course months before the conscript law was passed. The shift in the population's attitude concerning military service was reported by the press:

> The affecting scenes connected with the departure of Volunteers have given way to the heart-rendering sight of men torn away from their families by the strong arm of the law; heads of families, surrounded by weeping women and children, are forced into the army, their hopes and prospects blighted, if not forever ruined, under the plea of a military necessity, when, it will be remembered that, some eighteen months ago, we were told that secession would be peaceable, and a mere small job to be dispatched in the morning before breakfast.[35]

The emerging problems of conscription resistance, desertion, and the resulting need for cooperation between local and national authorities was publicly acknowledged by the war department in mid-July. Adjutant and Inspector General Cooper issued orders that substantially increased the responsibilities and administrative labors for enrolling officers and conscription bureau commanders.

Local sheriffs and jailors also became involved in conscription law enforcement:

> GENERAL ORDERS, NO. 49
> WAR DEPARTMENT,
> ADJT. AND INSP. GENERAL'S OFFICE
> Richmond, July 14, 1862.
>
> All persons engaged in enrolling conscripts are hereby authorized and required to arrest deserters from the Army and to deliver them to the commandant of the nearest camp of instruction, or to lodge them in the nearest jail, and to return their names, company, and regiment to the nearest Adjutant and Inspector General. Jailors are requested to detain them, and will be allowed fees and charges for the detention of prisoners prescribed by the laws of the State in which the jail is situated. Enrolling officers are also required to report to the Adjutant and Inspector General the names and address of all persons absent from the Army without leave, whether by the expiration of their leaves of absence, furloughs, details or otherwise; and where this unauthorized absence exceeds the time required to correspond with the War Department the enrolling officer will arrest the person and send him to the nearest camp of instruction, reporting the arrest to the Adjutant and Inspector General. Commandants of camps of instruction are required to forward deserters and persons absent without leave to their regiments, and have the powers of arrest conferred upon enrolling officers.
>
> By command of the Secretary of War:
> S. Cooper
> Adjutant and Inspector General [36]

General Order No. 49 made enrolling officers responsible for the administrative tracking of soldiers who were absent from their regiments in the Confederate Army. This would not be the last expansion of conscription officers' responsibilities and would eventually lead to the assignment of dozens of Confederate officers and enlisted men to conscription duties in each state.

Major Mallett ordered the militia colonels to assemble their regiments for enrollment on July 8. They were to bring all non-exempt men to Camp Hill or Camp Holmes on July 15. Militia officers ran newspaper notices to that effect for several weeks. Unfortunately, the initial gathering of conscripts would contain an unexpectedly large number of draft resisters.

The cooperation between the militia and Mallett's conscription bureau resulted in North Carolina's first enrollment being efficiently executed: in fact, too efficiently. Hundreds of conscripts began arriving at Raleigh and Statesville each week. Mallett had foreseen security problems, but he did not have a full compliment of camp guard and supporting force soldiers. His request for an additional infantry company to be temporarily assigned to Camp Holmes was approved by North Carolina's adjutant general on July 12.[37] Still, there were not enough guards to escort all the conscripts to their units. North Carolina officers were sent from Virginia to Mallett's camps for this purpose.

The log-jam of conscripts was worsened by the lack of trains to transport them to Richmond. Both camps became dangerously overcrowded. On July 25, Mallett reported "2,500 men ready and waiting transportation" at Camp Holmes.[38] Many of these men had arrived at camp frustrated and openly contemptuous of the conscript law. The next day, the combination of insufficient guards, crowded conditions, and hostility resulted in a mass desertion at Camp Holmes. In reporting the incident directly to the secretary of war, Mallett pointed to the circumstances that had produced the affair and requested a greatly enhanced security force for his camps:

> Headquarters Camp of Instruction
> Camp Holmes, July 27, 1862
>
> Sir
>
> I have the honor to acknowledge the receipt of your telegram of 26th yesterday. The difficulty is in getting transportation to Clarksville or even Weldon- the trains being crowded with troops. The officers sent out for Conscripts (only two from each Regt) are not willing to risk marching them through the country. The order desired from you was the privilege of one train to relieve the camp of 1000 men. I regret to report that 200 hundred men deserted last night having organized themselves and rushed the guards. We succeeded in preventing about 300 more in the same plot from escaping. Two of the deserters have been arrested and officers are now in pursuit of the others. It will require at least six companies well armed to guard this Camp and four [additional companies] at Statesville. With this force, detachments could be sent

> out immediately in pursuit of deserters, or to disaffected districts where compulsion will be necessary. I am using every precaution to prevent desertions, and respectfully request men and arms for that purpose.
>
> With high regard, I am sir,
> Your Obedient Servant,
> Peter Mallett
> Major, Commanding Post [39]

Between June 11, when Governor Clark ordered North Carolina Militia officers to assemble their regiments at Mallett's direction, and the desertion on July 26, Mallett had relied on state officers not only to gather their militiamen, but also to take them to the camps of instruction and to bring in those who refused to report for the enrollment. Mallett, like many conscription officers, had been surprised by the amount of resistance to the first enrollment. Militia officers had been drawn into conscription enforcement more deeply than anyone expected. Governor Clark regarded Mallett's use of the militia to have gone far beyond the authorization he had given. Clark used the opportunity presented by the mass desertion to complain directly to President Davis about Mallett's implementation of the first enrollment and his expanded use of militia officers.[a]

Clark's complaints put additional pressure on Mallett to get his security problems solved. Two weeks after writing to the secretary of war, Mallett communicated with the adjutant and inspector general and reiterated his desire for additional troops:

> Headquarters Camp of Instruction
> Camp Holmes Aug. 12, 1862
>
> I have to report that this camp was opened on the 15th [July]. There are 3,000 conscripts in camp- 1100 of whom are ready for the field, and waiting transportation.

[a] Clark also complained that he had not been consulted with regard to Mallett's appointment as the chief conscription officer for North Carolina (North Carolina Archives, GLB.46, Part II, p. 386-87). (The governor's letter copy clerk erroneously recorded the letter as being dated on July 21, 1862, but when responding, President Davis mentioned that it was dated July 31.) Davis assured Clark that his complaints would "receive prompt attention." Nothing came of the incident except for the additional tension created between Clark and Mallett (O.R., Series IV, v.2, p. 32).

> The delay has been caused for the want of transportation. I am now relieved in that respect and can furnish conscripts more rapidly; provided transportation can be had.
>
> The men generally will compare favorably with volunteers from this state.
>
> It will be absolutely necessary to have a regiment to Guard this Camp, to prevent desertions and for details in charge of officers almost daily necessary to send for men in different parts of the state, refusing to report for duty.
>
> With this force at my command, I am satisfied I can increase the list of Conscripts to at least 30,000. I therefore respectfully ask permission to organize a regiment of Conscripts for Camp Guard immediately. This will answer for both Camps....
>
> Very Respectfully,
> Peter Mallett
> Major Commanding Post [40]

Mallett was determined to assemble a camp security force that was large enough to prevent further embarrassment. He continued gleaning soldiers from incoming conscripts and stepped-up his efforts to build a solid officer corps for his bureau.

Among the officers selected by Mallett that summer were John McRae, Jr. and James Cameron McRae. Like Mallett, the McRaes were from a prominent Cumberland County family. A lawyer in civilian life, James Cameron McRae had served in the 1st North Carolina Volunteers early in the war. He then reenlisted in the 5th North Carolina State Troops and was promoted to lieutenant. He became the regimental adjutant during the winter of 1861-62 , but his health failed. He then sought a non-field assignment with Mallett.

John McRae, Jr. had been a lieutenant in the 20th North Carolina Troops. He was defeated for reelection when that regiment was reorganized in compliance with the conscription law. Mallett assigned John McRae to command Company B of the conscript battalion. Mallett had other plans for James.

As one of the more experienced officers in the bureau, James C. McRae quickly gained Mallett's confidence. He was promoted to captain and assigned to be the commandant at Camp Hill.[a] As such,

[a] The term "commandant" was often used to refer to commanding officers of military organizations and installations. Mallett was usually referred to as the "state commandant." His designees, while in command of the camps, also signed official documents as "commandant" or "acting commandant."

McRae was responsible for operating the North Carolina Conscript Bureau west of the Yadkin River. He conducted an enrollment for that part of the state on July 31.

Mallett sent Captain McRae to Statesville not only to gather conscripts for the army, but also to select additional men for his proposed regiment even though that permission had not been granted. Furthermore, Mallett did not have enough weapons to completely arm the men he had. As McRae began his assignment at Statesville, Mallett again pressed Richmond for more weapons and men:

> Headquarters Camp of Instruction
> Camp Holmes August 22, 1862
> Hon. Geo. W. Randolph
> Secretary of War
>
> Sir:
>
> In accordance with your instructions, I detailed one of my officers to go to Richmond for arms- five hundred muskets and accouterments- on the 9th instant, but he succeeded in getting only one hundred: and reported that Colonel Gorgas informed him that it would probably be a month before he could furnish the balance.
>
> I am greatly in need of them, and earnestly hope you will have them forwarded immediately, if possible. Send one hundred if no more- I am needing them daily. I shall need at least five hundred for each camp.
>
> It will be absolutely necessary, in order to get up the Conscripts and catch deserters- some of whom are bidding defiance to law and orders- to have at least two cavalry companies, in regard to which I have written to General Hill. [a]
>
> Please forward the arms by Express at the earliest moment...
>
> Yours, very respectfully
> Peter Mallett [41]

---

[a] After D. H. Hill's victory at the battle of Big Bethel, he was promoted to the rank of general. He replaced General T. H. Holmes as commander of the Department of North Carolina on July 17, 1862 (Barrett, *The Civil War in North Carolina,* p. 129). Hill had also been an early supporter of Mallett for the command of North Carolina's conscription bureau. Requests for troops by Mallett were reviewed by the department's commanding general. Camp Hill was most likely named for General Hill.

Mallett was beginning to realize that if the Confederacy was unwilling to give him additional troops, enhanced mobility of the troops he had might be the solution. His force could certainly reach farther if several of his companies were cavalrymen.

As Major Mallett and Captain McRae operated their camps and recruited men for their bureau, they would each be drawn into controversies generated by the interplay between state and Confederate authorities.

In order to induce volunteering and encourage compliance with the conscript law, the Confederacy and North Carolina allowed new recruits to select, with some restrictions, the regiments in which they wished to serve. The restrictions included which unit the recruit selected, whether the recruit had volunteered or was conscripted, whether or not the unit was at full strength, and the date of the soldier's entry into military service.

The new governor, Zebulon Baird Vance, who assumed office on September 8, 1862, instructed North Carolina's Adjutant General, James G. Martin, to issue orders stating that men who reported voluntarily to the camps of instruction "will be allowed to select the Infantry Regiments they wish to join, and unless full, they will be assigned accordingly."[42] During the early implementation of conscription, several different cut-off dates for volunteering had been announced. Furthermore, recruits could not know until after they reported to the camp of instruction whether or not the unit they had chosen was full. Military authorities and civilians alike shared confusion over the circumstances under which men could volunteer and select their units.

Hundreds of North Carolinians joined the army thinking that they could choose a specific unit, but were assigned elsewhere. The result was additional hostility for conscription in general and Mallett's bureau in particular. Governor Vance was bombarded with letters of protest from angry citizens and soldiers. He, in turn, exchanged contentious letters on the subject with President Davis. Major Mallett, while mindful of his primary responsibility to follow orders from Adjutant and Inspector General Cooper, tried in vain to operate within those constraints *and* honor the wishes of recruits entering the army. This controversy would continue through the end of 1862.

Similar conflict awaited Captain McRae in western North Carolina. By locating a conscription camp in that part of the state, Mallett was serving notice that his bureau would not be timid in an area that was known to harbor considerable anti-Confederate, anti-conscription sentiment. This region had shown early signs that conscription enforcement might be difficult. Furthermore, there was a legal issue to be settled. Mallett was aware that McRae's duties would precipitate a confrontation with other officers who were recruiting in the area.

One such officer was Robert G. A. Love, who was organizing companies in western North Carolina for the second time in a year. Love had originally enlisted in a Haywood County volunteer company in May 1861 and had been elected the captain. His company arrived in Raleigh and was assigned to the 6th North Carolina Volunteers. This regiment was later re-designated as the 16th North Carolina Troops. Captain Love was elected lieutenant colonel of the regiment when its organization was completed. When the 16th North Carolina Troops was reorganized in the spring of 1862 under the provisions of the conscript act, Love was defeated for reelection.[43] He had become another North Carolina officer who had lost his command as a result of the conscription law.

Love returned to western North Carolina and began raising companies for a new regiment. His efforts put him in contact with Augustus B. Cowan, who was organizing a company in Rutherford County. Love and Cowan agreed that Cowan's company of soon-to-be recruits would become part of the 62nd North Carolina regiment that Love was creating. Love's efforts to organize the new regiment put him in direct conflict with Captain McRae.

McRae was conducting conscription with the understanding that legal volunteering for all regiments that were not organized on or before April 16, 1862, was to have ceased on July 8 of that year.[44] He interpreted the law to direct that regiments organized after April 16 could not legally recruit men subject to conscription under any circumstances. Men for those regiments were to be supplied exclusively by conscription. Recruiting new regiments in violation of this procedure interfered with state and Confederate efforts to bring the formation of regiments and the assignment of recruits under control.

Both McRae and Mallett were of the opinion that all recruits should pass through the camps of instruction. They knew that men recruited outside the conscription system were often not subjected to the same scrutiny as those passing through the process. Their failure rate after reaching the army was higher. McRae had been sent to western North Carolina to gather men for the Confederate army *and* for the regiment that Mallett had requested. By interfering with the conscription process, Love was impeding both parts of McRae's assignment.

Love was either ignoring the cut-off date or was confused by the fact that notices for more than one such date had been circulated. May 17, July 8, and August 1 had all been given as final dates for volunteering for specific regiments and bypassing enrolling officers. The Confederate government had already fostered considerable confusion by allowing regiments in the field to send recruiting parties to their hometowns to recruit men without passing them through the camps of instruction. These recruiters and those like Robert Love, who were creating new regiments, all used the inevitability and shame of conscription to pressure men into joining their units. In the summer and fall of 1862, there was no clear consensus as to how the volunteer and conscription processes interrelated. Similar confusion existed in other Southern states. A great deal of unintentionally illegal recruiting occurred during this period. However, some officers ignored the law and enlisted any recruits they could attract. Intentionally or otherwise, in the summer of 1862, Colonel Love was in competition with the Bureau of Conscription. Men in western North Carolina would soon be caught up in this dispute.

On July 5, a baby was born at the Thompson farm on Cane Creek in Rutherford County. Thirty-two-year-old Albert G. Thompson nicknamed his new son "Bud." This was the family's fourth child in eight years: Elizabeth was eight years old; Ocran was age six; and Ulola Pandora, called "Dora," was four. Thompson's wife, Mary Catherine, known as "Cate" or "M C," had gotten through this pregnancy without problems. She and the new baby were healthy. Albert Thompson had waited for the birth of this child before taking the final steps to join the Confederate army. He was *not* an enthusiastic volunteer.

Older than the average early-war recruit by almost a decade and with a family that would suffer in his absence, Thompson had no desire to go to war. He was a successful farmer, operated a small roadside store, and owned a slave family, but the realities of his situation were inescapable. The war was not going to end soon. The conscript act was being aggressively enforced in Rutherford and surrounding counties from the camp at Statesville. Thompson was within the conscription age group, was not eligible for any type of exemption, and could not afford to hire a substitute even if he were inclined to do so. It was only a matter of time before he would be enrolled and sent to the camp of instruction and then to the army. He could either wait for the militia officers to come get him, or he could join the company that Augustus Cowan was organizing.

Many of Thompson's friends and neighbors had joined the army early in the war. Most were now in Virginia with the 16th, 34th, and 50th North Carolina regiments. The Long family lived across Cane Creek and several hundred yards down stream from the Thompson farm. Fifty-four-year-old Andrew Baxter Long was a family friend, was an elder at Thompson's church and was in the 16th North Carolina Troops. Nothing that Thompson had heard from Long or the other men had made him eager to enlist. Their letters were filled with reports of food shortages, sickness, and death. Thompson also read the casualty lists in the newspapers. The Union army's Peninsular Campaign had turned eastern Virginia into one large battlefield. Scores of North Carolinians were being killed and wounded at places called Mechanicsville, Savage Station and Malvern Hill.

Thompson had also heard stories about men who had been promised their choice of regiments only to find that when they left the camp of instruction, they had been assigned elsewhere by Major Mallett's bureau.[45] Thompson knew that if he waited to be drafted and tried to join a specific unit, there was no telling where he might be assigned. At least Augustus Cowan was a local man. In Cowan's company, Thompson could serve with neighborhood men, who, like himself, had managed to stay out of the war for more than a year. On July 21, he enlisted in Cowan's company of Colonel Love's 62nd North Carolina Troops. His association with that unit would be short lived.

Captain McRae knew that other Confederate officers were illegally soliciting volunteers among men covered by the conscript law. He knew that these officers were using the threat of conscription as leverage. He had also become convinced that Robert Love, in particular, was knowingly in violation of a widely published order on the subject issued by Major Mallett. This order reiterated war department directives that had been circulated weeks earlier. Some of the men who had been recruited for Love's new regiment were waiting at home for orders to report to their rendezvous point. They were now refusing to report to Camp Hill when ordered to do so by militia officers working with Captain McRae.

As soon as McRae felt he could prove that Colonel Love was disregarding orders governing conscription, he advised Mallett.

Mallett wasted no time in notifying Adjutant & Inspector General Cooper in Richmond:

> Headquarters, Camp of Instruction
> Camp Holmes, Aug. 10, 1862
>
> General:
> I have this day been informed that Col. R. G. A. Love is raising a regiment, composed mainly of Conscripts from the counties of Cherokee and Haywood.
> Has he the authority for raising a regiment by enlisting conscripts? If not, you will please give me an order on him for the men, as I understand the Regiment is about being organized, or has been organized within a few days past.
> This and similar organizations materially interfere with my operations, causing the conscripts to refuse to report themselves at the Camp of Instruction, and even to desert after reaching Camp. Waiting your instructions,
> Major Comding. Post [46]

Richmond reacted three days later. Adjutant and Inspector General Special Orders No. 188 contained seventeen different orders, reassignments, and directives. Item number twelve was the order that Mallett wanted:

> XII. Colonel R. G. A. Love will turn over all the conscripts which he enrolled in his regiment to Peter Mallett, commanding Camp of Instruction at Raleigh, N.C.
>
> By command of the Secretary of War:
> Jno. Withers
> Assistant Adjutant-General

Colonel Love had no choice but to comply with the order. Albert Thompson's status as an improperly recruited member of the 62nd North Carolina Troops was at an end. He was one of a number of soldiers removed from Love's command and enrolled at Camp Hill by Captain McRae.[a]

[a] McRae did not take "all the conscripts" from Colonel Love as Special Order No. 188 directed (*Special Orders, Adjutant and Inspector's Office*, v. 2, p. 343). However, he took a number of those recruited after July 8, 1862. Captain Augustus Cowan and the rest of his company remained in the 62nd North Carolina Troops. Colonel Love's health was not good and he was frequently absent from his regiment. He eventually resigned his commission (Johnston, *Vance Papers*, v. 1, p. 241).

Thompson was chosen to serve in Lieutenant John McRae's Company B of Mallett's battalion. One of Thompson's friends, Alfred C. Cowen, a distant relative of Augustus Cowan, was enrolled by Captain McRae on August 20. Cowen, who left behind his wife, Nancy, and their six-year-old son, William, was also assigned to Company B. Privates Thompson and Cowen began their service in Mallett's battalion guarding the perimeter of Camp Hill, making sure that their friends and neighbors did not desert.

Captain McRae remained at Camp Hill from late summer through early fall. Even while retaining several hundred conscripts for duty in their battalion, he and Mallett operated the most productive conscription bureau in the Confederacy. The secretary of war observed that "Major Mallett and Captain McRae in raising conscripts have been more successful than any other officers. They are sending 400 a day." [47] The increased number of guards at the two camps prevented any more incidents of mass desertion, although individual escapes were occasionally successful. Mallett diverted enough physically fit conscripts to build up the supporting force that would operate away from the camps.

The lack of reliable transportation continued to plague Mallett's efforts during this period. There were still not enough trains available to prevent overcrowding at the camps. An August 22 report lists more than one thousand conscripts present at Camp Hill.[48] The men were kept occupied by their drill instructors. They wrote letters in what little time-off they had, frequently expressing displeasure with their circumstances. One such soldier was a Gaston County conscript named William Dickson. He was living in a tent with five other men. Dickson wrote to his wife and described how the soldiers got passes, went into Statesville, and paid five dollars to have a "likeness" made. He complained that he and the other conscripts were "guarded here day and night with loaded guns." Dickson said that some of the substitutes were being paid as much as three thousand dollars. Cramped tents, the beating of drums, and sounds of passing trains reminded the men of how much their lives had changed.

On August 18, one of Dickson's tentmates, Marion L. Holland, wrote to his wife, Margaret, and described how some of the conscripts were getting ready to join regiments in Virginia while others were being selected to join Mallets camp guard battalion:

> Dear Wife
> I once more Seat myself to write you a few lines.... we have

orders to prepare three days rations to go to gordonsville va.... our company has just been caled together by the agetant [adjutant] from the Thirty Seventh regiment and give us orders to have our rations ready by three Oclock tomorrow morning Laban Quinn Chilian Bradley [and] Ben Bradley... will be left here with the special guard.... Margaret if [it] is gods will that I may never meet you and my children in this world I want us to live so we will meet in a world where there is no wars nor rumor of wars and whare we will have peace and hapiness I will have to stop riting for we have cooking to do and everything to pack up

M. A. Holland [a]

While the enrollments had produced a flood of conscripts in July and part of August, as September approached, the number of men reporting for induction dwindled to a steady and more predictable number.[b] Militia officers were still sending enrollees to the camps, but more often they were having to visit local communities and bring men in as opposed to simply putting a notice in the newspapers. Authorities were doing a better job of coordinating trains leaving from Raleigh for Virginia, although there were still occasional delays at Camp Hill. The number of conscripts at Camp Holmes was reduced to those being processed, awaiting legal or medical decisions, and those under arrest. Mallett saw an opportunity to reduce the costs of his bureau by consolidating two parts of its operation.

[a] An old copy of the original Dickson letter is in the possession of Mr. O. C. Stonestreet of Statesville, North Carolina, and is used with his permission. Three of the soldiers mentioned in Private Holland's letter, J. L. Quinn, Chilson Bradley, and B. G. Bradley served in Company D of Mallett's battalion *(Compiled Military Service Records of Confederate Soldiers* at the National Archives. The Holland letter is quoted through the courtesy of the Gaston County Museum of Art & History). The other soldiers went to the 37th North Carolina Troops. William Dickson was wounded at Gettysburg and, later, captured at Petersburg. He survived the war. Marion Holland was captured in Virginia in May 1864 and died three months later at the Point Lookout prisoner of war camp in Maryland (*North Carolina Troops 1861-1865 A Roster, v. IX, p. 571 and p. 573*).

[b] One "conscript" that arrived at Camp Holmes during this period was discovered to be a woman disguised as a man. She told authorities that she "had determined to accompany her friends in the perils of war, and avenge the death of a brother who fell in the fight near Richmond" (*Asheville News,* August 21, 1862).

He decided that the number of conscripts reporting for duty was no longer sufficient to justify two camps of instruction.[49] In addition, he had not received permission from the war department for the regiment that he wanted to guard both camps and to adequately staff his supporting force companies. He would have to accomplish his mission with a six-company infantry battalion and no cavalry.

Mallett sent word of his decision to Captain McRae in late August:

> Headquarters Camp of Instruction
> Camp Holmes, August 25, 1862
>
> Captain:
> Yours of the 20th instant is received.... In the meantime I shall make arrangements for discontinuing the Camp there as soon as practicable, and wish you to make all your arrangements accordingly. By thus consolidating the Camps, it will doubtless enable us to work more advantageously and with less trouble and confusion, now that the rush on both is over.
>
> Very respectfully,
> Peter Mallett
> Major & A.A.G. [50]

One week later Mallett reiterated his order and gave his captain an additional assignment:

> Headquarters Camp of Instruction
> Camp Holmes, Sept. 2nd, 1862
>
> Captain:
> Your communication of the 29th ult. is received.... You will use every effort as heretofore in bringing into Camp all the Conscripts you can get, and direct them to be sent here. You will discontinue the Camp at Statesville as soon as possible by sending the men here now in camp (unless ready to send off), and direct those arriving daily to proceed to this Camp. As soon as practicable you will take command of Co. "A" sent from this Camp, and proceed to Wilkes Co., to assist... in enrolling, and quell any outbreak or disloyal proceedings: arrest all deserters, and bring by force those refusing to obey the law. You will report weekly to these Headquarters.

Before proceeding to Wilkes, you will forward to this Camp a full report of men received, where from, to what Regt. sent, discharges, and desertions, to the 1st instant.

Very respectfully,
Your Obt. Servant
Major & A.A.G. [51]

Captain McRae had at his disposal the guards from Camp Hill and Company A of the Camp Holmes battalion to use in the sweep through Wilkes County. The mood of the population in this part of the state had started to turn against the Confederacy early in the war. This type of independent, company size assignment far from the camps would become routine for Mallett's company commanders. Mallett had foreseen this situation when he requested a full regiment and two cavalry companies.

Cate Thompson wrote to Albert when she heard that he and Alfred Cowen had been transferred from Camp Hill. She suggested a name for their new baby and informed him that their slave woman, Letty, had given birth to a son:

Rutherford Co N C Sept the 21

My Dear Companion I take my seat to answer your welcome letter which came to hand last Wednesday I was sorry to heare that you had not been well I was sorry to heare that you were gone from Stasville They will take you from one place to another untill they get you too the wors place of any perhaps you had better gone with Cowan [Captain Augustus Cowan] his men get to come home every once inawhile.... [Andrew] Baxter Long got wounded in the last battle.... all I want is for you all to get home and then I would be happy We are all well except Letty she had a fine son yesterday She had a hard time but is doing very well since She calls her babe Humbolt King buds name is William Albert Worth if you are willing he ways 15 pounds I started you a letter last Tuesday I do not know wether you will get it or not.... I must come to a close you know I have a heape to do just now put your whole trust in God may the Lord bless you....

M. C. Thompson

By September, incidents of noncompliance and outright resistance to conscription were becoming more frequent, especially in the mountains and foothills. Militia officers were having more difficulty locating conscripts and had to bring many of them in by force. Assaults on enrolling officers were common. Militia officers knew that the previous governor, Henry Clark, and Major Mallett had disagreed on the level of militia participation. Clark had said that he did not intend for militia officers to forcibly enroll and transport conscripts, but that they should only make cooperative conscripts available for the process. Mallett's orders seemed to require more. The increasing resistance made this a matter of grave concern to militia officers who needed legal justification to arrest resisters.

Governor Vance settled the question on September 13 when he issued General Order No. 7. He ordered militia colonels and their subordinates to physically deliver conscripts to Camp Holmes and granted them all necessary authority to do so. It also authorized courts marshal for militia officers who failed in this duty.[a] The order clarified militia officers' authority in the face of growing public opposition to compulsory military service.

North Carolinians who were considering evasion or resistance were emboldened by the activities of influential opponents of conscription. A prominent Raleigh newspaper, the *North Carolina Standard,* had gone on record against conscription from the very beginning, referring to the law as a "monstrous and dangerous measure."[52] An anti-conscription, anti-Confederacy, pro-Union culture began to take shape in parts of North Carolina, as well as in other Southern states.

[a] The militia's administrative network and newspaper publication of orders provided a reasonably rapid transmission of orders from the governor to local militia officers. Militia colonels throughout the state were issuing instructions to their captains for local enforcement of General Order No. 7 by September 22 as evidenced by a surviving hand written copy from Colonel B. G. Brown of the 86th North Carolina Militia regiment. The order is addressed to Mecklenburg County Captain Thomas Glewas. The document is held in the Latta Plantation historic site collection near Huntersville through the generosity of the Gluyas family. Governor Vance wanted North Carolinians to enforce conscription in his state, not Confederate officers from other states (Johnston, *Vance Papers*, v. 1, p. 176).

Amid these circumstances, Governor Vance took a firm public stand. His proclamation of September 18 revealed the seriousness of the situation and tried to shore up support for those charged with enforcing the unpopular law:

> A PROCLAMATION BY Z. B. VANCE
> GOVERNOR OF NORTH CAROLINA
>
> Whereas information has reached me that certain persons, unmindful of the calls of patriotism & forgetful of the duties of good citizens, are using their influence to prevent obedience to the law of Congress, known as the Conscription Law, and that others are attempting to organize an open resistance to its execution: whereas: such conduct, being not only in direct violation of the law, but also detrimental in the highest degree to the cause of our country, it becomes my sacred duty to prevent & repress the same by all the means in my power.
>
> Now, therefore, I, ZEBULON B. VANCE, Governor of North Carolina, do issue this my proclamation, warning all such persons to desist from such unpatriotic & criminal conduct: earnestly hoping that all, who are disinclined to defend their homes themselves, either by reason of age, infirmity or cowardice will cease to dissuade those who are willing: and notifying positively all persons contemplating an armed resistance to the law, if there really be any such misguided & and evil-disposed persons in our midst, that they will commit the crime of treason according to the laws of Congress, and must not expect to escape its penalties- Whilst thousands upon thousands of our best & bravest have obeyed the law & by their patriotic valor have driven the enemy back to the Potomac, it would be an intolerable outrage upon them, to permit others to shirk or evade the law, or worse still, to resist it by open violence. Let no one therefore be deceived, the law will be enforced, & I appeal to all loyal & patriotic citizens to sustain those who are charged with its execution.
>
> Given under my hand and attested by the Great Seal of the State- Done at the City of Raleigh the 18th day of September 1862.
>
> Zebulon B. Vance [53]

As Governor Vance was writing his proclamation, the battle of Antietam near Sharpsburg, Maryland, was raging. North Carolina soldiers, many only recently conscripted, suffered heavy casualties in the Confederacy's first attempt to invade the North.

As the public's mood against conscription deepened, Mallett went ahead with plans to streamline his bureau. Camp Hill was closed in September although the bureau would maintain a limited presence there until the end of the year. Thompson, Cowen, and the other conscript guards from Camp Hill arrived in Raleigh and began building their barracks. Like the conscripts they guarded, Mallett's soldiers lived in tents while they built permanent quarters.

Mallett's men worked on construction projects, stood guard on the camp's perimeter and guardhouse, and escorted groups of conscripts to Virginia. They also kept busy with the routine of life at a military base: camp maintenance, company and battalion drills, barracks inspections, morning roll-call, evening dress parade, and weekly uniform and equipment inspections. Occasionally, they were called upon to provide honor guards at funerals for high ranking North Carolina officers who had been killed in Virginia. They also had to do combat with hundreds of rats that infested the camp, especially around the stables.

The city of Raleigh provided Mallett's officers with opportunities to purchase additional clothing and have their uniforms tailor-made. The *Raleigh Register* and other newspapers carried advertisements placed by local merchants for socks, drawers, shirts, shoes, blankets, and more. At M. Grauseman's Large Military and Civil Clothing Manufactory, officers could purchase cloth for uniforms in "North Carolina Gray," "Confederate Gray Cloth," and "Confederate Sky Blue Cloth - very fine." From W. L. Pomeroy's mail-order bookstore, officers could buy the latest in military manuals, including "Hardee's Tactics" by W. J. Hardee, "Bayonet Exercise and Skirmishers Drill" by R. Milton Cary, and "Gilham's Manual for the Volunteers and Militia of the Confederate States."[54] A somewhat less stylish commercial district grew up near Camp Holmes. There, soldiers could buy food, soap, candles, writing material, and personal items that could make camp life more comfortable.

Raleigh's soaring wartime population spurred commercial activity and created a boom-town atmosphere. Thousands of troops traveling back and forth between Virginia and the Deep South passed through the city. The influx of thousands of men, many away from home for the first time, also fueled commercial activity of a less desirable nature. Newspapers reported on soldiers' misadventures in the less fashionable parts of Raleigh. Life in an army camp town could be dangerous:

> FATAL AFFRAY
>
> An affray occurred at a house of ill-fame near the Central Depot in this city on Friday last, by which two men lost their lives. A man named James Robinson, a conscript substitute, ripped out the bowels of a soldier named Willoghby Davis, a member of the 56th regiment, when he, in turn was instantly shot dead by one of Davis' companions. Davis lived but a short while after being carried to the hospital.[55]

While killings were not common, barroom brawls, public drunkenness, and disorderly conduct by soldiers were frequent. Deserters from anywhere in the South could be found in Raleigh. Mallett realized that proper policing of the city was in the best interests of accomplishing his mission. He would soon have to help keep Raleigh under control.

Comparatively naive men from remote parts of North Carolina were exposed to the unique coarseness that army life generated. On one occasion, Thompson wrote to Cate saying, "I have seen so much of the badness of man and woman that I am worse than ever on the thoughts of the like." He related an incident involving a prisoner in the guardhouse who was visited by two women who "come in and hang round him and set in his lap.... then in a few days here come his wife...." Thompson felt sorry for the wife, "for she look like she was a lady." He promised Cate that he would "rather bin ded" than to have her think of him acting that way. [56]

Camp Holmes was tolerable for soldiers who did their work and kept out of trouble. The camp stayed busy as men from all around the state were brought in. Thompson and Cowen often had the opportunity to visit with Rutherford County soldiers who were passing through. Eight such men had joined Colonel Love's 62nd North Carolina Troops during the summer. They had stayed with that unit when Thompson left, but they now arrived in Raleigh as prisoners. Ben Lovelace, Drury Greene, Albert Toney, and five other Rutherford County men were locked-up in the Camp Holmes guardhouse, charged with desertion.[57]

The Confederate Congress made a series of adjustments to the conscription laws in September and October. President Davis was authorized to extend the upper draft age limit from thirty-five to forty-five years of age. An examining board of three surgeons was to be appointed for each congressional district. A large number of job exemptions were added in order to increase wartime production. Workers in a variety of manufacturing and agricultural occupations were exempted from military service, provided that their employers complied with government price controls. Among those exempted were shipbuilders, factory owners, miners, tanners, salt producers, postal workers, railroad employees, blacksmiths, and mechanics. Plantation overseers who were responsible for twenty or more slaves were exempted under certain conditions, as were several religious groups upon the payment of an exemption fee.[58]

These changes reflected the Confederacy's need for comprehensive management of its resources. The first conscription law did not provide enough exemptions or production coordination for a national war effort. The result was an avalanche of requests for deferment from military service, each having to be investigated and ruled upon. The new procedures were intended to provide a systematic solution to this problem. On the negative side, if abused, these exemptions could provide thousands of legal hiding places for the growing number of men wishing to avoid military service.

While congress enlarged and strengthened the bureaucracy, Major Mallett was trying to build a positive relationship with Governor Vance. Relations between the two men were strained by the on-going controversy over the assignment of North Carolina conscripts to regiments in the field. Mallett was caught in the middle of this problem. He knew that without Vance's help and goodwill, his job would be next to impossible. He occasionally called on the governor in Raleigh. By early October, Mallett felt confident enough about the condition of his camp and battalion to send the governor an invitation:

> Headquarters Camp of Instruction
> Camp Holmes, October 2nd, 1862
>
> Sir:
>
> In my hurry this morning I neglected to invite you to the Camp. I shall feel highly honored and particularly gratified if you will do me the favor of coming out to dress parade this evening about 5 o'clock.
>
> You have never seen the Battalion and as you propose visiting Richmond tomorrow, I shall regard it as a compliment and personal favor if you can conveniently comply with my request.[59]

While Mallett maneuvered to have the governor take a favorable impression of the North Carolina Conscript Bureau to Richmond, Albert Thompson found time to write home. He mentioned one of the recent changes in the conscription law and described conditions at the camp:

> Camp Holmes Near Raleigh Octo the 26 1862
> My Dear Cate I with much pleasure take my seat this Sabbath morning to answer your very welcome letter which came to hand the 24 inst.[this month].... I would be glad to come home and see you once more and get a straw tic to lion for we have not got blankets to keep us warm.... We have commence clearing of a new camp to put up winter quarters we are going to make little cabbons to stay in this winter We will have a heap to do now for a while.... I want you to knit me a pair of gloves and send them to me.... M C you may tell the rest of the men they will have to come from 18 to 40.... I am on duty to day and have just come in out of the rain and am about half wet and cold....

Thompson's acceptance of his situation was not shared by all of the men in the battalion. As the weather turned colder, conditions in the camp became more harsh. Most of the soldiers were still living in tents. There was a shortage of shoes and winter clothing, especially among poor soldiers. Mallett often had to furlough men for the sole purpose of obtaining additional clothing. Governor Vance ordered every militia captain in the state to visit each family in his district to purchase or accept donations of clothing, shoes, blankets, and socks for needy soldiers.[60] Letters home during this period often spoke of the hard times. N. N. Patterson of Company D was not happy with life at the camp:

> Camp Holmes, Raleigh, N.C.
> Nov 15th 1862
> Dear Sister Mary Ann
> I am on the sick list today I never will be able to stand Camp life we are treated wors than mangy dogs we don't get anything to eat hardly.... the soldiers are talking of killing the hogs that stay round the camp....[61]

The soldiers hurried to complete their living quarters as an unusually cold winter set in. With their other duties, this work fell behind schedule. Dozens of soldiers had to be detailed to unload and distribute the large amounts of fuel consumed by the camp. Firewood was needed to cook meals, heat buildings, and supply campfires for the soldiers still living in tents. Wood was unloaded from railroad cars nearby and brought to the camp in wagons. Fuel costs were part of the annual operating expenses of the camp. The amount of fuel consumed each month had to be recorded and justified. Since camps of instruction were authorized by an act of congress, the Confederate government had to approve all expenditures and authorize the payment of bills.

Major Mallett saw little need for a rigid distinction between the two functions of his battalion, at least where the enlisted men were concerned. The camp guard and supporting force needed to trade men back and forth even though the assignments had different responsibilities. This flexibility allowed the two assignments to draw men from each other as needed. Less capable or sickly men could be directed toward less demanding tasks. Eighty soldiers were needed to secure the camp perimeter and watch the guardhouse around the clock: forty on duty at a time. While on duty, the guards carried shotguns or muskets loaded with buckshot and were issued ponchos and special "guard caps" for inclement weather.[a]

While Mallett directed the conscripting and enrolling functions of his bureau, he put Captain McRae in charge of the camp and escorts. McRae charged his lieutenants with the daily supervision of the camp guard. A differentiation of assignments was more necessary for officers than for the enlisted men. While officers were held responsible for specific tasks, it was not uncommon for an enlisted man to work a shift at a guard post, have eight hours off, then be sent to Richmond with a group of conscripts. The number of men present in camp in Mallett's companies at any given time fluctuated significantly due to these assignments. The number of conscripts in camp also varied from several thousand during the summer to just a few dozen at times during the fall.

Mallett's soldiers organized themselves into small groups of "messmates." Messes were informal groups of from four to eight men and were also common in field armies. The typical mess at Camp Holmes consisted of several soldiers who served in the same

[a] An ordnance records book (North Carolina Archives, AG No. 27, p. 254) shows that ordnance issues at Camp Holmes often list buckshot and "shotgun percussion caps." A Special Requisition Form 40 signed by Captain McRae on Jan. 21, 1863, is for forty ponchos and forty guard hats.

company, lived in the same tent or cabin, and shared cooking and cleaning responsibilities.[a]

In late November, Thompson wrote to his family and described part of the military routine that would be his life for the foreseeable future:

> Camp Holmes Near Raleigh November the 27 1862
> My dear wife and children.... I received your letter this morning which cherd me up.... If we cannot see each other I want us to still write to eachother.... Sunday is as bisey a day as we have here we have to put... cleane close in [our] Knapsack[s] and march out to the field and there be inspected I went up and tried for a furlow he said he would give me one in a few days but that is the chat always

Thompson was growing accustomed to the army routine and to the fact that his company officers, and the more distant battalion officers, controlled his life with their pronouncements. The voice of one officer in particular, Lieutenant E. N. Mann, became familiar to Thompson and the rest of the camp. Major Mallett had appointed Mann to be the battalion adjutant. As such, he addressed the soldiers during morning formations, evening parades, and at Sunday inspections, passing along daily orders and information. According to army regulations, the adjutant is an administrative assistant to the commander. He maintains personnel files, attends to much of the routine paperwork, and acts as an intermediary in order to insure good communications between the company commanders and the battalion commander. Although there is no such thing as a non-combatant in an infantry battalion, Mann's position as adjutant was as close as any.

The September and October conscription law revisions were implemented by General Order No. 82 from the adjutant and inspector general's office on November 3. The expanded list of deferments from military service increased the administrative workload for enrolling officers as thousands of men all over the Confederacy began applying for job-related deferments. Another procedural change gave the commander of the Trans-Mississippi region authority over conscription that was not granted to generals east of the Mississippi River. East of the Mississippi, commandants of conscription, like Mallett, continued to bypass area generals and report to the secretary

[a] Albert Thompson's messmates were Alfred Cowen, Caleb Goodnight, Joseph Scoggins, N. F. Butler, William Walker, and W. A. Davis.

of war through the adjutant and inspector general's office. This distinction would later prove to be significant.

Mallett was ultimately responsible to the secretary of war, but he was almost entirely dependent on the governor and the state's adjutant general for the militia officers who enforced conscript laws at the local level. While his bureau headquarters was at Camp Holmes along with the camp's administrative offices, Mallett was spending more and more time in Raleigh maintaining his relationship with state government. Changes made by congress in the conscription process would soon begin to reduce part of this dependency.

North Carolina militia officers had gathered all of the eighteen-through thirty-five-year-old men that had been enrolled in the president's first call. But reliance on the militia had not worked well in several other states. As resistance to conscription increased, militia officers in North Carolina and elsewhere were often assaulted and occasionally killed. Many of them became less inclined to clash with their neighbors over the unpopular law.

The adjutant and inspector general's November orders required state commandants to assign three surgeons and an army officer to each congressional district. In North Carolina, this meant ten such officers and thirty surgeons. The commandants were also authorized to assign disabled enlisted men to each county, city, or town for conscription duty. The transfer of men from the field to the conscript bureau had to be made by the "commanding generals of armies in the field." They were to order disabled, but otherwise qualified officers and men to "report to the commandant of conscripts in their respective States...." [62] These disabled soldiers would eventually replace the militia officers. The change-over would take some time to complete, but Mallett could foresee a time when most local conscription work would be done by native North Carolina Confederate officers and enlisted men who were under his command, not by militia officers controlled by the governor. The militia officers had done an excellent job in North Carolina, but their ability to operate in the increasingly hostile environment was eroding.

Mallett was promoted to colonel in November.[a] In December, he began appointing the ten disabled captains and thirty surgeons that the recent changes required. He also had to implement President

[a] Mallett's promotion was never confirmed by the Senate, but he was not informed to revert to the rank of major until after June 1864. Former North Carolina Governor, U.S. Senator, and Confederate Attorney General Thomas Bragg interceded on Mallett's behalf (Johnston, *Vance Papers*, v. 1, p. 175).

Davis's next call up of conscripts, those between thirty-five and forty years of age, on December 20.[a] Militia officers would handle this call as they had the first one. Mallett issued his orders during the last week of November:

> HEADQUARTERS, CAMP OF INSTRUCTION
> CAMP HOLMES,
> November 29, 1862. SPECIAL ORDERS, NO. 12
>
> I. Commanding officers of militia regiments are required to assemble all persons subject to the provisions of the Act entitled, "An Act to amend an Act to provide further for the public defense," approved September 26, 1862 and enroll the same.
>
> II. An enrolling officer and an examining board will be appointed for each congressional district, who will give due notice to commanding officers of regiments to bring the conscripts to the county seats of their respective counties for examination. Immediately upon examination, the said commanding officers of regiments will conduct all conscripts not having received certificate of exemption, to the camp of instruction near Raleigh.
>
> III. All persons who may desire to volunteer must do so before December 20, the day set apart for enrollment, and must join companies which were in the service of the Confederate States on April 16, 1862.
>
> IV. Applications for exemption must, in all cases, be made to the enrolling officer of the district, duplicate copies of said application being made in writing, duly sworn to before an acting Justice of the Peace, and bearing the certificate of the clerk of the court, given under the county seal and sent through the colonel of the regiment. An appeal may be taken from the decision of the enrolling officer to the Commandant of Conscripts.
>
> V. All conscripts engaged on government works will be enrolled and returned to their said work.
>
> In issuing the above orders for the enrollment of conscripts between the ages of eighteen and forty, the commandant avails himself of the opportunity to thank the state officers for their untiring and laborious efforts in the discharge of their duties and the efficient and ready assistance rendered to him in their official capacity heretofore.

[a] The new conscription law authorized President Davis to call all non-exempt men up to the age of forty-five into military service. He chose to only to take those up to age forty at this time. The law also allowed for a brief period of voluntary enlistment in companies of the recruit's choice.

> The importance and absolute necessity of renewed energy and prompt action in executing these orders faithfully is fully expressed in His Excellency Governor (Zebulon Baird) Vance's General Orders No. 10.
>
> The efficiency of the army and the safety of our country depends in a great measure upon their faithful discharge of these duties.
>
> By order of,
Colonel Peter Mallett,
Commandant of Conscripts in North Carolina,
E. N. Mann
Adjutant.[63]

The process that was to be used on December 20 was essentially the same as the first enrollment. Colonel Mallett instructed the militia colonels to have their regiments gather at designated times and places, usually long-established militia parade grounds or county seats. Notifications were placed in newspapers throughout the state. Militia captains and lieutenants made sure that the population within their geographic areas of responsibility was notified. The conscripts were assembled, given medical examinations, and afforded the opportunity of applying for exemptions or work related deferments called "details." Those who were not excused for medical, religious, or job related reasons were transported to the camp of instruction. Upon arrival at camp, the conscript's name, where, when, and by whom enrolled were recorded, along with his physical description, known as a "descriptive list." Each recruit was given a final medical exam and vaccinated. Any particular suitability for assignment to the cavalry, artillery, or navy was determined. He was then issued a uniform and non-ordnance equipment: knapsack, canteen, blanket and haversack.[a] Groups of conscripts were then assigned to members of the camp guard, who accompanied them on the trip to Virginia. Depending on train schedules, the recruits' stay at the camp of instruction was usually only a few days.

This was a much shorter process than originally intended by the adjutant and inspector general. Gone were the days when newly organized regiments could be sent to the coast for several weeks of training and acclimation prior to being sent to the seat of war. When he assumed that the training process for conscripts would be same

[a] Conscripts were not issued their stand-of-arms or ammunition until they arrived at their regiments in the field.

as for the volunteers of 1861, the adjutant and inspector general had authorized camps of instruction to be staffed with drill instructors to teach companies and regiments of recruits the skills of soldiering. However, the immediate need for troops in Virginia during and after the Peninsular Campaign and the Confederacy's decision to maintain troop strength in existing regiments rather than organize new ones eliminated most of the instructional responsibilities of the camps. Conscripts were pushed through the system as quickly as possible.[a] The novice soldier learned his trade on the job under the watchful eyes of hardened veterans.

The camps of instruction became processing centers that collected, guarded, outfitted, and escorted conscripts. This shortened process was much more efficient than the initial plan. Replacement soldiers were delivered to depleted regiments more quickly, guards could more easily and safely escort small groups of conscripts over the long distances involved, and small groups or individual conscripts were less likely to voice anti-conscription and anti-government attitudes in their new units. They arrived as strangers, outnumbered by veterans who had developed a culture of discipline and conformity.

The shortened process was not without its disadvantages. The brief period of time between enrollment and assignment in the field meant that soldiers arrived in their new units without having contracted the usual camp diseases. Many of them became ill within a few weeks of their arrival and had to be cared for in the field, where many of them died. Others were sent to Richmond for treatment. Hundreds of others had to be given medical furloughs and sent back home, taking up needed bed space in wayside hospitals along the railroad lines.[b]

However, the timing of this change in the responsibilities for the camps of instruction was fortuitous. Increasing desertion and

---

[a] During the Peninsular Campaign, then Secretary of War Randolph contacted Mallett and the conscription commandants in Virginia, South Carolina, and Georgia. He ordered them to send conscripts to Richmond "as rapidly as you can get them in. We have no time now to prepare them for the field...." He also recommended that drill instructors be sent along with the untrained troops (*O.R.*, Series I, v. 11, pt. 3, p. 631).

[b] Conscripts sent to the 37th North Carolina Troops in September of 1862 serve as an example of this problem. Twenty-two percent of them died of disease during their first twelve months in the army (Hardy, *The Thirty-Seventh North Carolina Troops*, p. 104).

conscription resistance necessitated a reallocation of resources by state commandants. The reduction in the need for drill masters occurred simultaneously with the rising need for officers in the camp guard and supporting forces. Supporting forces needed to be strengthened for deserter-gathering operations that often required one or more companies to be sent away from camp. Captain James C. McRae had already conducted one such operation the previous September in Wilkes County. This altered job description for Mallett's battalion would not be last such change.

Early in November, Mallett decided to go after deserters and resisters in Alamance and Chatham counties, just west of Raleigh. He intended to personally lead the mission and wanted it completed well ahead of the conscripts who would arrive at Camp Holmes beginning on December 20. He selected two companies for the assignment and issued the orders:

> Headquarters Camp Holmes
> November 3rd, 1862
> Lieut. Thos. S. Robards
> Comding. "Co. D"
>
> Lieut:
>
> You will receive today two weeks rations for your men. On Wednesday you will start towards Chatham County taking with you guides from the Alamance [Militia] Regiment and request the Colonel of the Regiment to accompany you and assist in arresting conscripts in his regiment. He will also order his company officers to accompany and assist you through their districts, or further if necessary. On Thursday morning you will commence operations in Chatham. As far as possible make all conscripts whom you arrest, furnish their own rations. You will send immediately upon reaching Chatham to the Company officers of the Chatham militia, requiring them to meet you with guides and assist you. You will endeavor to drive the whole Country as you advance into Chatham, arresting all men between 18 and 35 who have not satisfactory papers, and who are able to come to Camp. Incline toward your left, so as to form a junction with [me] on Friday or Saturday. I will march in through the country from Durham's, and will communicate with you probably on Thursday. Do not send off squads of less than ten men and place them under the most reliable officers or non

commissioned officers whom you have. Instruct your men to be kind to everyone and treat all the inhabitants with the greatest circumspection. Any act of Wantonness on their part will punished with the greatest severity.

It is to be hoped, as it is believed, that they will conduct themselves in a dignified manner, worthy of soldiers of the Confederate States Army.

By order of Major Mallett

P.S. Let the conscripts know that if they report themselves to you, they will be well treated, but that you intend to take them at all hazards.[64]

Mallett's professional and commonsense approach to conscription enforcement was evident in the wording of his orders. Even so, "Wantonness" would soon enough become commonplace in the conscription business.

While their colonel was in Chatham County, most of Albert Thompson's company remained at camp. Albert wrote to Cate and gave her all the news:

Camp Holmes Near Raleigh Nov. the 19 1862

My Dear wife and children.... I am well and at Raleigh yet but don't know how long I will stay here There is too companies gon out to hunt up conscripts now but we are still here yet.... I received your letter the 16 of November I would have answer your letter before now but I was gon to Richmond with some prisoners and got detained I started on Tuesday and return on Sunday.... We have got our houses up but not covered You was writing to me something about when I thought peace would be made I don't beleave peace will be made till Linkons time is out.... We are all well except Scoggins and Goodnight and they are in the hospital in Raleigh I heard the other day that Sam Norville had run away from his regiment They are bringing in runaways every day here we have some twelve or fifteen in the gard house at this time We have some thirty negros here that was taken from there masters There masters was to thick with the yankey they was selling cotton to the yankey and while they was gone with there stuff to the yankey we got there negros and are going to sell them and put it to the use of

> the government There was one of the little negros died this morning with the sore throat.... [a]

Even in the midst of busy Camp Holmes with its deserters and sickness and no roofs on the cabins, Thompson considered himself to be comparatively fortunate. On November 20, a young relative of Joseph Scoggins, one of Thompson's messmates, was passing through Raleigh heading back home to western North Carolina. Seventeen-year-old John Scoggins was an early-war volunteer who was being discharged from the army for being underage, as allowed by the conscript act.[65] While Thompson and others in Mallett's battalion were still living in tents because their cabins weren't finished, young Scoggins reminded them that his regiment, the 34th North Carolina Troops, had neither cabins nor tents.

As Mallett completed his Chatham County operation and Camp Holmes was readied for the call-up of conscripts planned for December 20, the Union army was preparing to attack inland. This move would seek to accomplish an objective that had been set almost a year earlier: the destruction of the railroad bridge at Goldsboro.

In the ten months since the capture of Roanoke Island on February 8, 1862, the Union army had made steady progress along the North Carolina coast and had mounted a second attempt to take Richmond. Edenton, North Carolina, was captured in February. New Bern fell on March 14. The towns of Washington and Morehead City were occupied later in March. Three thousand Union soldiers were sent to obstruct the canal system that connected the Virginia and North Carolina waterways in April. They were defeated by the 3rd Georgia Infantry and the First Brigade of the North Carolina Militia at the battle of South Mills.[66] Fort Macon, near Morehead City, surrendered to Union forces on April 26 after a thirty-four day siege.

General Burnside established a base of operations at New Bern. While Burnside fortified New Bern, General McClellan landed one hundred and twelve thousand Union troops on the Virginia peninsula in March, waited for the weather to clear, then began his move toward Richmond on April 4. It was the presence of this huge army and its movement toward the capitol that had compelled the Confederate Congress to pass the first conscription act. McClellan wasted so much time laying siege to Yorktown that General Joseph Johnston was able

[a] John Samuel Norville, a Rutherford County conscript and Thompson family friend, was returned to the 35th North Carolina Troops. Captured later in the war, he died in the prison camp at Elmira, New York (*Roster*, v. IX, p. 447).

to assemble a sixty thousand man force between the Union army and Richmond. Many of these Confederates had been kept in the army by the conscription law, and additional untrained conscripts were rushed to Richmond directly from the camps of instruction.[a]

At the same time, General Burnside was ordered to push inland from New Bern toward Goldsboro in support of McClellan's Peninsular Campaign. The Union plan was for McClellan to defeat the Confederates at Richmond. If the Confederate army escaped, McClellan was to push them south as they retreated along the railroad lines. He could trap them near Raleigh or Goldsboro as Burnside's troops advanced from the coast. Burnside's movement was also intended to keep Confederate troops in North Carolina tied up defending Goldsboro rather than being sent to assist Johnston on the peninsula.[67]

The Union plan went well, albeit slowly. General Johnston's outnumbered Confederates fought delaying actions until May 31, when they attacked the divided Union forces at Fair Oaks, Virginia. Johnston was wounded in the fighting and was replaced the next day by General Robert E. Lee, who had been serving as a military advisor to President Davis. The two armies maneuvered against each other during the month of June until Lee attacked at Mechanicsville on June 26. The Confederate plan was poorly executed, and the fighting ended after nightfall. The next day, Lee attacked at Gaines's Mill, where poor coordination again thwarted his plan. The result was a total of fifteen thousand casualties for the two armies. Lee continued to maneuver and struck at the now retreating Union forces at Savage Station on June 29 and again at Frayser's Farm the next day. McClellan, now thoroughly intimidated, pulled his forces back and occupied a strong defensive position on Malvern Hill.

During the last part of the Peninsular Campaign, President Lincoln became fearful of a complete disaster. In early July, he ordered General Burnside to cancel his push toward Goldsboro and instead sail from New Bern with part of his army to reinforce the hard-pressed McClellan. Rather than meeting McClellan's victorious army near Raleigh, Burnside was being sent to save him from destruction at the hands of Robert E. Lee. Burnside put General John

---

[a] It is likely that without the first conscription law keeping the one-year volunteers in service through this period, the Confederate army would have disintegrated as it retreated up the peninsula. The war could have ended with the Union occupation of Richmond by mid-summer.

Foster in command of the Union troops that remained at New Bern and sailed for Virginia with seven thousand men.

On July 1, the Confederates attacked Malvern Hill. Lee's continuing inability to coordinate his forces resulted in five thousand more Southern casualties, bringing the campaign's totals to more than twenty thousand Confederates killed, wounded, and captured. There were more than fifteen thousand Union casualties. McClellan had been sufficiently battered. He retreated to Harrison's Landing and dug in. What had started out as McClellan's long awaited campaign to take Richmond ended up with victorious Confederate regiments, many from North Carolina, having "Seven Days Around Richmond" painted on their battle flags. The Union plan of attacking Goldsboro in support of a Virginia offensive would have to wait. During the Peninsular Campaign and for the remainder of the summer, conscription began to supply thousands of additional troops to Lee's army. The North's best opportunity to win a short war was gone.

General Foster, with the New Bern garrison reduced to approximately nine thousand men, began conducting raids along the North Carolina coast. He also employed hundreds of African-Americans as laborers to further improve defenses around the town. When complete, these fortifications were considered to be practically impregnable, consisting of cleared flat lands, impassable swamps, and well-placed artillery positions, all under the protection of Union gunboats. The town was so well protected that President Lincoln appointed a Military Governor of North Carolina who made New Bern his "capitol." The army also established a rendezvous to recruit North Carolinians who wanted to fight for the Union.[a] As Foster was reinforced and became more aggressive, he pushed considerable distances inland, using the rivers and the Union navy for transportation and support.

Governor Vance called on the Confederacy to expel the invaders, but General Lee would not weaken his army in order to push Foster out of the state. A number of North Carolina towns were attacked, and a great deal of property damage was inflicted. North Carolinians, already displeased with the Confederate government over conscription, could not understand why such a large part of their state was being left defenseless while Peter Mallett sent even more

---

[a] The Union army established recruiting centers in all areas of the occupied South. By the end of the war, more than three thousand white and five thousand African-American North Carolinians had been recruited to fight for the Union (McCaslin, *Portraits in Conflict*, p. 44).

North Carolinians to Lee's army. They knew that of the fifty-three regiments North Carolina had contributed to the war effort, all but six of them had been sent to Virginia.[68]

Several thousand more troops were sent to Foster during the fall of 1862. By December, his army was again preparing to act in concert with a Virginia offensive. This time, the plan called for the Army of the Potomac, now under the command of General Burnside, to attack Lee's Army of Northern Virginia at Fredericksburg.[a]

Union forces at New Bern were again ordered to advance on Goldsboro. They were to move as rapidly as possible, keep Confederate forces occupied, and burn the railroad bridge near town. Destruction of the bridge would prevent North and South Carolina troops from reinforcing Lee's army. In conjunction with the land force, a small fleet of gunboats was to steam up the Neuse River on Foster's far right flank as he advanced.

If Union forces were successful at both Fredericksburg and Goldsboro, Foster could go on to Raleigh or turn and strike at Wilmington. If General Burnside failed at Fredericksburg and both Union armies had to withdraw, the destruction of the railroad bridge at Goldsboro was still part of the long-term Union goal in the state. The frequent raids in eastern North Carolina always targeted railroad depots and bridges.

As Mallett's conscription bureau prepared for the December 20 enrollment, Union soldiers were called out of their comfortable Sibley tents and wooden barracks around New Bern.[69] General Foster would lead them deep into the state.

---

[a] General George McClellan was replaced as the commander of the Army of the Potomac for failing to press Lee's army after the battle of Sharpsburg (Boatner, *The Civil War Dictionary,* p. 524).

Chapter Four

No Fun In A Battle

December 1862

It was common knowledge among his troops that General Foster liked to use artillery to clear the way for his infantry. For the Goldsboro expedition, Foster assembled a force at New Bern that was heavy in artillery.[70] His plan was to move inland as quickly as possible to keep the Confederates from gathering in any one place long enough to counterattack. His superior strength in artillery was intended to silence Confederate guns and break up troop concentrations. His infantry could then attack before the Confederates' next defensive position was established. While the Confederates were retreating, Union cavalry units would keep up the pressure and inflict as much damage as possible on the railroad system. To clear any obstructions that might be placed along the line of march, a pioneer brigade of African-Americans accompanied Foster's army.[71] The campaign depended on rapid movement and superior firepower.

Foster chose a route that would take his army westward, parallel with the Atlantic and North Carolina Railroad line. The route was well south of the Neuse River and would lead him thirty-five miles to Kinston, then another twenty miles to Goldsboro. This approach bypassed Confederate fortifications north and east of Kinston and allowed the Union gunboats to advance simultaneously up the Neuse River. The navy could provide additional firepower and supplies when Foster's army reached Kinston. In preparation for the campaign, Union cavalry cut telegraph lines to interfere with Confederate communications. By the time Foster's army left New Bern, the district's Confederate commander, General Gustavus W. Smith at Petersburg, had to send messages by locomotive to Southern forces in the region notifying them of the Union movement inland. On December 10, Foster, mindful of the disgraceful conduct of his soldiers during a raid at Fort Branch and the nearby town of Hamilton in early November, issued strict orders to his army forbidding the pillaging of civilian property.[a]

[a] Foster's troops had marched into the deserted town of Hamilton, North Carolina, and proceeded to steal and damage a great deal of civilian property. A number of private residences were also burned (Barrett, p. 138).

More than ten thousand Union infantrymen, forty pieces of artillery, and six hundred and forty cavalrymen left New Bern on the morning of December 11. Lead units in the column had only gone about eleven miles when they ran into Confederate pickets. The Confederates had known about Foster's plan long enough to cut down dozens of trees in order to block the road where it passed through a large swamp. They had chosen the spot well. Foster's soldiers had gotten far enough into the swamp that they were not able to bypass several hundred yards of obstructed roadway. The artillery units could not move without the road. Most of the force halted for the remainder of the day and set up camp while the pioneer brigade went to work clearing the obstructions.[72]

During the bitter cold night, the 9th New Jersey infantry bypassed the obstructions and pushed through the swamp toward the town of Trenton. Their mission was to ascertain the Confederates' location and strength. Skirmishing broke out between this regiment and Confederate pickets and continued until the rest of Foster's army arrived in mid-morning on December 12. The small force of Confederate infantry and cavalry was forced to retreat. From this point on, the opposing forces skirmished almost constantly as the Confederates fell back toward Southwest Creek.

Union soldiers found that the few roads leading toward the creek were blocked by felled trees and destroyed bridges, all of which had to be cleared or bypassed. The Union force had to leave detachments at crossroads to guard against surprise attacks. The column was also plagued with straggling, which further sapped its strength.

News of Foster's advance reached both Raleigh and Richmond. The Confederate capitol was already busy reacting to General Burnside's move in Virginia. Any troops that Richmond could spare were being sent to Lee's army at Fredericksburg. Confederate generals in North Carolina would have to organize a defense somewhere between Southwest Creek, several miles south of Kinston, and Goldsboro, using troops that were already in the state. Units close enough to be of help included the 61st North Carolina Troops at Kinston, part of General Clingman's brigade at Wilmington, Mallett's battalion at Raleigh, and General Nathan G. Evans's South Carolina brigade, also in the Kinston area.[a]

[a] General Clingman's brigade had just been organized and consisted of the 8th, 31st, 51st, and 61st North Carolina infantry regiments. General Evans's brigade contained the 17th, 22nd, 23nd South Carolina infantry regiments and the Holcomb Legion of South Carolina Volunteers stationed at Greenville, North Carolina (*Roster*, v. XIV, p. 600 and Barrett, p. 140).

Consolidating these units would take time. Mallett's battalion could start moving pretty quickly, as could the 61st North Carolina Troops. The South Carolinians were close but were not ready for a hard fight. They had lost half of their twenty-one hundred men at Second Manassas and Sharpsburg and had been sent south to recuperate and rebuild. After riding on flatbed railroad cars through the ice and snow, the brigade arrived at Kinston only a few days before Foster left New Bern. Evans's soldiers were a threadbare, weak, and miserable group of men who needed rest. They and the 61st North Carolina Troops started toward Southwest Creek to intercept Foster. Clingman's brigade headed for Goldsboro.

The Confederates made a stand on December 13. The natural barrier of Southwest Creek gave them their first opportunity to put up a serious defense. If they could hold on long enough for all of Clingman's and Evans's regiments and artillery to be brought up, both Kinston and Goldsboro might be saved. The Confederates knew that the railroad bridge near Goldsboro was Foster's main target.

The 61st North Carolina and 17th South Carolina regiments and a four-gun artillery battery defended a partially dismantled bridge over Southwest Creek. This force occupied earthworks dug across the road and along the creek bank. Union cavalry made initial contact and the opposing forces fired back and fourth across the creek. General Evans arrived at ten a.m. and began to direct the Confederate forces personally. After an hour of fighting, enough Union artillery had arrived and opened fire that the Confederate artillerymen were driven from their guns. When the Confederate cannons stopped firing, the 9th New Jersey and the 85th Pennsylvania Volunteers crossed the creek and outflanked the Confederate infantry, pushing them from their earthworks.

The Confederates retreated slowly, skirmishing along the way. They made another stand late in the afternoon with two regiments and two artillery pieces. Again, Union infantry engaged them until enough artillery was brought forward to shell them into withdrawing. Evans had not been able to gain enough time to concentrate the rest of the Confederate forces during these two engagements.

Evans decided to withdraw and make another stand closer to the Neuse River. He wanted to fight Foster south of the river instead of crossing the bridge and making a stand on the Kinston side. If the bridge was destroyed with the Confederates north of the river, Evans would not be able to re-cross and pursue Foster as he continued on toward Goldsboro. While the Confederates retreated late in the day, Foster's troops camped several miles from Kinston. The Union gunboats that were moving upstream on the Neuse River had been hampered by low water levels and then stopped by Lieutenant Colonel Stephen D. Pool's battalion of the 1st North Carolina Artillery. Pool's heavy guns were mounted in earthworks two miles below Kinston near a bend in the river.

As Evans's troops fought at Southwest Creek and retreated toward Kinston, Mallett's men were preparing to leave Camp Holmes. The battalion was issued one hundred and seventy-eight rifles, 242 muskets, and 32,000 rounds of ammunition.[73] The men secured belongings that would be left behind in their quarters and packed their knapsacks with blankets, food, and personal items that they would need in the field. They had no idea how long they might be gone.

Mallett took as many of the guard and supporting force soldiers as his camp could spare. A small contingent stayed behind to watch the prisoners and prepare for the thirty-five-to forty-year-old conscripts. They would begin arriving in less than a week. When the battalion was ready to leave, it consisted of nineteen officers and four hundred and sixty men. They marched to the railroad near camp and boarded the cars. The ride toward Kinston was uneventful, except for speculation about the crisis that lay ahead.

The train arrived at the Kinston station at seven o'clock on December 14, a cold and clear Sunday morning. General Evans met Colonel Mallett in town amid screeching train whistles and a fearsome beating of drums as the battalion formed its ranks. Evans wanted Union scouts across the river to hear the commotion and think that a large force had arrived to reinforce his command.[74] Mallett and Evans marched the battalion through town to Herritage Street, turned south, and headed for the bridge over the Neuse River less than a mile away. By eight-thirty, Mallett's men were occupying trenches near the river in support of Captain Robert Boyce's South Carolina artillery unit. They heard the battle begin just a few minutes later.[75]

On the other side of the river, the Union army, with its skirmishers several hundred yards out in front, was moving toward a small country church known as Harriette's Chapel. Foster's regiments were deploying on both sides of the road. Earlier, at eight a.m., General Evans had ordered two companies of his South Carolinians to leave their positions and move forward until they made contact with the enemy. Evans's far right flank was not yet well protected and he wanted to draw the lead Union regiments toward his center and left where he was anchored on the river. This area was defended by his

South Carolinians and several companies of the 61st North Carolina Troops. Evans supported these troops with Captain J. B. Starr's and Captain S. R. Bunting's batteries of North Carolina artillery.

The opposing skirmishers made contact with each other shortly before nine a.m. and fired the initial volleys of the battle. Sporadic fighting continued as the South Carolinians retreated (as Evans had instructed), slowly drawing the Union infantry toward the Confederate position.[76]

Evans knew that his left and center could hold, but on his right there was open ground leading toward a large swamp. He decided to secure this area by bringing up Mallett's battalion, his last available troops.

At nine-fifteen a.m., one of General Evans's aides delivered a message to Colonel Mallett on the Kinston side of the river. Mallett formed his companies and marched them at the double-quick across the bridge. The soldiers passed between buildings on either side of the road, then executed movements to advance in a battle line. As the battalion moved forward, Lieutenant John McRae's Company B was on the far right flank. Artillery shells fired toward the bridge by distant Union batteries burst overhead. The battalion marched across open fields for about three hundred and fifty yards, suffering its first casualty of the day from shrapnel.[a]

The battalion halted in front of a fence that ran around to the right along the edge of the swamp. Mallett could see Union regiments on the far side of the swamp and ordered his battalion to open fire on them. Union firing, rather than intensifying as if to signal an attack, slowed after an hour or so.

There was a slight hill several hundred yards to Mallett's left. He could not see any further in that direction than Harriette's Chapel. He could hear that the artillery, some of the South Carolinians, and part of the 61st North Carolina Troops were heavily engaged near the chapel but were apparently holding their ground.[b] The other South Carolina regiments, farther to the left, were also resisting determined Union attacks between the hill and the river. Before noon, orders from

---

[a] During this early part of the fighting, Union batteries were positioned too far away to see their targets. Union gunners were firing in the general direction of the Kinston bridge and setting the shell fuses based on range estimates provided by a "guide" (*O.R.*, Series I, v. 18, p. 63).

[b] The ten companies of the 61st North Carolina Troops had become separated at Southwest Creek the day before and were fighting as two separate battalions in this battle (*Roster*, v. XIV, p. 597).

General Evans were delivered to Mallett: "COLONEL: Let me know if the enemy are in your front. If not, join me at the bridge." [77]

By this time, Union firing in front of Mallett's position had ceased entirely. He could see no sign of enemy activity on the far side of the swamp. Still hearing the sound of serious fighting to his left, he determined that his command should return to the bridge in compliance with General Evans's instructions. Mallett withdrew his battalion in good order. When he arrived back at the bridge, he could not find the general and realized that the artillery that had been guarding the bridge was gone. He assumed that Evans had withdrawn part of his force and retreated to high ground on the far side of the river. Mallett led his men across the bridge and headed toward Kinston.

General Evans had indeed crossed the river and was observing the battle from an artillery position about halfway to town, but he had not withdrawn any of his regiments. He watched Mallett's battalion cross the bridge. He could now see Union infantry preparing to enter the swamp across from the position that Mallett previously occupied. Evans's South Carolinians on the left and center were still holding, but his right flank was again unprotected. If Union infantry got through the swamp and advanced across the open ground on the right of the Confederate line, they would be able to capture the bridge and trap most of the Confederates against the river.

Mallett's battalion had not gotten far toward town when one of Evans's officers rode up and ordered them to re-cross the river and return to their former position. The battalion counter-marched at the double quick and headed back across the same field, through the same artillery barrage, and opened fire on Union regiments that were making their way through the swamp. Between the difficulties presented by the swamp and the intense firing coming from Mallett's men, the Union advance stalled. Union soldiers fought stubbornly, taking cover in the thick vines and trees and standing waist deep in water. During this fighting, part of the 61st North Carolina Troops came up to reinforce Mallett's right flank. He ordered them to assist the troops closer to Harriette's Chapel. Mallett could see fighting around the church and heard the battle intensifying toward the river.

After two hours of fighting, Mallett felt confident enough about his position to send his far right company, Company B, around behind the rest of his troops to reinforce the units near Harriette's Chapel.[a]

[a] Company B was protected by the swamp in front and to its immediate right and was not in position to be of much use in this part of the fight.

Thompson, Cowen, and the rest of Lieutenant McRae's men made this end-run and were immediately thrust into some of the most intense combat of the day.[a] As Mallett's soldiers fought for the next three hours, their ammunition supply dwindled. Meanwhile, the tide of battle was beginning to turn against the Confederates beyond Harriette's Chapel.

This part of the Confederate line stretched for almost a mile to the river. Here, the South Carolinians were under sustained and heavy attack. They had held their ground well for several hours, but as the day wore on, their ammunition ran dangerously low. As the first units to be engaged, they were the first to exhaust their cartridge boxes and had not been sufficiently re-supplied. Several units that began to withdraw were ordered back into the fight by General Evans, then retreated again. As one regiment began to retreat, the next unit in line, not wishing to be out flanked by Union infantry, would also withdraw. The situation was deteriorating more rapidly than General Evans could send orders to fix it.

The Confederate line gave way one or two units at a time from the river to Harriette's Chapel. Near the chapel, men of Bunting's battery, the 61st North Carolina Troops, and Lieutenant McRae's company observed the approaching collapse of their entire left flank. The officers realized that without more ammunition and reinforcements, they would have no choice but to withdraw to the river, cross the bridge, and make a stand on the Kinston side. These units began their retreat in good order. Mallett saw them begin to fall back and realized that he could not stay where he was for much longer. He, too, was low on ammunition and concerned about being outflanked and cut off from the bridge. His battalion began an orderly withdrawal toward the river, pausing to fire volleys into the 85th and 103rd Pennsylvania regiments as they emerged from the swamp. The lay of the land prevented Mallett from seeing how bad things were getting on the Confederate far left and at the bridge.

Retreating South Carolina troops, now crossing the bridge, were met by couriers from General Evans and ordered to return to the fight. They turned and tried to re-cross the bridge only to collide with other units who were being pressed by advancing Union infantry.

---

[a] A South Carolina soldier noted that "Col. Mallett's battalion of N.C. Troops... charged the enemy on our right and drove them back some distance...." (Silverman and Thomas, *A Rising Star of Promise,"* p. 64). Another South Carolinian described the fighting around Harriette's Chapel as "the hottest fighting of the day...." (*North Carolina Argus*, Jan. 15, 1863).

The confusion caused a bottleneck of troops on both sides of the river. Some soldiers began to drop their weapons and accouterments so they could swim across the river if the situation on the bridge was not brought under control.

Evans, from his distant vantage point, watched the South Carolinians' retreat turn into a rout with Union troops in close pursuit. He realized that the battle on the far side of the river was lost and that he needed to save his army by destroying the bridge after his troops got across. He had previously placed turpentine-soaked cotton bales on the bridge just in case such a situation should arise. He now gave orders to have the bales ignited.

Most of the South Carolinians managed to get across the burning bridge along with part of the 61st North Carolina Troops and Company B of Mallett's battalion. The rest of General Evans's brigade was approaching the bridge as the fire took hold. As the last Confederate unit to begin its withdrawal, Mallett's other five companies were still several hundred yards from the bridge when they realized that it was on fire. Their stubborn retreat became a rout as they too dropped their weapons and knapsacks and ran toward the river. By the time they arrived, the burning bridge was crowded with terrified troops. In the smoke and confusion, Union *and* Confederate artillery fired on the southern approach to the bridge, killing and wounding friend and foe alike.[a] Union infantry, which had been chasing the South Carolinians, lined up along the river bank about two hundred and fifty yards downstream and began firing into the Confederates as they crowded onto the bridge.[b] Colonel Mallett was one of many casualties near the bridge, receiving a painful bullet wound that broke his left leg. He turned command of the battalion over to Captain James McRae.

Some South Carolinians and a number of Mallett's men swam the river or got across the bridge before the flames drove the rest back. The advancing Union soldiers ceased firing into the trapped Confederates when they saw a white flag waving in the crowd. One hundred and sixty-two South Carolinians from four different regiments and the Holcomb Legion were taken prisoner. Sixty-six

[a] One report indicates that General Evans, thinking that Mallett had already retreated, ordered the shelling Mallett's position even before the battalion withdrew toward the bridge (Trotter, *Ironclads and Columbiads,* p. 181).

[b] Some of the Union infantry was only fifty yards behind the fleeing South Carolinians as they raced for the bridge. Evans's artillery on the Kinston side of the river could not fire directly at the nearest Union troops for fear of hitting Confederates (*North Carolina Argus*, Jan. 15, 1863).

members of the 61st North Carolina Troops were taken along with six North Carolina artillerymen. Mallett's battalion lost seven killed, eight missing, twenty-two wounded, and one hundred and eighty-three captured, including both Colonel Mallett and Captain McRae.[78]

Union soldiers herded the captured Confederates off to one side. They extinguished the bridge by kicking the burning cotton bales into the river and dousing the flames using buckets found in nearby buildings. They discovered the bodies of several badly burned Confederates on and under the bridge.[79] Union artillery batteries advanced quickly, set up new positions along the river bank, and shelled the retreating Confederates all the way through Kinston and beyond. Shells exploding in the town started several fires and terrified the few residents that had stayed behind.

The defeated Southerners passed beyond Kinston and regrouped about two miles west of town where they were safe from the artillery. The 47th North Carolina Troops arrived from Weldon at this time and joined Evans's command. Evans received a surrender demand from Foster, which he rejected. Foster began to deploy his troops for a follow-up attack. Evans stalled for a while, expressing concern for civilians that were still fleeing the town, then withdrew his forces again, ending the battle.

Lieutenant Colonel Pool's artillerymen spent the day listening to the battle and keeping the Union gunboats at a respectful distance down river. When Pool realized that Kinston had fallen, he ordered his guns to be dismounted and had most of the ammunition dumped in the river. He then abandoned the earthworks to avoid being captured. Some of Mallett's men who managed to swim across the river during the battle linked up with Pool's men and they all headed for Goldsboro.[80]

Foster halted his army for the night. Soon, Kinston's streets were lined with long rows of stacked rifles. Tents covered the fields around town. Townspeople began returning to their homes under a flag of truce, often escorted by sympathetic Union soldiers. Some officers took up residence in homes that were still abandoned.

During the night, Foster's men began searching the town for valuables. Many families were forced back out of their homes by the looters. Some Union officers tried to control the situation, but the theft of personal property continued. Food, money, and jewelry disappeared from homes. There was widespread vandalism, and livestock was needlessly slaughtered. A shop near the center of town was set on fire. Private Henry Guy of the 43rd Massachusetts infantry wrote to his family and described the end of the battle and his stay in Kinston:

> There was plenty of guns of every description lying around and boxes which afforded amusement for the boys. The rebels couldn't stand the fire of our cannons nor will they face us in an open fight, but they run and conceal themselves behind brush and breastworks. We camped for the night in the village and during the evening the soldiers were busy about town. Every store was cleaned out in a hurry but the stock was very small.... all got plenty of tobacco. Several houses were burnt to the ground. I went into several buildings and everything was turned upside down on the floor. Suffice to say, we had plenty of pillows to sleep on that night.... We took several hundred prisoners but paroled them in the morning....[81]

General Foster telegraphed news of his victory to Washington: "This morning I advanced on this town, and found the enemy strongly posted. After five hours hard fighting, we succeeded in driving them from their position." [82] In return, Foster received news of Burnside's terrible defeat at Fredericksburg. He knew that Confederate reinforcements would soon be sent from Virginia.

General G. W. Smith was already en route from Weldon. He had ordered eight infantry regiments and three batteries from Richmond to meet him at Goldsboro. Clingman's brigade was coming from Wilmington. Foster knew that he would have to do what damage he could in the next few days and withdraw. He had been warned not to let a reinforced Confederate army catch him too far from New Bern.[a]

Foster led his army out of Kinston the next morning, crossed back over the blackened bridge, then burned it to keep Evans's command north of the river.[83] The expedition headed toward Goldsboro by way of White Hall, reaching that town on December 16. Union artillery fired across the river and there was a half-hearted attempt to burn a Confederate ironclad that was under construction nearby. Foster continued along the south side of the river toward Goldsboro. By the next day, General Smith and several Confederate regiments had arrived at Goldsboro. They were determined to save the Wilmington and Weldon Railroad bridge.

[a] Nearly a year earlier, General McClellan cautioned Foster's predecessor, General Burnside, about going too far inland and allowing Confederates to quickly send reinforcements using the railroad (Barrett, p. 68-69). This was still a concern.

The 51st and 52nd North Carolina regiments advanced toward the covered bridge but were driven back by intense fire coming from five of Foster's regiments. Several Union soldiers dashed forward and set the bridge ablaze. Artillery batteries opened fire and kept the Southerners from extinguishing the flames. General Foster realized that his enemy was finally beginning to concentrate troops in the area. Feeling that the fire would complete his mission, he ordered his army to begin moving back toward New Bern. To cover the withdrawal, he detached a brigade under Colonel H. C. Lee. Lee posted his force in a line stretching for a mile and a half behind a railroad embankment.

The Confederates now had enough troops to launch a counterattack. Generals Clingman and Smith were attempting to coordinate their movements with General Evans. Clingman ordered an attack on the right side of Lee's line. The 8th North Carolina State Troops and remnants of the 61st North Carolina regiment and Mallett's battalion fixed bayonets and advanced for half a mile toward the railroad embankment. Upon arriving at the Union position, they found that the enemy had retreated four hundred yards to take shelter under the protection of their artillery. The Confederates halted and were shelled until nightfall when the Union artillery withdrew.[84]

Meanwhile, General Evans ordered the 51st and 52nd North Carolina regiments to attack the part of the Union line that was approximately two-thirds of a mile in front of them. The two regiments charged to within three hundred yards of the Union position before the attack stalled under heavy artillery fire. The effect of the cannon fire caused Private Guy to write:

> The enemy was met with a veritable storm of grape and canister shot such that they were all mowed down in heaps. I hope that they killed a thousand of them for they are a sneaky, cowardly and treacherous foe and they deserve no lenience....

Colonel Lee's brigade soon withdrew and followed the rest of Foster's army. There was no serious attempt by the disorganized Confederates to interfere with Foster's return to the coast. By December 21, he and his army were safely behind their defenses at New Bern.

General Foster reported to his superiors that the campaign was "a perfect success" and had accomplished its goals. Northern newspapers gave favorable front-page treatment to the expedition in the wake of Burnside's disaster at Fredericksburg. However, most of the damage done to North Carolina's railroad system was repaired within two weeks. A number of Foster's men felt that the Goldsboro expedition had been nothing more than a waste of time that generated nearly six hundred Union casualties.[85] On December 24, all Union troops in North Carolina were designated as the Eighteenth Army Corps. Foster was named as the corps commander.

The 1862 campaign season in Virginia ended with the battle of Fredericksburg.[a] Interrupting supply lines from North Carolina to Virginia, even temporarily, was a substantially less important goal during the winter.

Colonel Mallett's conscripts had borne the brunt of the Kinston bridge defeat. Counting those captured, his battalion had lost two hundred and twenty men, almost half its strength. Most of those captured were paroled the day after the battle. In compliance with the prisoner exchange program, they could not perform military duty until they were declared officially exchanged.[b]

Controversy soon developed around General Evans's performance at Kinston and Goldsboro. His force of approximately two thousand men was outnumbered five to one, but he had chosen a good defensive position. The nature of the countryside on the approaches to the Confederate line had prevented Union artillery from being fully utilized during the fight.[86] Evans had skillfully drawn the initial Union attack toward the strongest part of his position. Had he arranged for a reliable supply of ammunition, his small army might have held on until General Clingman's brigade arrived. Failing that, Evans should have timed the withdrawal of his troops with their use of the available ammunition rather than ordering his men back into battle with empty cartridge boxes. A properly supplied and managed retreat by the South Carolinians would have provided time for a systematic withdrawal of all the Confederate forces. Most importantly, Evans should have been close enough to the battlefield to

---

[a] The hapless General Burnside started two more campaigns, one in late December that President Lincoln canceled and another in late January that was stricken prostrate by two days of torrential rain and forever after referred to as "The Mud March" (Boatner, *Civil War Dictionary*, p. 573).

[b] The on again, off again prisoner exchange program was administered by a cartel of Union and Confederate representatives. Captured Confederate soldiers signed paroles agreeing that they would "not take up arms against the United States or serve in any military capacity whatsoever against them until regularly discharged according to the usages of war from this obligation...." Captured Union soldiers signed paroles with similar wording (Boatner, *Civil War Dictionary*, p. 620).

ascertain whether all his force had crossed the bridge before ordering its destruction. Instead, half of his troops were on the far side of the river, caught between the rapidly advancing enemy and the burning bridge. Including Colonel Pool's abandoned guns, eleven pieces of artillery were lost in addition to the infantry casualties. After starting the affair well, General Evans's mistakes had turned a manageable situation into a panic-driven stampede.

One possible explanation for Evans's poor performance was drunkenness. He was known as a hard drinker and was never far from his private stock, even during battle. Some South Carolina officers complained that Evans was drunk when the Kinston bridge was set on fire and again later when he ordered the 51st and 52nd North Carolina regiments to make their ill-fated counterattack at Goldsboro. Relations between Evans and officers of his brigade deteriorated after the Kinston affair. In February, he was tried by a military court on several counts of drunkenness but was exonerated.

As bad as Kinston and Goldsboro had been, Mallett's soldiers had passed the test of battle. The unit fought well at Kinston. They pulled back in good order, stubbornly fighting their pursuers until they caught sight of the burning bridge. Those who escaped at Kinston had regrouped and participated in the counterattacks at Goldsboro. The defeat they suffered and the majority of their casualties were the results of mismanagement at higher levels. Their officers had directed the unit well and had suffered their share of casualties along with the men in the ranks. Colonel Mallett was wounded and captured. Second in command, Captain James McRae, was also captured. Two lieutenants in Company A, J. J. Reid and Robert K. Williams were killed, along with Lieutenant Joseph A. Hill in Company C. Lieutenants Jesse McLean, Frank Hahr, James J. Speller, John Little, Walter Bullock, and E. B. Goelet were all taken prisoner.[a]

Newspaper reports of the battalion's performance were glowing. The *Fayetteville Observer* stated that "Col. Mallett's Regiment went into the fight this morning cheering." The *Raleigh Progress* reported, "Col. Peter Mallett's Battalion was in the fight yesterday, and fought gallantly and sustained considerable loss." A *Raleigh Journal* correspondent wrote that "Men who were in the fight speak in the

---

[a] Lieutenant John McRae and most of Company B got across the bridge before it was blocked by the flames. Their position in the battle near Harriette's Chapel resulted in several men in the company being killed, wounded, or captured, but they began their retreat before the rest of the battalion realized that the Confederate left flank had collapsed.

highest terms of Col. Mallett's Regiment of Conscripts. They fought like veterans."[87] The experience had a sobering effect on the men who endured it. Albert Thompson wrote to Cate the same day that Foster's army returned to New Bern:

> Goles Burrow N C December the 21 1862
> My dear wife and children I take this eavening my pen in hand to drop you a few lines to let you know that I am still safe and sound As yet I have been in too Battles since I left Ralleigh. I am proud to say that I am sound whild several has fell by my side and me not hurt. there was to of our liutenants kill[ed]. Our col[onel] was shot in the leg. They was not one of our mess kill[ed]. Well Cate I tell you there is no fone in a Battle we had to retreat cross the River and I lost both of my Blankets and I have nothing to cover with only my over coat and there is no chance to ceap warm these nights. We are here in the courthouse now but I don't know how long we will Stay here we are garding the town and the railroad. we have a find place to stay these nights when we are not on gard but we haf to go on every other night well dear Cate you must do the best you can with out me for I don't know when I will be at home whether ever or not but I hope I will get to come home some time. I don't know how I misd being kill[ed] but I gave it up to the Lord and he Brought me through it safe So I will do my duty and if I am kill[ed] it will be all right....

What was left of Mallett's battalion was back at Camp Holmes a week later. At their first morning formation the men were shocked to see how badly the unit had suffered in the campaign. Most of the companies were greatly reduced in size, some almost entirely absent. Officers were missing from their usual places. Even the sound of morning orders was different. The battalion's adjutant, E. N. Mann, was among the dead.

Chapter Five

The System In Conflict

January-August 1863

Mallett's battalion began the new year with less than half its number available for duty. Most of the men had to work double shifts: half on duty and half off for twenty-four hours at a time. With the incoming thirty-five- to forty-year-old conscripts, all of the guard posts around the camp and guardhouse had to be manned. Most of the paroled soldiers from the Kinston fight reported to Camp Holmes in late December but were sent home to await the completion of the prisoner exchange process. Others headed for home without notifying their superiors of their whereabouts.[a] Captain McRae was briefly present at the camp in January, but Colonel Mallett was bedridden in Fayetteville with his leg wound. Both officers were still paroled prisoners who had not been declared exchanged. Like the men in the ranks, they were not allowed to perform their normal duties.[88]

On January 12, the adjutant and inspector general appointed Colonel Thomas P. August to replace Peter Mallett. August was a Virginian who had been disabled by wounds earlier in the war and was of the appropriate rank for the assignment. A North Carolina infantry captain, Lucius Johnson, was also assigned to the bureau and assumed Captain McRae's duties.

The forty-two-year-old Johnson, an attorney in civilian life, had been a company commander in the 17th North Carolina Troops. He and most of his regiment had already been captured and exchanged twice, once at Hatteras and again at Roanoke Island. The regiment was reorganized and went into winter camp near Hamilton, North Carolina, in early December. Johnson was assigned to the conscript bureau on December 16. He arrived a few days later and began

[a] Hahn, *The Catawba Soldier of the Civil War*, p. 367. General Smith threatened to have newspapers publish the names of Mallett's paroled soldiers that had not reported to Camp Holmes, listing them as deserters (*North Carolina Argus*, Jan. 15, 1863).

handling McRae's duties and those of Colonel August, who would not arrive for several weeks.[a]

Johnson took an early opportunity to alienate Captain Augustus Landis, one of Mallett's enrolling officers in Granville county. Captain Landis, formerly of the 12th North Carolina Troops, was one of the first officers to be transferred to the North Carolina Conscript Bureau as a result of being wounded in battle and disabled from field duty.[89] Shortly after the battle at Kinston, Landis inquired about Colonel Mallett's wound and prisoner status. Captain Johnson's reply was unnecessarily hostile:

> Headquarters Camp of Instruction
> Camp Holmes, Dec. 23rd, 1862
>
> Captain:
> Your communication of the 18th instant, inquiring whether Col. Mallett was wounded and a prisoner has been received; and in reply I have to say that he is. But the fact of his being a prisoner does not change your position or interfere with your duties as enrolling officer. I would, therefore, suggest the propriety of proceeding with your work....[90]

Less than two weeks later, Captain Johnson reported to the recently appointed Superintendent of Conscription General Gabriel J. Rains on the morale of Mallett's troops and the condition of the camp when he arrived:

> Headquarters Camp of Instruction
> Camp Holmes near Raleigh
> January 7th, 1863
>
> General:
> Be pleased to find enclosed [the] monthly report inclusive of 31st Dec. 1862. I am free to say that it does not appear very satisfactory, but it is as near the truth, as I have been able to get after a great deal of labor and investigation....

---

[a] *O.R.*, Series IV, v. 2, p. 379. The date of Johnson's assignment to Mallett's bureau makes it unlikely that he was sent to fill the vacancy left by the capture of Captain McRae only two days before. Johnson's transfer by Adjutant and Inspector General Special Order No. 294 was intended to be permanent. The same special order also assigned Brigadier General Gabriel J. Rains as the first superintendent of conscription for the Confederacy (*Special Orders, Adjutant and Inspector General's Office, v. 2*, p. 581).

> Upon taking command here, I am constrained to state, I found this camp in a most deplorable condition of demoralization and confusion.
>
> This condition of things resulted perhaps in part from the absence of Col. Mallett, who it seems was ordered from this place with a very large portion of the men usually kept here.... Col. M. was wounded and taken prisoner and paroled at the Kinston fight, with a number of his men and officers....
>
> The Winter quarters for this Camp of Instruction are still incomplete, I am using what disposable force I have to complete them as fast as I can.
>
> The men now here of the Camp Guards when not off escorting parties of deserters etc., are employed in the guard and Camp duty, and in working on Winter quarters.
>
> I flatter myself that the condition is somewhat improved....[91]

Johnson wrote to General Rains again, just two days later, spreading his indictment of Mallett's conscription enforcement statewide:

> Headquarters Camp of Instruction
> Camp Holmes, near Raleigh, N.C.
> January 9th, 1863
>
> General:
>
> In my communication of the 7th inst., I reported to you the "deplorable conditions of demoralization and confusion" I found upon taking command here. It existed not only in this camp, but out of it, and through the state in regard to the conscription business.... But that you may more fully understand the condition of affairs, permit me to call your attention to certain facts, which I feel it my painful duty to submit to you, as having a vast deal to do with the demoralization above mentioned.
>
> A strong impression seems to have been made upon the public mind... that the Honorable Legislature of this State are determined to place the State of N. Carolina in antagonism with the Confederate States authorities.... The action of that honorable body in regard to a certain bill to raise a body of State Troops, irrespective of the Conscript Act.... Then Col. Mallett... was ordered into the field for active operations against the enemy, leaving only a drill-

> master in command, whom, when I took command, I did not find at his post: and there were not men enough, even by putting them on duty (part serving double duty, the balance off one day and on the next,) to guard safely the Camp property, deserters, conscripts in camp, negroes — men, women and little children — sent to camp to be taken care of, political prisoners sent by state authority, prisoners of war and traitors caught in arms against the Confederate States.... The effect of the impression first mentioned, coupled with the then inefficient condition of the Camp of Instruction and the effect of sending Col. M. and his command into the field... and being kept in the field until the very last of December, giving coloring to the very common report that Mallett's Battalion, as it was called, would never return to conscript duty, seems to have created a belief that the Camp of Instruction had already, or was about to go down, and in fact that the Conscription business in N.C. is at an end....
>
> I flatter myself that the condition of things is now improving and that if sustained and assisted in my labors, instead of being interfered with, I may yet be able to organize and render efficient the beautiful system intended by the Conscription Act....
>
> Trusting, General, you will pardon the length and multiplicity of my communication, because of my zeal in the service, I beg to remain,
>
> Very respectfully,
> Your Obt. Servant, [92]

Not satisfied with casting aspersions on Colonel Mallett and the state legislature, Johnson intentionally offended the representative of an even higher authority. Apparently feeling that the battalion was lacking in spiritual guidance, Johnson sent a curt note to Reverend Fitzgerald, the camp's chaplain, ordering him to be present "with us on Dress Parade every evening at sundown."[93]

While Captain Johnson annoyed Mallett's officers and curried favor with the new superintendent in Richmond, the enrollment that began on December 20 had to be completed. Several personnel matters initiated by Mallett before the Kinston battle were still pending. The congressional district enrolling officers had to be selected from among disabled North Carolinians. These appointments were approved by the military district's commanding general and usually given to officers who had requested assignment to Mallett's bureau.

In another matter, Mallett's choice for an officer to organize a provost company for the city of Raleigh had to be finalized. Captain Samuel B. Waters, who commanded a company of guards at the Salisbury prisoner of war stockade, was assigned to Mallett's bureau, but he had been delayed in reporting for duty.[a]

The battalion's officers had to rebuild their companies and replace lost equipment while at the same time preparing the incoming conscripts for assignment to regiments in Virginia. Replacements for the men killed and wounded at Kinston were taken from among the new arrivals. Fortunately, the prisoner exchange process was accomplished quickly. As was the practice, once both sides agreed on the prisoner exchanges, notifications were printed in newspapers. On January 15, Captain Johnson notified 1st Lieutenant E. B. Goelet of the battalion that "you are included in the 'Goldsboro list' and will therefore report as soon as practicable." [94]

By January 19, Johnson had become irritated, as had General Smith, with the lack of speed with which Mallett's men were returning to duty. He began issuing orders to militia colonels to facilitate the process:

> Headquarters Camp of Instruction
> Camp Holmes, January 19, 1863
>
> Colonel:
> You will please arrest, or cause to be arrested and delivered at these Headquarters, John Ward, a paroled prisoner belonging to Mallett's Battalion. This will be considered as applying to any member of this command, absent without proper leave. They have all been exchanged and orders issued for their return to duty.
>
> Very Respectfully,
> Your Obt. Servant,
> (signed) L. J. Johnson
> Capt. Commanding Conscripts [95]

---

[a] Waters was a twenty-eight-year-old Beaufort County resident who had served with Mallett in the 3rd North Carolina State Troops as a lieutenant in Company I. He transferred to the 18th North Carolina Troops as that regiment's adjutant but was wounded and disabled on June 30, 1862, when he was "knocked from his horse by an exploding shell." He was discharged from field service the following September, but by then he was on duty at the Salisbury prison (*Roster*, v. VI, p. 306 and Compiled Confederate Service Records Group 109, National Archives).

In mid-January, newspapers published "Exchange Notice No. 4," which declared as legally exchanged "All Confederate officers and men captured and paroled at Goldsboro, N.C. in December, 1862."[96] Some of Mallett's parolees who were at their homes may have not been aware of their change of status until the end of the month.

Private James Miller of Company D had been wounded but was well enough to return to camp at the end of January. He wrote to his wife when he got back to his company, but he did not seem to notice the low morale that Captain Johnson had reported to Richmond:

> Camp Holmes N.C. Wake Co.
> January the 31st, 1863
>
> Dear loveing wife I seat myself to inform you that I am well... and hope that these lines will find you all in good health. We found the company well and in good spirits. I tried to git a furlough in Salisbury but I could not git one. The doctor told me that I would have to report and we came on. we was to late to git on the cars at Statesville. I reported to Captain R[obards] and he said it was all right and he said I shouldn't be put on duty for some time or not till I got sound and well and that will be sometime yet. My thigh is very sore this morning. We have got the same mess only not the same tent we are in the old cloth kind yet and I don't know when we will git out.... Write soon as this comes to hand.... your loving husband
>
> James C. Miller [97]

Colonel August arrived at Camp Holmes at the end of January. He found that the December 20 enrollment had not been productive due to the capture of Mallett's battalion and the widespread rumor (accurately reported by Captain Johnson) "that the Conscription business in N. C. is at an end...." [a]

Colonel Mallett's officers kept him informed about Colonel August, Captain Johnson, and conditions at the camp. One such officer, Captain George Baker of the Conscript Bureau's Quartermaster Department, wrote to Mallett in late February:

[a] General Robert E. Lee observed that the December enrollment was not very productive and complained to the secretary of war that January's delivery of conscripts to his army had not kept up with attrition (*O.R.*, Series III, V. 5, p. 695).

Camp Holmes
Near Raleigh, N.C. Feby 22nd 1863

My Dear Col.

Yours of the 11th Inst was duly recd.... I'm truly glad to hear that your "Game Leg" is improving.... how boring your confinement must be to you, and how anxious we officers & men are to see you here again. Col. You have not the most remote idea how much the men respect and love you and how anxious they are to have you here once more and particularly at this time....

Capt. Johnson has at last discovered that I know more about my business than he does & we get on much more pleasantly, than before, but tis far from pleasant yet.[98]

While Captain Johnson's presence in the bureau was a personal annoyance for Mallett's officers, Colonel August's assignment was not well received for political reasons. Consistent with the views of his predecessors, Governor Vance wanted a native North Carolinian in charge of conscription in his state. He began to protest August's appointment even before the disabled Virginian could get settled at Camp Holmes:

State of North Carolina
Executive Department
Raleigh Jany. 26th. 1863
Hon. James A. Seddon
Sec'y of War
Richmond, Va.

Sir

I had the honor to complain to his Excellency the President, and your immediate predecessor Mr. Randolph in regard to the manner of enforcing the Conscript Act in this State, & of disposing of men in regiments, during the month of October last. I am compelled again, greatly to my regret, to complain of the appointment of Col. August as Commandant of Conscripts for North Carolina, who has recently assumed command here.

Merely alluding to the obvious impropriety and bad policy, of wounding the sensibilities of our people by the appointment of a citizen of another State to execute a law, both harsh & odious, I wish to say Sir, in all candor that it smacks of discourtesy to our people to say the least of

> it. Having furnished as many (if not more) troops for the service of the Confederacy, as any State, and being, as I was assured by the President, far ahead of all others in the number raised under the Conscription law - the people of this State have justly felt mortified in seeing these troops commanded by citizens of other States....
>
> Most respectfully
> Yr. Obt. Svt.
> Z. B. Vance [99]

Vance's dissatisfaction with the Confederate government was growing. North Carolina had supplied well over fifty thousand volunteers and conscripts, yet there were precious few North Carolina generals in Lee's army. The state's militia had done an excellent job of gathering conscripts while the militias of other states had failed miserably at the same task. While most North Carolina troops were being sent to Virginia to defend Richmond, Union Generals Burnside and Foster conquered much of North Carolina's coast and raided inland at will. Robert E. Lee, a Virginian, had refused to send any troops to help. South Carolinians under General Evans tried to defend North Carolina, but they had been unable to keep Foster from sacking Kinston. Foster's raid did not end until North Carolina troops arrived at Goldsboro. Under the circumstances, the appointment of a Virginian to conscript North Carolinians was more than Vance could tolerate.

As the governor sparred with Richmond and Colonel Mallett's eventual return to duty remained in doubt, a fundamental flaw in the Confederate conscription process resurfaced. This was the "October last" complaint to which Vance referred: the assignment of conscripts to units in the field. During the first two months of 1863, philosophical struggles emerged within the Confederacy that would last into 1865. These conflicts would threaten Mallett's battalion and eventually reshape the whole process of Confederate conscription.

While many Southerners had not been eager to join the army in the summer and fall of 1862, they had realized that under the conscription law, they would eventually end up at a camp of instruction and from there be assigned to a regiment in the field. They could either be enrolled and report to the camp when notified to do so, or they could wait at home until militia officers or conscript bureau soldiers came and arrested them. Either way, they had no idea as to which regiment they might find themselves assigned.

In North Carolina, shortly after taking office, Governor Vance directed state Adjutant General Martin to issue orders that allowed the recruits to select the regiment in which they would serve when they left Camp Holmes.[a] This option was intended to make military service less objectionable to conscripts and to motivate more of them to report voluntarily for enrollment. While *some* unit selection was allowed by the war department, more often than not Colonel Mallett assigned conscripts under guidelines that reflected the demands of the army.[b] Vance, feeling that the interests of his citizens had been ignored by Richmond, engaged in a running war of words with the Confederate government. Mallett continued to assign soldiers in compliance with his instructions from the secretary of war.

Given the choice of an undesirable assignment either by reporting to camp voluntarily or by waiting to be arrested, many Southerners joined specific regiments through recruiters, thus bypassing the conscription process and camps of instruction. In this way, a hesitant recruit could avoid the stigma of conscription, collect one or more cash bounties, and choose a unit filled with family and friends. If he chose carefully, perhaps he could end up in a regiment that was unlikely to see combat. Consequently, the conscription law was responsible for having forced these men into the army, but the military authorities had lost control over assigning them to any specific unit. Without sending them through a camp of instruction, there was no control over the selection, training (such as it came to be), or equipping of these troops, much less an accurate reporting of their number.

Colonel Mallett had widely circulated his orders forbidding the bypassing of the camps of instruction the previous summer:

> Headquarters, (Camp Holmes,)
> Camp of Instruction,
> Near Raleigh, N.C., July 19, 1862
> General Order
> No. 3
>
> All persons subject to the provisions of the Act of Congress entitled "An act to provide for the public defense, approved April 16," are hereby warned not to join or enlist in any regiment or company whatever. They

---

[a] Vance maintained that conversations with both President Davis and the secretary of war had led him to believe that he could issue such an order (Johnston, *Vance*, v. 1, p. xlv).

[b] For instance, during October, 1862, Mallett was acting under orders from the secretary of war that required him to send all North Carolina conscripts to General S. G. French at Petersburg, Virginia (Johnston, *Vance*, v. 1, p. 251).

> must report to the commandant of this Camp for duty or be considered as deserters. All officers are hereby notified not to recruit or enlist in this State men enrolled or liable to conscription. All persons enlisted by officers for any company or regiment in the State or Confederate service, since enrollment under said Act, must be returned to the commandant of this camp.
>
> Officers refusing to comply with this order will be reported to the War Department. By order:
> Peter Mallett [a]

Like Mallett, conscription commanders in other states tried to suppress direct volunteering throughout the summer and fall of 1862. They felt that widespread bypassing of the conscription process would subvert the national military effort. Both the national and state governments were torn between trying to stimulate volunteering, while at the same time, refining a system of compulsory service. The problem continued into 1863 and was then made worse by the adjutant and inspector general.

The Confederate army needed to prepare for the approaching spring and summer campaign season. This meant getting as many men as possible assigned to units in the field, having them over their camp illnesses, and settled in their regiments before May. To accomplish this, the adjutant and inspector general's office issued orders to generals in the field that completely legitimized the bypassing of the conscription process:

> Circular
> ADJUTANT AND INSPECTOR GENERAL'S OFFICE
> Richmond, January 8, 1863
>
> SIR: Your attention is called to the great necessity which now exists for strenuous exertions in securing men to fill up the commands of the Army within a reasonable time. You are therefore desired to detail from your command such suitable officers and men as can be spared to proceed at once to those sections of the country in which their regiments were raised, for the purpose of gathering conscripts and conducting them to their commands, without passing them through the camps of instruction in the ordinary manner. [100]

---

[a] *Semi-Weekly Raleigh Register,* July 30, 1862. This order and Confederate Adjutant and Inspector General's Special Order No. 188 (series 1862) formed the authority under which Captain James McRae relieved the 62nd North Carolina Troops of the recently enlisted A. G. Thompson and others in August 1862.

The order went on to require recruiters to generally follow all other conscription procedures. None of the conscription commandants was naive enough to believe that would happen.

General Lee immediately dispatched "Details of officers and men... from all N.C. regts to visit the State to obtain recruits & absentees." [101] He issued similar orders to his regiments from other states. Other generals, who commanded brigades or divisions not assigned to Lee's army, sent out recruiters of their own.[a]

The commandants were not pleased with this legalized circumvention of their conscription networks or with General Lee's apparent enthusiasm for it. They had organized their bureaus and were being held personally responsible for productivity. What started as an informal bypassing of conscription in the spring of 1862 had grown into an illegal circumvention by summer. Now, in January 1863, the same activity was officially adopted by the Confederate government.

As a result of Lee's orders, several states were quickly swamped with recruiting officers sent by their regiments. Not only were these officers in competition with duly appointed enrolling officers, they were in competition with each other. In North Carolina, some of these officers claimed that the conscription law had been temporarily suspended throughout the state, but still used the threat of eventual conscription to coerce recruits into their units.[b] In February, no less than four infantry companies and one cavalry regiment ran competing advertisements in the same issue of a Wadesboro, North Carolina,

[a] The enthusiasm with which the order was received and implemented by generals in the field is revealed by General Clingman in the Department of North Carolina. A scant five days after the circular was issued, Clingman sent orders to South Carolina district commander, General States Rights Gist, to "forward to this office, with the least possible delay, the names of one officer in each company of your command — An intelligent, energetic and popular officer — for detail upon recruiting service...." (Southern Historical Collection, No. 157, Clingman Papers).

[b] In fact, four North Carolina state senators and twelve representatives from the fifteen western counties petitioned President Davis for a suspension of conscription in the 10th Congressional District (O.R., Series IV, v. 2, p. 247). Their request was denied. However, the conscript laws *were* suspended in the eastern counties of the state that were occupied by the Union army. The Confederacy's all encompassing conscription law, as opposed to a series of drafts, gave the Union army the legal justification to arrest, as a prisoner of war, any Southern man not specifically exempted from military service whether or not he was in the military. As the age groups that were covered by Confederate conscription were expanded to men thirty-five to forty-five, and later to the seventeen-year-old and forty-five-to fifty- year-old men, Union authorities in the occupied South had the option of mass arrests at their disposal (*O.R.*, Series 2, v. 7, p. 793).

newspaper. The ads declared that prospective recruits could join any company they wanted, could be paid up to one hundred dollars in bounties, and would be allowed generous furlough time to make preparations to leave home. The ads also referred to the unpleasant alternatives: "Those who fail to Volunteer, will undoubtedly be conscripted" and suffer the "disagreeable necessity of being sent to a Camp of Instruction." One advertisement placed by Lieutenant Samuel T. Wright of Company A, 23rd North Carolina Troops stated that "There is no getting out of this thing. You must go to the war, peaceably if you will, forcibly if you will not. This is no time for skulking." Lieutenant Wright even alluded to Governor Vance's recently published amnesty for deserters. Wright's advertisement further stated that "Absentees and Deserters will report to me, if they wish to avoid the death penalty, which will assuredly be visited upon them."[a] These notices were effective and resulted in hundreds of recruits leaving home to enlist in North Carolina regiments in Virginia. They often left without notifying their local militia officers or the conscript bureau. Enrolling officers wasted considerable time and effort looking for men who were already in the army.

Commandants of conscription responded to this situation by arguing to the war department that gathering men from the general population and sending them directly to units in the field was inefficient. The quality control and assignment authority exercised by the conscription bureau was lost. Physically or mentally unfit men could end up in the service and then have to be discharged, wasting valuable resources. Thousands of men could go to units where they were not needed. The re-enlistment of deserters under assumed names, which was already a problem, was growing worse. A soldier could desert from one unit, commit any number of crimes, enlist in another unit under an assumed name, and collect bounties along the way. In short, men recruited in this manner were not passing through the clearinghouse process that centralized conscription provided.

Only one month after the January circular, the war department issued a clarification in response to the commandants' objections:

[a] The competing ads were placed by the 59th North Carolina Troops, Company A of the 23rd North Carolina Troops, Company K of the 26th North Carolina Troops, and Companies H and I of the 43rd North Carolina Troops (*North Carolina Argus,* Feb. 12, 1863).

ADJT. AND INSP. GENERAL'S OFFICE
General Orders No. 16
Richmond, February 7, 1863

I. The special measures instituted in the circular from this office of the 8th of January, ultimo, were intended to aid, and in nowise to supersede the operation and rules of the regularly established system of conscription. Reports have been received that officers thus sent from the Army have been practically setting aside the system, decisions, and exemptions established under the authority of the commandants of conscripts in the respective States, and are neglecting to make to those officers any returns of the conscripts gathered by them. It is hereby ordered that all officers acting under the authority of the circular in question shall refrain from interference with any conscripts already in the custody of the officers regularly on conscription duty, and shall assert no claim over them, otherwise than by estimates on the commandants for the quota to which their regiments shall be entitled, under the principle of pro rata distribution; also, that they shall respect certificates of exemptions issued by regular enrolling officers, reporting for decision of the commandants any case in which the exemption may appear to them to have been improperly granted; that in no case shall they themselves grant certificates of exemption or detail; that in all doubtful cases or cases of appeal from their decision, they shall refer to the regular enrolling officer or the commandants, and that they shall furnish to the local enrolling officers, or the commandants of conscripts for the State, descriptive lists of all persons within conscript ages recruited or gathered by them.

II. The commandants of conscripts, in making their reports to the Bureau of Conscription, will return separately the conscripts gathered and reported to them under the system instituted by the circular above referred to.

By order:
S. Cooper,
Adjutant and Inspector General. [102]

This attempt at compromise did more harm than good. The revised procedure depended on cooperation and disclosure of information between two competing elements of the military: conscription officers on one hand and recruiting officers from field units on the other. The procedure encouraged recruiters sent by the army to second-guess and appeal exemptions and details made by local conscription officers. The commandants would be the judges in such cases, but this was a time-consuming additional responsibility that they did not need. Additionally, commandants were required to send statistics to Richmond that they could not verify, supplied by officers they did not command. The new procedure increased administrative work for everyone involved.

Difficulties generated by competition within the Confederate military continued through the spring/summer campaign season of 1863, which included the costly battles of Chancellorsville and Gettysburg. Casualties produced by these battles further weakened Lee's Army of Northern Virginia. During the same period, Superintendent of Conscription Gabriel Rains was transferred to other duties. In August, the newly appointed Superintendent John S. Preston assumed his duties fully aware of the issues. He had commanded the camp of instruction at Columbia, South Carolina.

In a lengthy report to Secretary of War Seddon, Preston made a number of recommendations. He wanted to complete the assignment of disabled army officers and enlisted men to every county in the nation, thus eliminating the use of militia officers. He also wanted to secure the assistance, as opposed to the competitive interference, of army commanders. In this same vein, he described the adjutant and inspector general's circular of the previous January 8 that sent swarms of recruiters into the states as "The first severe and almost death-blow..." struck against the efficient operation of the Bureau of Conscription. As a remedy, he offered a rewritten version of a conscription order from late 1862. Preston's rendition was designed to unify the system:

> All impressments, recruiting, or volunteering of persons between the ages of eighteen and forty-five years, under any pretense or authority, are strictly prohibited, it being the design of the Department, from which there will be no departure, to supply the Army exclusively through the Bureau of Conscription. [103]

The assistant Secretary of War, John A. Campbell, agreed with Preston's assessment and recommendations.[a] He felt that competition

[a] Before the war, Campbell was an associate justice of the United States Supreme Court. He opposed secession although he believed that it was not illegal under the United States Constitution. He worked diligently to prevent the outbreak of hostilities (Boatner, *Civil War Dictionary*, p. 116).

between recruiting officers from individual units had done more to demoralize the army than to strengthen it. Campbell was familiar with several abuses stemming directly from the activities of recruiters sent by the army. Hundreds, perhaps thousands of men had been given extended furloughs, some as long as ninety days, for volunteering to serve in specific companies. These furloughs were intended to allow recruits time to prepare to leave home. The recruit would then produce his furlough document as grounds to refuse to report to the local enrolling officer. When the furlough expired, the recruit could then sign up with another company and repeat the whole process. Also, local courts were getting involved. When conscript officers made arrests, the enrollees hired lawyers, and weeks of legal maneuvering ensued. The net result of this and other conscription dodges was that the army was deprived of much needed manpower. Army morale suffered in the absence of decisive government action to end the malingering.

Preston and Campbell were advocating conscription as the sole means for supplying men to the military. They and others in the government felt that only in this manner could the Confederacy develop a systematic process of inducting, equipping, and assigning troops. Zebulon Vance, never at a loss for an opinion, entered the controversy on the same side as the superintendent and assistant secretary. Vance complained that the recruiters were not only enticing conscripts away from Mallett's officers, but they were also taking recruits from authorized military units within his state. Siding squarely with views long held by Mallett and Captain James McRae, Vance told Secretary of War Seddon that the army should be supplied with recruits by "proper enrolling officers alone And the military authorities should not be permitted to interfere with their duties, except simply to render aid when required in making arrests." [104]

The controversy was beginning to draw clear philosophical battle lines within the government. While one faction pointed to the large number of recruits being supplied by army recruiters, the other side observed that no one really knew which units were benefiting from that method and which units were not. Lack of decisive government action allowed the confusion to persist. In October 1863, various newspapers printed excerpts from war department circulars that were written to reduce the confusion:

> From late orders issued by the War Department at Richmond, we make the following extracts; "Information

> having been received of repeated misconstructions and violations of previous orders, it is reiterated that no person liable to conscription will be permitted, under any circumstances, to volunteer in regiments, battalions or companies organized since the 16th of April, 1862, except such as were organized under the provisions of the Act of Congress of that date, entitled, 'An act further to provide for the public defense.'
>
> "It shall be the duty of the commandants of conscripts, on information of persons being received contrary to the provisions of this order, to make immediate requisition for such persons on the officer commanding, and on failure of the officer to return the persons so received to the camp of instruction, the commandant shall report the matter, with the facts of the case, to the Bureau of Conscription, to be decided.
>
> "No officer commanding, whose company reaches the maximum allowed by regulation, shall be permitted to receive recruits either as volunteers or in any other form.
>
> "No officer commanding shall accept or muster in persons of conscript age, unless such person shall first exhibit a certificate approved by an enrolling officer, stating that he has volunteered and selected his company, which company is allowed to receive recruits. [105]

Such clarifications were of little help. As long as the war department allowed direct volunteering *and* conscription, the confusion and abuse would continue. Try though it may, the government could not fix this problem by creating more paperwork.[a]

In January 1864, almost a full year after Circular No. 8 and the first attempts to repair the damage it had done, General Robert E. Lee tried to influence the situation. After initial participation in the problem, he became concerned about the effects of operating two competing systems. For the entire year of 1863, non-front-line units

[a] While the war department tried to combine the two competing systems, Preston was proving that he was serious and knowledgeable about his new assignment. In the fall of 1863, he initiated measures designed to enhance communications and quality control within the bureau. He tried to foster professionalism among commandants and congressional district enrolling officers and urged them to develop closer relationships with their respective state governments. He required every state commandant to assemble his district officers each month in order to discuss conscription issues and to make recommendations to him. He appointed inspection officers who had the authority to remove incompetent conscription officers. Preston personally made an inspection tour in October (Moore, *Conscription and Conflict,* p. 218).

had filled with men wishing to avoid combat. Lee voiced his concerns regarding North and South Carolina:

> Headquarters Army of Northern Virginia
> Col. J. S. Preston, January 13, 1864
> Superintendent Bureau of Conscription, Richmond, Va.
>
> Colonel: I consider it very important to use every exertion to strengthen the armies in the field at once by the regular operation of the conscript law.... Very few conscripts are being received in this army at present. I feel that the privilege of volunteering is abused. In the State of South Carolina I am informed that a single company, called the Rutledge Cavalry, was increased by volunteering beyond its compliment until it was divided into two and afterward four companies. The regiments from that State in this army are much reduced, and I think that all men who have gone into organizations forbidden by law and orders, and all who are in excess of the compliment of old companies, should be sent to armies in the field. In the State of North Carolina a similar state of things is said to exist, men volunteering in the heavy batteries at Wilmington and in cavalry companies upon the coast.... If you desire it, I can send you at present some officers from this army, to aid the enrolling officers in the different States either to collect conscripts generally or those intended particularly for this army, which needs them very much. I have the honor to be, your obedient servant,
>
> R. E. Lee
> General. [106]

That same day, Lee wrote to President Davis and expressed similar concerns regarding military units in Virginia.[107] As commander of the Army of Northern Virginia, Lee was again worried about the approaching campaign season. In order to prepare his army, he was offering to assign some of his officers to work under the direction of conscription authorities in the states, rather than being in competition with them.

The conscription controversies of 1863 uncovered a second and deeper division within the Confederate government. In the autumn of 1862 after the first conscription laws were enacted, the secretary of war made a procedural distinction between the states of the eastern and central Confederacy and the western states of the Trans-Mississippi

Department. The difference pertained to the control of conscription in the respective areas: the military department commander or the civilian government in Richmond.

In order to organize military operations, Jefferson Davis divided the Confederacy into geographic military departments in 1861. The configuration of these departments varied somewhat during the course of the war as Confederate strategy evolved.[a] The departments were contiguous and were subdivided into military districts. Each department was commanded by a lieutenant general or major general. The districts within were commanded by brigadier generals. The generals were responsible for routine military operations within their areas: defense, communications, intelligence gathering, etc. Troops were assigned to them for these purposes. Department commanders were expected to accomplish their mission with the troops that were assigned to the area. They were also charged with supporting and cooperating with any of the South's several armies that might conduct operations within their respective areas.

East of the Mississippi River in the central and eastern Confederacy, Southern forces initially controlled large and reasonably secure geographic regions. Stable conscription bureaus could operate in these areas. Militia officers and county sheriffs were available to support enrolling officers. During 1863, the conscription role of local militia officers decreased as they were replaced by disabled army officers. The army officers set up permanent offices, assembled staffs, and ran more professional conscription services. Enrollees were gathered and examined by the medical boards, newspapers printed the necessary public notices, and communication with state commandants and Richmond was maintained. East of the Mississippi River, commandants of conscription reported to the secretary of war through the superintendent of conscription and his superior, the adjutant and inspector general. The military department and district generals had no authority over conscription activities within their areas other than approving the assignment of disabled officers and enlisted men to conscription duty. The generals were specifically

[a] In June 1863, there were nine such departments: the Department of Northern Virginia, the Department of North Carolina and Southern Virginia, the Trans-Allegheny Department, the Department of Richmond, the Department of East Tennessee, Department No. 2 (comprised of central and west Tennessee and Alabama), the Department of South Carolina-Georgia-Florida, the Department of Mississippi and East Louisiana, and the Department of the Trans-Mississippi (Current, *Encyclopedia of the Confederacy,* p. 73).

warned by General Order No. 82 issued on November 3, 1862, that conscription authorities "will not be interfered with by generals commanding departments or armies in the field." [a]

Conscription west of the Mississippi River was a different matter. The Trans-Mississippi Department was larger than the other eight departments combined. Its size precluded a defensive strategy that could provide stability and the region was too far from Richmond to be efficiently controlled by the superintendent of conscription. The Trans-Mississippi was too large, too sparsely populated, and did not contain the infrastructure required by Richmond style conscription: reliable mail service, telegraphs, railroads, etc. In order to solve this problem, the same order that told generals east of the Mississippi to stay out of the conscription business put the lieutenant general of the Trans-Mississippi in charge of conscription within his department:

> West of the Mississippi they [commandants of conscription] will report to and receive instructions from the commanding general of the Trans-Mississippi Department, who will require them to conform as nearly as possible to this order and to the regulations prescribed for commandants east of the Mississippi. [108]

All communication from commandants of conscription in the Trans-Mississippi were to be directed to the department commander who would then report to Richmond. However, in practice, because of the great distances involved, the Trans-Mississippi Department commander directed conscription and other governmental activities pretty much on his own authority. As a result, the commander of this department exercised a level of control over conscription in his area that was not tolerated east of the Mississippi River.[b] As the process evolved, Trans-Mississippi conscription became more mobile, contained fewer bureaucratic levels, and was more independent of

---

[a] *O.R.*, Series IV, v. 2, p. 163. Needless to say, this order was ignored throughout 1863 as generals sent recruiters all over the eastern half of the nation in compliance with the circular of January 8.

[b] The exclusion of department and district generals from conscription activities evolved during 1862 and culminated in the wording contained in General Order No. 82. Prior to the Circular of January 8, 1863, the war department seemed to be serious about keeping generals east of the Mississippi River out of conscription. In October 1862, General James Martin, then in command of a district in General T. H. Holmes's Department of North Carolina, was advised by then Secretary of War Randolph that he was not to become involved in the assignment of conscripts who were sent by Mallett's bureau (*O.R.*, Series I, v. 18, p. 752-53).

local court rulings than in the east. Conscripts who were gathered west of the Mississippi River were often assigned to regiments there or in the central Confederacy.[a]

The relative stability of the eastern and central Confederacy, upon which the secretary of war had partially based his east/west distinction of conscription enforcement, was short-lived in the central Confederacy. Early in the war, large parts of Tennessee and Mississippi came under Union control. For most of the war, Union and Confederate armies fought back and forth over much of this area and, later, northwest Georgia. The frequent movement of opposing armies across large areas tended to displace the population and disrupt communications and transportation systems. In this much more fluid environment, Army of Tennessee commanders Braxton Bragg and Joseph Johnston came to exercise a great deal of control over the conscription process, even to the extent of open competition with enrolling officers appointed by the conscription bureau in Richmond.

When the circular urging army generals to gather conscripts and deserters "without passing them through the camps of instruction in the usual manner" was issued on January 8, 1863, General Braxton Bragg was in command of the Army of Tennessee. He already wanted more control over conscription and less interference from Richmond, local politicians, and the courts. The circular gave Bragg all the authority he needed. On January 16, he created the Volunteer and Conscript Bureau of the Army of Tennessee and chose his friend and subordinate, General Gideon Pillow, to rebuild the depleted army.

General Pillow enthusiastically embraced his new assignment and was circulating printed orders within twenty-four hours of his appointment. He directed that a captain and six lieutenants from each regiment and three field officers and two cavalry companies from each army corps should be assigned to conscription and deserter apprehension duty. Bragg also allowed Pillow to use all officers who were without assignments due to the consolidation of regiments.[b] These officers, working under General Pillow's tireless direction, raised twenty additional companies of mounted troops, including

---

[a] Like conscripts in the eastern Confederacy, men liable to conscription in the Trans-Mississippi often bypassed the camps of instruction and joined specific regiments from their home states wherever they were stationed.

[b] Troop strength in some regiments had gotten so low that occasionally two regiments were combined, leaving nearly a full compliment of officers with no troops to command.

numerous conscripts, to be used for conscription and deserter apprehension. Cavalry commander Nathan Bedford Forrest eagerly assisted in Pillow's efforts.

General Pillow created a highly mobile conscription force that operated wherever General Bragg's army controlled territory. As the army moved in and occupied an area, even if for only a brief period of time, the Volunteer and Conscript Bureau troops went to work. They searched the countryside for stragglers, deserters, and anyone else that they felt needed to be in the army. When the army moved on, they simply took their activities to the next area of operation.[a] In March 1863, General Pillow even sent his conscription cavalry into western North Carolina to recruit "without the shadow of law and in defiance of proper authorities," prompting threats of "bloodshed" from Governor Vance. [109]

Many local civilian authorities, as well as regularly appointed conscript officers, objected to Pillow's bypassing of the courts and the conscription bureau's appeal process. State courts had ruled on a variety of conscription related cases, stating that they had jurisdiction because of the involvement of state citizens. The governors, while usually supporting the Confederate war effort, often agreed that their state judges had jurisdiction. While at odds with the courts over the issue of jurisdiction, the superintendent of conscription argued that his bureau's hierarchy of appeals was a necessary part of the procedure and was needed to safeguard civil rights. Generals Bragg and Pillow knew that thousands of men all over the South were using the two coexisting appeals processes to escape military service.

Using both processes allowed men to delay their assignment to the army indefinitely. The system became clogged with endless appeals as more and more Southerners decided that they did not want to go to war. Most of them were allowed to remain at home while their cases were waiting to be heard. Others had to be held under arrest at camps of instruction at government expense. In the meantime, the conscription law often changed, allowing lawyers representing conscripts to repeat the entire process.

Pillow's approach solved many of these problems by simply ignoring the right of appeal. Conscripts either went to the army or to jail. As a result, Pillow was credited with supplying thousands of troops to the army. Nevertheless, his heavy-handed tactics and the

[a] General Pillow's bureau had rendezvous and outposts in the more stable areas of Alabama and Mississippi. These installations were fewer in number than in eastern states and to each was assigned a cavalry company (*O.R.*, Series IV, v. 2. p. 821).

criticism that he generated caused the government to curtail much of his activity in March 1863. But during the summer, the fortunes of war would put Pillow back in charge.

The loss of Vicksburg in July and other military reverses in central Tennessee caused a dramatic rise in desertion in the Army of Tennessee. The new commander, General Joseph E. Johnston, felt that Richmond-style conscription could not significantly strengthen his army. He received permission from the secretary of war to direct conscription in Alabama, Tennessee, Mississippi, and Florida.[a] Johnston delegated this authority to none other than General Gideon Pillow, who immediately resurrected his tactics *and* the accompanying controversy.

Pillow was again very effective. His ever-expanding bureau (in terms of the number of soldiers assigned to conscription duties) operated for the rest of 1863. By the end of the year, Pillow may have supplied as many as twenty-five thousand men to the Army of Tennessee and other Deep South Confederate forces. [110]

Philosophical questions raised by the struggle for control over conscription set two factions within the Confederacy firmly against each other. The Richmond establishment, represented by Superintendent Preston, much of the war department, and North Carolina's Governor Vance, wanted to preserve the civil rights protection provided by the courts and the conscription bureau's appeals process. This approach was more consistent with the Confederate Constitution and the philosophy of a limited and civilian controlled central government, as opposed to military control. The military side was represented by Bragg, Johnston, and many field commanders like Gideon Pillow. They argued that if the war was lost due to lack of manpower, arguments as to who controlled the conscription process would have been pointless. They advocated ignoring all other considerations in order to win the war.

In December 1863, the Confederate government again bowed to the intense criticism that General Pillow was generating. Responsibility for all conscription east of the Mississippi River was returned to Superintendent Preston. Pillow was assigned to other duties. While it may have appeared that the Bragg-Johnston-Pillow philosophy had been defeated, such was not the case.

The Confederacy was losing the war almost everywhere during

[a] This left the Confederate superintendent of conscription in charge only in Virginia, North Carolina, South Carolina, and Georgia.

1863. Lee's army was holding its own in Virginia, but the Army of Tennessee suffered a series of defeats. Large parts of the central Confederacy and Trans-Mississippi fell to the Union. The blockade was beginning to have an effect on the South's ability to survive a protracted struggle. The Union army still occupied parts of coastal Virginia, North Carolina, South Carolina, Georgia, Florida, and the Gulf Coast. Southern strategists realized that the Confederacy was sure to loose a long war.

The South's slowly deteriorating situation and the conflict over how to supply recruits to the army combined to threaten Mallett's battalion. General D. H. Hill had been detached from the Army of Northern Virginia in early 1863 and assigned as the department commander of North Carolina. Union forces at New Bern were again becoming active as spring approached, making attacks on Kinston and Goldsboro likely. Hill was also anticipating attacks at Wilmington and Charleston.[111] He wanted more troops to defend eastern North Carolina and to go on the offensive if possible. Using the January 8 circular, he bypassed the conscription bureau in gathering troops for his coastal regiments.[a] He was one of many generals who could see no reason why Mallett's battalion and similar units should have hundreds of men assigned to conscription duty while army recruiters, with their attractive incentives, were supplying more troops to the war effort.[b] A plan gained favor in Richmond to disband Mallett's unit and send most of his soldiers, except a small camp guard force, to regiments near the coast. Mallett had been advised of the plan to reduce his battalion in February while he was still bedridden. Orders were issued and the reassignment of his men began in March.

Mallett was in the process of returning to Raleigh from Fayetteville. He was bringing his pregnant wife, Annabella, and their children to live with him. Ideally, he wanted to be reinstated

---

[a] In March and April, General Hill's forces unsuccessfully attacked both New Bern and Washington, North Carolina. In April, there was a Union naval attack on Charleston.

[b] At the time, this was likely true. With army recruiters offering cash bounties, choice of assignments, and generous furloughs, the only conscripts that enrolling officers could get were the ones that weren't paying attention. General Hill was known to complain that too many able-bodied men were used in non-combat roles "while the ranks of the army are daily becoming thinner" (*O.R.*, Series IV, v. 2, p. 670-71). Still, Camp Holmes was by no means idle. A "Record of Recruits examined at Camp Holmes" lists thirty-one enrollees as having been examined by camp surgeons on April 1-2, 1863. Seventeen of these were approved for military service (Manuscripts Department, Wilson Library, U. N. C., Chapel Hill).

as conscript bureau commander and keep his battalion together as before. Failing that, if his men were to be transferred, they wanted to be sent to the front as a group. Mallett communicated these wishes to fellow North Carolinian, General Robert Hoke, whose brigade was serving with Lee in Virginia. Hoke responded that "nothing would give me more pleasure than to have Col. Mallett with his officers and men in my Command." [112]

Mallett was unsure at the time if he would ever recover sufficiently from his wound to assume a field command. Whether in command or not, he wanted the battalion to stay together so his officers could keep their commissions. He contacted Governor Vance, who agreed to help. Together, they mounted an effort to keep the battalion intact and at Camp Holmes with Mallett in command. The positive relationship that existed between Governor Vance and Colonel Mallett was about to pay off for both men.

Mallett headed for Richmond armed with a letter from Vance to the secretary of war:

> State of North Carolina
> Executive Dept.
> Raleigh, March 5th, 1863
> Hon. Jas. A. Seddon,
> Secy. Of War
>
> Sir
>
> I beg leave to ask your favorable consideration in the case of Col. Mallett, late commanding the Camp of Instruction near this place, who will hand you this, and make known the circumstances of his case.
>
> His conduct whilst in command, I believe, gave general satisfaction: He organized a Camp Guard of some 600 men, who were duly officered by his assistants and drill masters and rigidly disciplined. Ordered suddenly into the midst of the severe conflict at Kinston, their conduct was such as to elicit the praise of veteran troops and the whole country. Their heavy losses show the gallantry of their bearing and their leader. Col. Mallett was severely wounded, from which he is now only slowly recovering. On hobbling back to Raleigh, he finds himself superseded by Col. August, and an order directing his command to be disbanded & placed in various regiments as Conscripts! What is to become of him? I respectfully submit that it is a great hardship on these brave men and their officers, after

having been associated for eight to ten months and fought together on the field, to now be scattered among strange regiments, their officers conscripted and their efficient and gallant Commander turned out of the service.

In view of the hardship of the case and the meritorious conduct of both men and officers, I am constrained, in spite of my general indisposition to form new regiments, to ask you first to retain Col. M. in command of the Camp as heretofore, whence he could be easily sent to any point where he might be needed; or if this cannot be done I ask that he may be sent into the field with his entire command, having Col. August to form a new guard from the new Conscripts.

It is one of the finest bodies of men in the Southern Confederacy and on their own account should not be separated.

Very respectfully
Yr. Obt. Svt.
Z. B. Vance [a]

In the meantime, the reassignment of Mallett's men had already begun. Companies A and C were disbanded and the soldiers were assigned to other regiments by the end of March. Many of them were sent to North Carolina regiments along the coast. Albert Thompson, while relating the details of his latest trip to Virginia, commented on the harsh life endured by some of his friends in the army and mentioned the breaking up of his unit:

Camp Holmes Near Raleigh April the 9 1863

My Dere wife and children I this morning with much pleasure take my seat to answer your kind letter which came to hand the other day I was glad to here that you all attended to fast day we all did keep that day here we did not drill any that day we had preaching here on that day.... well Cate I just got back from Frederick Burg I saw all the boys from N.C.... I stayed one night in the sixteenth regiment.... The boys sees hard times there they just get one quarter of a pound of Bacon a day and you now that is little a nuft that is all we get now of Bacon we mout as

[a] Mobley, *Vance*, v. 2, p. 81-82. Some of Mallett's officers had received their commissions for assignment to the conscript bureau only. If these officers were reassigned, they were likely to revert to the rank of private.

> well see hard times as aney body   last Sunday I marched through Snow from five to six inches deepe and we walk from 15 to 20 miles.... The most of the soldgers has now [no] tent cloth but they make a tent by digging a pit in the ground and covering it with dirt   They look just like possoms coming out   I also saw the yankeys Balloon up last Monday   we have hard times now   We have to stand guard every other night since the Battalion Busted up....[a]

While Thompson and the rest of Mallett's soldiers waited to hear if they too would be transferred, Governor Vance kept up the pressure to save what was left of the battalion. He had also given Mallett a letter for the North Carolina congressional delegation:

> State of North Carolina
> Executive Department
> Raleigh, March 4th, 1863
> Hon. T. D. McDowell
> Richmond Va.
>
> Dear Sir
> Our mutual friend Col P Mallett who will hand you this will also show you an unsealed letter to Mr. Seddon which will show what I have asked to be done for him - He can himself explain the whole matter. It is a hard case indeed, and I desire you to see Mr Dortch, Mr Davis and if necessary the whole of our delegation and ask them to oblige me and a gallant officer by seconding my request.
> It is a splendid body of men, well equipt, well disciplined, and fought with desperate gallantry, at Kinston. Every body here would grieve to see them scattered & and their individuality lost. Besides, there are a number of high spirited young officers who would be entirely thrown out and reduced to ranks.
>
> Very truly & respectfully yours
> Z. B. Vance [113]

Instead of being adversaries as might have been expected, Mallett and Vance worked reasonably well together. The politics of

[a] Albert to Cate, April 9, 1863. The "fast day" referred to by Thompson was one of numerous days of "fasting and humility" decreed by President Davis during the war in order to invoke God's intervention on the side of the Confederacy. In the North, President Lincoln issued similar decrees on behalf of the Union.

national compulsory military service had caused immense friction between the Confederate government and several governors. Vance was second only to Joseph Brown of Georgia in his adversarial relationship with Richmond. As the conscription bureau's ranking representative in the state, Mallett was likely to collide with the governor on a variety of issues.

Vance seemed often to seek disagreements with Confederate authorities. He continuously railed about slights, both real and imagined, made against his state. He insisted that North Carolina regiments should serve together in the same brigades. He then insisted that these brigades should be commanded by generals from North Carolina. He routinely became involved in Confederate army personnel matters and troop movements and corresponded endlessly with President Davis, the secretary of war, and Robert E. Lee. He quarreled with the war department and with Peter Mallett over the assignment of North Carolina troops. He even recommended to the secretary of war that a newspaper reporter be allowed to travel with North Carolina regiments to insure adequate reporting of their accomplishments.[114] Zebulon Baird Vance was a tireless and irritating champion of state's rights in the midst of a war effort that could no longer afford the luxury.

While Mallett's primary responsibility was to the Confederate military, he was mindful of his dependence on Vance for the accomplishment of his mission. Mallett and the Confederacy still needed Vance's militia to gather conscripts and deserters. Mallett was slowly replacing most of the militia enrolling officers with disabled army officers, but that process would take at least a year to complete. Even after that, Mallett's officers would need the experience and cooperation of the militia as conscription resistance and desertion increased. True, Vance had consistently refused to allow the Confederacy to conscript his militia officers, but just as consistently, he had required those same officers to assist Mallett's bureau. Mallett knew that the gain far outweighed the loss.

Vance, likewise, needed Mallett's cooperation. The commandant's skill and energy had made North Carolina the leading supplier of conscripts to General Lee's army. That accomplishment resulted in significant influence for Vance in Richmond. Furthermore, Mallett could delay the enrollment of individual conscripts or categories of conscripts for extended periods of time. The ability to influence the conscription process through Mallett translated into political power for the governor.[115] This relationship was interrupted when Mallett was wounded and replaced by Colonel August. Prior to that, Mallett and Vance had managed to fulfill their respective responsibilities without seriously alienating each other. Neither of them was interested in a change in the status quo.[a] Aside from all the efforts to keep Mallett and his battalion in Raleigh, a legal development may have tipped the scales.

North Carolina Supreme Court Chief Justice Richmond Pearson rendered a decision that threatened to undo the partnership between Vance's militia and Mallett's bureau. The original incident occurred in February. Fifty militiamen had gone to arrest more than a dozen draft dodgers who were hiding in a Yadkin County schoolhouse. A shootout ensued in which two members of the militia and two resisters were killed. Judge Pearson ordered the resisters to be freed on the grounds that the state militia had no legal authority to arrest individuals who were suspected of violating a national law, i.e. conscription. Vance seized on the incident to use as compelling leverage to preserve Mallett's battalion:

> Raleigh March 26th, 1863
> Hon. Jas. A. Seddon
> Secty of War
> Richmond Va
> A recent decision of our Chief Justice on a Habeas Corpus renders it impossible for me, without further legislation to aid in arresting conscripts with Militia. I therefore advise that Col Mallett's battalion not be diminished, for the present, as the whole execution of the law will devolve on him.
> Z. B. Vance [116]

Faced with the possibility of a breakdown of conscription in North Carolina and with the further alienation of the state's combative governor, the war department relented. No more soldiers were taken

[a] The Mallett/Vance relationship was not always one of mutual respect. Controversy surrounding the conscription of men who had previously hired substitutes for army service reached a crisis in early 1864. After the provision allowing substitution was abolished, Mallett was caught between orders from the Confederate government to conscript these men and Judge Pearson's ruling to the contrary. Governor Vance supported Pearson. Vance did not want a controversy with Mallett and wrote during the period, "... I am on the verge of being forced into a conflict with Mallett. He lacks brains - But I shall act cautiously and hope to steer safely." On that occasion, Vance got Mallett to agree not to send men who had hired substitutes to the army until a definitive legal decision was rendered (Yates, *The Confederacy and Zeb Vance,* p. 60-61).

from Mallett's battalion. Colonel August was transferred and Mallett was reinstated as North Carolina's conscription commander.[117]

By the time he returned to his duties, Mallett was living in Raleigh with his family. He moved his conscription headquarters from Camp Holmes to a suite of offices in town where he could finish recuperating from his wound and stay in close contact with Governor Vance. Day-to-day activities at the camp were delegated to Captain McRae or to one of the several lieutenants upon whom Mallett had come to rely. Although conscription was in a transitional period, the business-like approach that Mallett had originally established for his bureau had survived the brief tenures of Colonel August and Captain Johnson, who returned to his regiment in May. The conscript bureau continued to supply men to the Confederate army, although the numbers varied according to how active the competing army recruiters were. Also, the returning of deserters to the army was becoming an increasingly more significant part of the bureau's mission.

The replacement of militia officers with disabled army officers coincided with an increase in administrative responsibilities for conscript officers. By spring 1863, conscript officers were spending a great deal of time assigning enrollees to civilian jobs that were considered essential to wartime production. Textile workers, miners, mechanics, harness makers, shoe makers, government employees, and others had to be excused from military service yet mobilized to contribute to the national war effort. In every state of the Confederacy, thousands of applications for these assignments had to be investigated and verified. These "details" which allowed men to avoid military service were much sought after and widely abused. Once granted, details were good for periods of from sixty days to one year, then the assignment had to be renewed. Further complicating the process were court decisions and changes in law passed by congress that forced conscript officers to periodically reexamine and reclassify large numbers of men.

The amount of clerical work generated by conscription and related activities was unprecedented. Dozens of new forms and reporting procedures were developed. The war department frequently issued orders attempting to standardize reporting formats and a considerable amount of time and energy was expended on perfecting administrative processes.

Mallett's headquarters staff handled large sums of money to keep the bureau running. Battalion officers and men not only had to be paid their regular salary, but they also had to be reimbursed for expenditures incurred in the performance of their duties. Rent for office space, feed for horses, room and board, and travel expenses all had to be verified and payments made. The congressional district medical boards had to be kept staffed with surgeons, each of whom was paid through Mallett's office. Orders, desertion notices, procedural changes, and inquiries to and from Richmond were all funneled to Mallett's headquarters. His clerks logged the individual items and referred them to a congressional district enrolling officer, usually a captain, who sent them to the appropriate county officer, usually a lieutenant, for action. When the investigation was completed, the item was sent back through the same chain of command. Accounts were kept for theses activities, and Colonel Mallett paid post office and telegraph bills quarterly.

Administrative files that were required to track thousands of conscripts through enrollment, medical examinations, issues of uniforms and equipment, and final assignment were maintained at Camp Holmes. Engineer and naval officers occasionally arrived looking for conscripts with an aptitude for those branches of service.[a] Records on individual exemptions, details, and desertions were kept at Mallett's headquarters, as were most of the financial records. Copy books of all postal and telegraph correspondence were maintained at headquarters, Camp Holmes, and at the congressional district offices. Congressional district and county conscript officers also maintained files on all local enrollees. This clerical activity documented the process whereby thousands of men were transformed from civilians to soldiers. It tracked them if they deserted and settled their accounts when they died.[b]

During the course of the war, more and more soldiers were back in their hometown communities for various reasons. Furloughs, illness, wounds, and other types of leave peppered each county with soldiers who were legally away from their regiments. Upon arriving at home, each soldier was required to report to his local conscript officer, present his furlough document, and make his presence in the

[a] Mallett's success in gathering men for the Confederate States Navy was noted by Commander John M. Brooke, who reported in 1863 that Camp Holmes was providing more sailors than any other camp of instruction. The next year, another report stated that "Camp Holmes, N.C., continues to give the largest number of recruits, 613 having been enlisted there from January 1 to October 30, 1864" (*O.R.,Union and Confederate Navies*, Series II, v. 2, p. 754).

[b] The unpaid wages of deceased soldiers, minus any deductions, were payable to the next-of-kin through a tedious application and probate process (*Carolina Watchman,* Sept. 1, 1862).

county known.[118] When his furlough expired, the soldier had either to apply for an extension, return to his unit, or be declared absent without leave.

Each month, county conscript officers compiled a "return" (any report that was submitted on a regular basis or updated existing information) containing the names of all soldiers on leave within the county. These reports recorded each soldier's regiment and army assignment, when, where and by whom he was furloughed, and for what period of time. The soldier's physical description was noted in order to discourage disabled imposters from appearing in place of soldiers who were well enough to return to their units. Consolidations of the county returns were prepared by the congressional district officer's staff. These reports were sent to Colonel Mallett's headquarters where they were again consolidated and sent to the superintendent of conscription in Richmond. All of these returns, like most reports in the army, were filled out in duplicate or triplicate. The Camp Holmes assistant quartermaster, Sergeant James Marcom, acquired a printing press and supplied Mallett's bureau with printed forms. Occasionally, hand-written reports were used when printed forms were not supplied to outlying offices in a timely manner.

County conscript officers were charged with arresting men who failed to report for duty and soldiers who had deserted or overstayed their leave. Usually, they had only the local sheriff and militiamen for protection. The rise of violent draft resistance seriously weakened this support. When the safety of local conscription officers became a serious concern, squads or companies of Mallett's battalion were sent to the area in question.

During 1863, the problem of desertion from Confederate armies and conscription resistance came to threaten the South's war effort. While the first conscription law provided few job-related exemptions, subsequent amendments allowed a variety of ways to escape military service. The hiring of substitutes and an exemption for slave overseers on plantations were also allowed. Various exemptions, deferments, and details enabled thousands of Southerners to delay or avoid conscription and fueled the "rich man's war, poor man's fight" argument. This attitude took hold in western North Carolina, as well as in most mountainous regions of the Confederacy where there were few large plantations and thousands of small family farms. Entire communities had been stripped of their farm workforces by the combination of early-war volunteering and conscription laws. Families left behind often faced starvation. These conditions combined with anti-Confederate sentiment and growing Union army influence from Tennessee. The result was public discontent and, finally, violence in western North Carolina. As civil unrest increased, local authorities became less capable of maintaining the peace.

For soldiers from eastern North Carolina where the Union army occupied or conducted raids in twenty of the state's eighty-nine counties, the issue of family safety was also a real concern. The Confederacy's inability or unwillingness to expel the enemy from this area generated additional discontent with the national government. At both ends of the state, families separated from their men by war were at the mercy of the enemy and society's meanest elements.

Thousands of North Carolina soldiers were torn between the desire to care for their families and their sense of duty. Most soldiers could not afford to hire substitutes, did not have the expertise to get a work detail, and did not live in an area where the overseer exemption applied. These circumstances, along with Confederate impressment laws and tax-in-kind levies, deepened the class-conflict element of the public's discontent.

Impressment was the process that allowed Confederate officers and local officials to seize private property needed by the army: food, livestock, etc. There was a complicated procedure to evaluate and reimburse the owner. He was often paid weeks or months after the seizure, at below-market prices, with inflation-riddled currency. The tax-in-kind law, or tithe tax, required farmers to turn over to the Confederate government ten percent of all crops and livestock produced each year. These measures were particularly hard on subsistence farm families who had already lost their workers to the army.

While not all North Carolinians were affected to the same extent by this combination of circumstances, practically everyone understood what was happening and had an opinion as to why. Even comparatively prosperous soldiers like Albert Thompson were not immune to the attitudes that were taking shape. From his vantage point as a conscript who guarded other conscripts, he observed that "a man that is out of the ware don't cere for those that are in the ware or that has friends in the ware   They don't cere if the ware holds on ten years." [119] Thousands of North Carolina soldiers shared Thompson's feelings. As 1863 wore on, they began to desert from the army in large numbers.

The state's desertion problem was further aggravated by a series of rulings from state judges. Habeas corpus appeals increased dramatically after Judge Pearson's initial ruling in the Yadkin County case and in another case involving the question of substitutes in the army. Governor Vance agreed that state judges had jurisdiction in these cases. Still, he searched for ways to circumvent Pearson's opinion that the state militia could not enforce conscription. He ordered his militia officers to "aid" Confederate conscript officers and to act as an unofficial "posse when requested." [120] This was little more than a gesture, but it was all Vance could do in the short term. President Davis wrote to Vance in May 1863 and recommended that he form a separate enforcement organization to apprehend deserters and conscription resisters.

In July, the North Carolina legislature authorized the Guard for Home Defense. The law provided that most men in the militia were also to be classified as members of the "Home Guard."[a] The new organization was designed to satisfy Judge Pearson's legal objections to state enforcement of national laws. Vance planned to use the Home Guard to assist Mallett with conscription resistance and to continue using militia officers in non-coercive conscription assignments. Judge Pearson then promptly disqualified the Home Guard from most conscription enforcement. Months of maneuvering between the three branches of state government had resulted in no help for Mallett in collecting conscripts, no protection for the population from lawlessness that the war had generated, and few options left for the governor. Newspapers were quick to point out that Judge Pearson's decision rendered the governor powerless to combat the outrages being committed by deserters. It wasn't until the end of the year that the legislature was able to pass a law that satisfied Judge Pearson's requirements.

By then, the damage was done. As early as the previous April, about the time Mallett returned to duty, desertions from North Carolina regiments had reached epidemic proportions. The highly respected General Dorsey Pender described the effects of North Carolina's legal tug-of-war in a memo to General Lee:

> HEADQUARTERS PENDER'S BRIGADE
> April 23, 1863
>
> I would beg leave to call the attention of the commanding general to the state of affairs that exists in

[a] Membership in the North Carolina Militia and Home Guard was concurrent for most men. An individual could be an officer or enlisted man in both organizations or hold a different rank in each (Cook, *The Last Tarheel Militia*, p. 5-6).

the North Carolina regiments of the army, and the causes which, in my opinion, have brought it about. I think I am safe in saying that at least 200 men have deserted from the Twenty-fourth North Carolina Regiment in this corps within the last thirty days. This, sir, I fear is not the worst of it, for unless some prompt measures be taken to arrest those already deserted, and severe punishment inflicted after they shall be caught, the matter will grow from bad to worse.

In my humble opinion, the whole trouble lies in the fact that they believe when they get into North Carolina they will not be molested, and their belief is based upon the dictum of Judge Pearson, chief justice of the State, in a recent trial of persons who killed some militia officers while in the discharge of their duties. I have not seen the judge's proceedings in the case, but our men are of the opinion that he held that the conscript law was unconstitutional, and hence they draw the conclusion that enrolled conscripts will not only be justified in resisting the law, but that those who have been held in service by the law will not be arrested when they desert.

This conclusion is borne out by the facts. I have heard from a reliable gentleman that the conscripts and deserters go unmolested in Yadkin County, North Carolina, and Sergeant Grose, of my brigade, who has just returned, was told by the militia officers of that county that they should not arrest any more deserters in the face of Judge Pearson's holding unless protected by the government, and the boldness of the deserters there proves that they are acting up to their word. Letters are received by the men urging them to leave; that they will not be troubled when they get home.... What I have stated concerning Yadkin, I fear, holds elsewhere, and, unless some check is put upon it, will work great and serious injury to the cause. I would suggest that a regiment be sent to that section of the State to arrest deserters. Any effort to arrest them between here and home must only be partial at best, and, when we get on the march, totally impracticable. Unless something be done, and quickly, serious will be the result. Our regiments will waste away more rapidly than they ever have by battle.

When forwarding Pender's memo to Richmond, Lee added his endorsement: "General Pender states to me that the men go off with their arms in squads. They can thus band together in the State with other malcontents, produce great trouble, defy the law, &ct."[121] Governor Vance agreed with Pender that the rumors about Judge Pearson's ruling were doing more damage in the army than the decision itself. Naturally, Vance wrote directly to the president:

> ....news of Judge Pearson's decision went abroad to the Army in a very exaggerated and ridiculous form, soldiers were induced to believe that it declared the conscript law unconstitutional and that they were entitled if they came home to the protection of their civil authorities - Desertion.... broke out again worse than before.[122]

Judge Pearson's rulings could not have done more damage to North Carolina's ability to strengthen Lee's army. The state militia and Home Guard were faced with enforcing an unpopular law against their friends and neighbors. If assaulted or killed in the process, the offenders would be released on Pearson's legal technicality. What little enthusiasm the militia and Home Guard still had for conscription work was further reduced. North Carolinians in the army deserted by the hundreds, confident that no one would bother them once they got back home.

Sharing mountainous borders with four other states, the western part of North Carolina attracted men from three sides and from its own Quaker Belt in the Piedmont. The result was increasing political unrest, lawlessness, and violence. Sooner or later, something would have to be done.

As the situation in the western half of the state worsened during 1863, Mallett rebuilt the two companies of his battalion that were disbanded before he and Vance could get the process stopped. The arrival of spring meant increased conscription efforts to prepare Lee's army for summer fighting. The unsuccessful statewide enrollment of the previous December was reinitiated on a staggered schedule between mid-January and April 16. Thirty-five-to forty-year-old men arrived at Camp Holmes at a steady rate during the period. Even with the competition from army recruiters, Mallett's militia colonels brought in a respectable number of conscripts. However, Judge Pearson's decisions meant additional difficulty in forcing deserters back into the army. When Albert Thompson wrote to Cate from

Camp Holmes in late March, he mentioned how the desertion problem affected his duty at the camp:

> Well Cate I got my butter and fruit and apples and the leather that you and father sent me and I thank you very kindly for them for my shoos have needed mending very bad.... My eyes has got better and my throat is well.... There is still some sickness here there was one man died in Co. D the other day with the fever.... we have a heap of conscript coming in here at this time some of them trie to runaway and some of them dus runaway when one runaway they make us stand [guard] too days at a time....[123]

As the 1863 campaign season approached, Mallett's battalion faced an expansion of its responsibilities. The battalion's noteworthy performance at Kinston and the timeliness of its arrival there made the unit a logical choice for similar assignments. While use as a rapid deployment force against the Union army was not part of their initial responsibility, Colonel Mallett had little doubt that such occasions would arise again. Department of North Carolina forces were neither quick enough nor strong enough to keep General Foster at bay; Kinston and Goldsboro had proven that. Even before the Kinston fight, the use of Mallett's battalion for emergencies as far away as Richmond had been suggested by General Martin.[124] Governor Vance had suggested this use of the battalion as a reason not to disband it.

Not surprisingly, when Union forces threatened the railroad junction and bridge at Weldon in May, the governor and General D. H. Hill asked Mallett to send reinforcements. Mallett put two of his companies and Captain James McRae on a train and sent them to join other troops already there. Albert wrote to Cate when he arrived. He had heard about the battle of Chancellorsville near Fredericksburg, Virginia:

> Weldon N.C. May 8th 1863
> Dear Cate.... We are here at Weldon rite on the Bank of the Roanoke River we came here last night I don't know how long we will stay here there is several regiments here and one Batry I don't know whether the enimy will attack us here or not but we must keep a sharp look out for them till we hear whare they are they have been [with]in seventeen miles of Richmond and have tore up some of the railroad and it is thought that they will give Weldon a trial.... Some

> say we will stay here and gard the Bridge but we can here anything here but the truth.... Well Cate our men has gain at grate victory in Va Ginerl Stone Wall Jackson got wounded in the fight he had his left arm ampitated just above the elbow joint I am very sorry to here of it for he is a grate man.... direct your letters to Camp Holmes the same as you did and I will get them....

Three days later, Thompson wrote again from a different camp location. Rumors about the casualties at Chancellorsville were making the rounds:

> Halifax Cou N C. May the 11 1863
> My dear wife and children... I have had the flu for a few days but I think I am better this morning than I have been.... I am at Halifax ferry garding the ferry the ferry is on the Roanoke River below Weldon 12 miles We are all tolerable well satis fied at this place We are rite in the woods in a cedar grove We have no tents here nothing only one blanket but we have made a tent out of cedar brush and I think it will turn water I don't know how long we will stay here... the steamboats pass up and down the river every day.... I have been trying to find out the pirtickulars of fredrick Burg fight but I cant I beleave that I herd that we lost six or seven thousan men and that the enemy lost twenty or thirty thousan I think there has bin men a nuft kill[ed] for the ware to stop.... some times I think they want us all kill[ed]....

Captain McRae and his two companies stayed in the Weldon area until the middle of June when Acting Superintendent of Conscription G. W. Lay insisted that they be returned to Raleigh.[a] They would soon be on the move again.

[a] Over General D. H. Hill's objections, Superintendent Brigadier General Gabriel J. Rains had ordered McRae and the two companies to be returned to Raleigh in mid-May, but the order was not carried out until June due to changes at the superintendent's office. Rains was replaced by Brigadier General C. W. Field on May 25. A week later, Field was replaced by Lieutenant Colonel George W. Lay who held the position until July 29 (*O.R.*, Series IV, v. 2, p. 1074). Governor Vance, General Hill, and Colonel Mallett apparently took advantage of the confusion and kept McRae's men at Weldon.

General John Smith Preston
1809-1881
Bureau of Conscription
Superintendent
Museum of the Confederacy
Richmond, Virginia

Lieutenant General
Theophilus Hunter Holmes
1804-1880
Department Commander
& General of the Reserves
Library of Congress

General Samuel Cooper, 1798-1876
Confederate Adjutant
and Inspector General
Author's Collection

Major Franz J. Hahr, 1825-1878
North Carolina Bureau of Conscription
Courtesy of Shelly and Russell Dooley
Hendersonville, North Carolina

Private James C. Miller, 1829-1863
Company D, Mallett's battalion
Courtesy of Mrs. Mildred Miller
Stoney Point, North Carolina

WAR DEPARTMENT,
ADJ'T AND IMSPECT. GENERAL'S OFFICE,
Richmond, August 19th, 1862.

GENERAL ORDER,
NO. 58.

I. The following rules, in relation to the examination of Conscripts, are published for the guidance of enrolling and medical examining officers:

1. At each camp of instruction and at such military stations, and other points as may be designated, an experienced army Surgeon, from a different section of the country will be detailed to examine Conscripts.

2. All Conscripts capable of bearing arms will be received.

3. Conscripts not equal to all military duty may be valuable in the Hospital, Quartermaster's or other staff departments, and if so will be received.

4. Blindness, excessive deafness and permanent lameness, or great deformity are obvious reasons for exemptions.

5. Confirmed consumption, large incurable ulcers, and chronic contagious diseases of the skin are causes for exemptions.

6. Single reducible hernia, the loss of an eye, or of several fingers will not incapacitate the subject for the performance of military duty.

7. A certificate of disability of a Conscript, given by a private physician, will not be considered unless affidavit is made that the Conscript is confined to bed, or that his health and life would be endangered by removal to the place of enrolment.

8. But when a Conscript is incapacitated by temporary sickness, he must present himself, so soon as recovered, to the enrolling officer, or to the nearest school for Conscripts.

9. No previous discharge, certificate, or exemption from any source will be acknowledged.

10. Medical officers of the army are not allowed to examine Conscripts, and give certificates, unless they are regularly detailed for that duty.

By command of the Secretary of War.

[Signed.] S. COOPER,
Adjutant and Inspector General.

Adjutant and Inspector General Order No. 58, August 19, 1862, established medical guidelines for the examination of conscripts. Even as early as the second summer of the war, significant physical defects did not excuse Southern men from military service. Hundreds of general orders (procedural directives) and special orders (personnel advisories) were issued by the Adjutant and Inspector General's office each year. They were reprinted by the thousands and distributed throughout the army. Surviving examples are often perforated along the left margins. Army officers frequently kept them in loose leaf notebooks for easy reference. Document shown in actual size. Author's collection.

No. 40.

SPECIAL REQUISITION.

(1) One Cap	$2.-
(1) One Jacket	12.
(1) One pr Pants	9.
(1) One Shirt	3.
(1) One pr Drawers	3.
(1) One pr Shoes	6.
(1) One pr Socks	1.
(1) One Knapsack	4.50

I certify that the above requisition is correct; and that the articles specified are absolutely requisite for the public service, rendered so by the following circumstances: the man is to be sent into the field -

J R McLean 1st Lt. P.A.C.S.

Capt G. B. Baker A.Q.M. Quartermaster North Carolina Army, will issue the articles specified in the above requisition.

J. C. McRae Capt
Commanding.

Received at Camp Holmes, the 18th day of July, 1863, of Capt G. B. Baker A.Q.M. Quartermaster North Carolina Army, One Cap, One Jacket, One pr Pants, One Shirt, One pr Drawers, One pr Shoes, One pr Socks, One Knapsack in full of the above requisition.

[SIGNED DUPLICATES.]

J R McLean
1st Lt P.A.C.S.

The Special Requisition Form No. 40 was one of the most widely used forms in the Confederate military. They were printed in several slightly different formats. A single Form 40 could be used to outfit one soldier or several hundred. For budgetary control, the government's cost for each issued item was usually listed. As manufacturing costs soared, the prices were updated by successive general orders (see next page). This particular requisition was filled-out at Camp Holmes on July 18, 1863, by Lieutenant Jesse McLean and was approved by Captain James C. McRae. Courtesy of the National Archives.

Adjutant and Inspector General's Office,
Richmond, Nov. 9, 1863.

GENERAL ORDERS, }
No. 146. }

I. The subjoined statement of the cost of clothing for the army is published for the information and guidance of all concerned:

Statement of the Cost of Clothing for the Army of the Confederate States, for the year commencing January 1*st*, 1864.

Cap complete, - - - -	$2 00
Cover, - - - -	38
Jacket, - - - -	14 00
Trowsers, - - - -	12 00
Shirt, - - - -	3 00
Drawers, - - - -	3 00
Shoes, pairs, - - - -	10 00
Socks, pairs, - - - -	1 00
Leather stock, - - - -	25
Great coat, - - - -	25 00
Stable frock (for mounted men), - -	2 00
Fatigue overall (for eng'rs and ord.), - -	3 00
Blanket, - - - -	10 00

II. From the time this takes effect, and until further orders, soldiers will be charged and credited on account of clothing to which they are entitled, as provided in General Orders, No. 100, last series, at these rates, and *not* at invoice prices.

By order.

S. COOPER,
Adjutant and Inspector General.

General Order No. 146 was circulated only a few months after the Special Requisition from the previous page. In that brief period of time, the government's costs had risen significantly on uniform jackets, pants, and shoes. If a soldier negligently lost or damaged an item, his account was charged using the prices in effect at the time. The amount was usually deducted from his pay by his company commander. If a soldier died without having received items due him, his next of kin could apply for reimbursement. Dimensions: 5 x 8 inches. Author's collection.

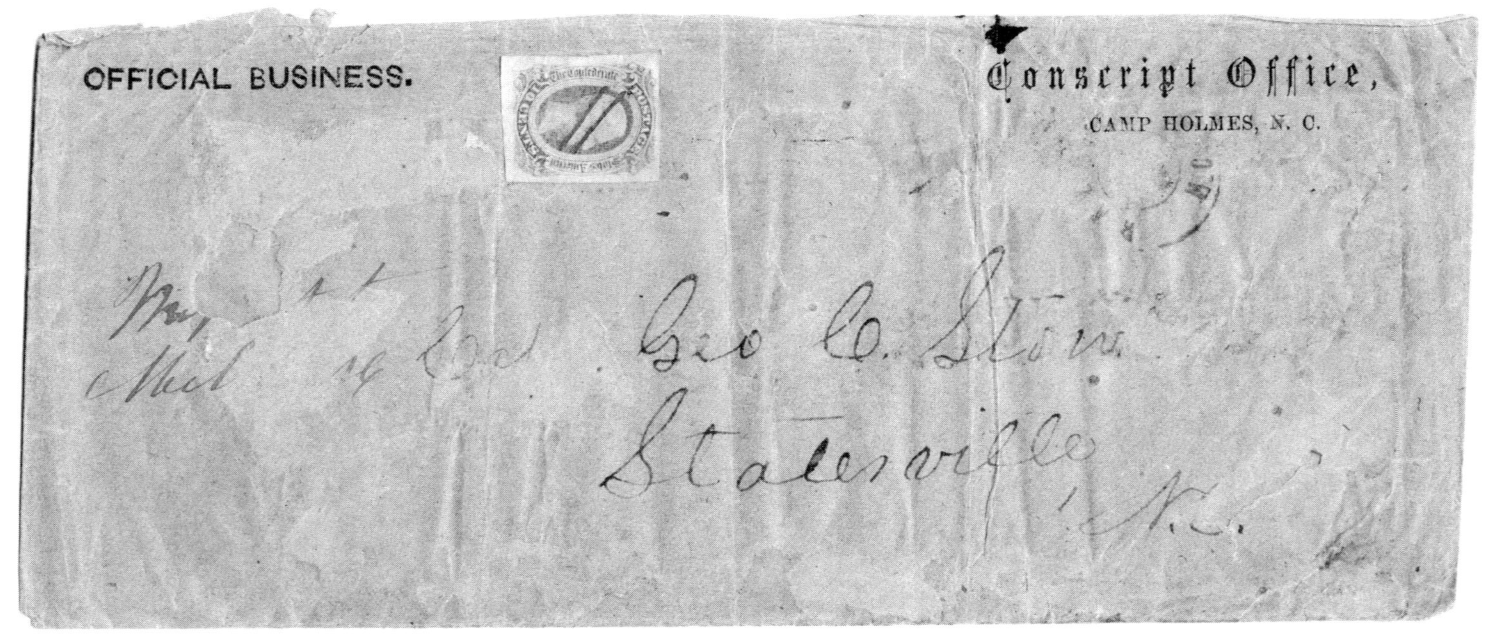

This conscription office envelope is typical of postal covers used for official correspondence throughout the Confederacy. This particular cover was sent to Captain George C. Stowe during the summer of 1863 while he was an enrolling officer at Statesville. Previously, Stowe commanded Company I, 33rd North Carolina Troops. He had been wounded ("thumb shot off") in 1862. He returned to duty but was captured and paroled in December that same year. Stowe was then assigned to conscription duty until he was transferred to Major James C. McRae's battalion. Later, he served as the lieutenant colonel of the 5th North Carolina Senior Reserve regiment. Dimensions: 3 3/4 x 9 inches. Author's collection.

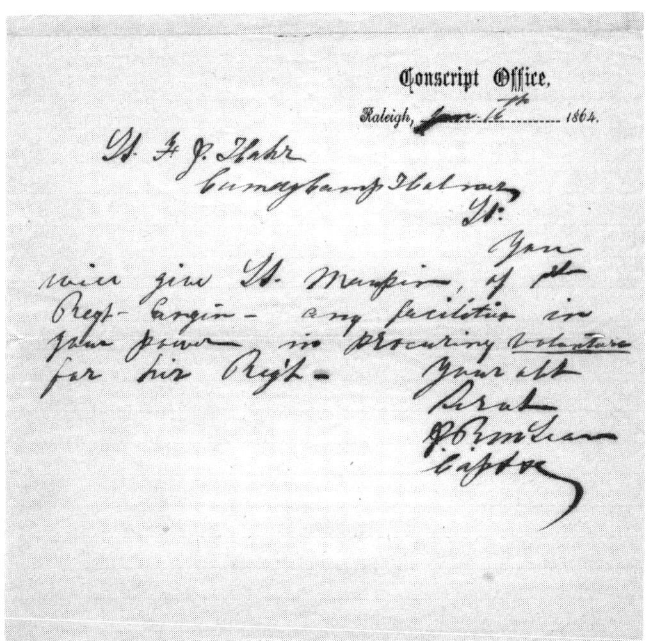

Conscript Office,
Raleigh, Jan 16th 1864.

Lt. F. J. Hahr
Cmdg Camp Holmes
Lt.

You will give Lt. Maupin, of the Regt. Engin- any facilities in your power in procuring volunteers for his Regt. -

Your obt
Servt
J. B. McLean
Captn

The above memorandum was sent by Captain Jesse McLean at Mallett's Raleigh headquarters to Lieutenant Hahr at Camp Holmes on January 16, 1864. The message directs Hahr to assist Lieutenant Maupin of the 1st Confederate Engineers in locating volunteers for his unit from among conscripts then in camp. Dimensions: 7 x 7 inches. Authors collection.

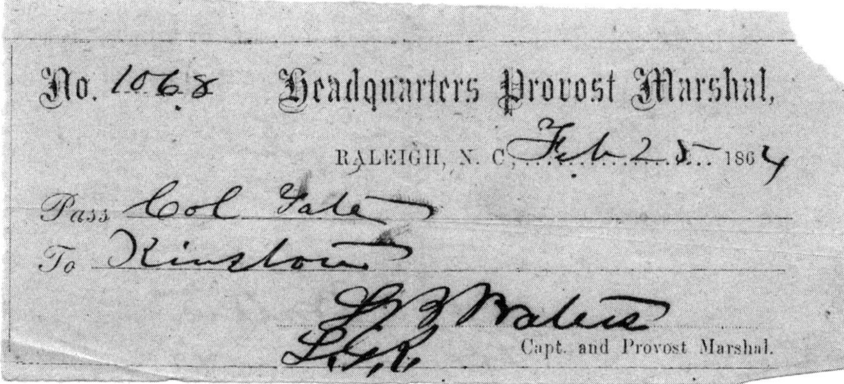

No. 1068 Headquarters Provost Marshal,
RALEIGH, N. C., Feb 25 1864

Pass Col Tate
To Kinston

S. B. Waters
Capt. and Provost Marshal.

Once Captain Samuel B. Waters organized his provost company, even officers like Lieutenant Colonel Samuel McDowell Tate were required to carry passes when they traveled through Raleigh. This pass was issued to Colonel Tate on February 25, 1864. Tate had been wounded the previous October and had been furloughed to his home in Morganton. In February, he was traveling to visit his regiment, the 6th North Carolina State Troops, at Kinston. Tate's regiment was part of General Robert Hoke's brigade, which was preparing to attack New Bern. Dimensions: 5 1/4 x 2 1/4 inches. Author's collection.

This image, depicting the closing moments in the battle of Kinston, was published in a history of the 43rd Massachusetts Infantry in 1883. Several 20-Pounder Parrot guns of the 3rd New York Light Artillery are shown along the south bank of the Neuse River. They are firing over the heads of advancing Union infantry at General Evans's fleeing Confederates on the far side of town. North Carolina Collection, University of North Carolina Library at Chapel Hill.

This engraving, published in the January 10, 1863 issue of Harper's Weekly magazine, shows the bridge over the Neuse River at Kinston during the December 1862 battle. Mallett's battalion is depicted in the upper left corner holding its position near the swamp. Author's collection.

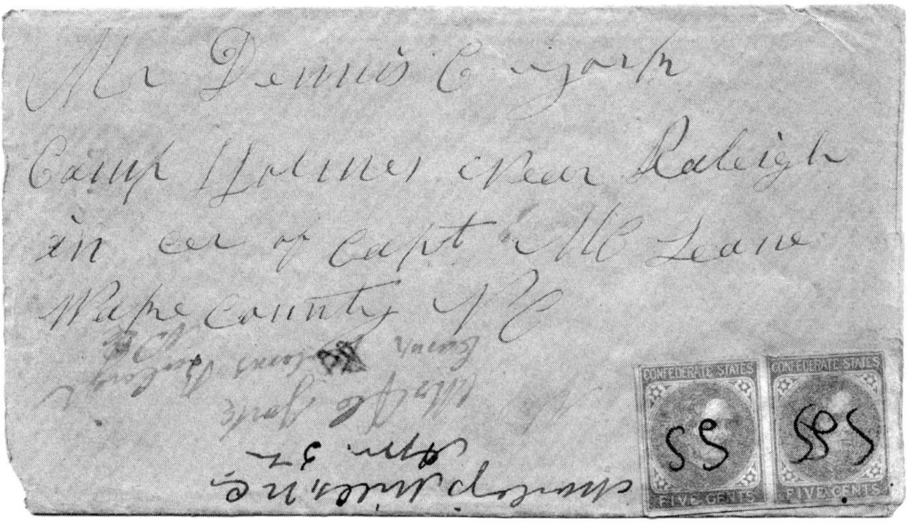

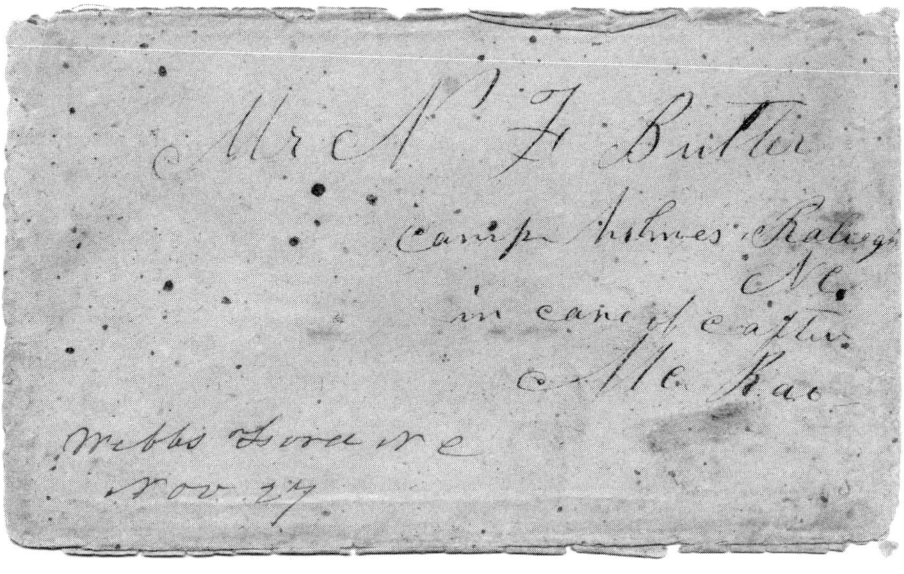

Thousands of letters were sent to and from soldiers at North Carolina's conscript camps. Most were handled by the Confederate postal service, but hand-carried envelopes with no stamps were also widely used. The envelope shown at the top of the page was used at least twice to send letters to Dennis C. York, a musician in Mallett's battalion. On the first occasion, the letter was mailed with two five-cent Confederate stamps attached to the lower right corner. Later, the envelope was turned around, readdressed, and hand-delivered to York. The second envelope was mailed from Webb's Ford, North Carolina, on November 27, 1862, to one of Albert Thompson's messmates, Private N. F. Butler. Two five-cent stamps were used to seal the back of the envelope. Dimensions: both covers are 3 x 5½. inches. Author's collection.

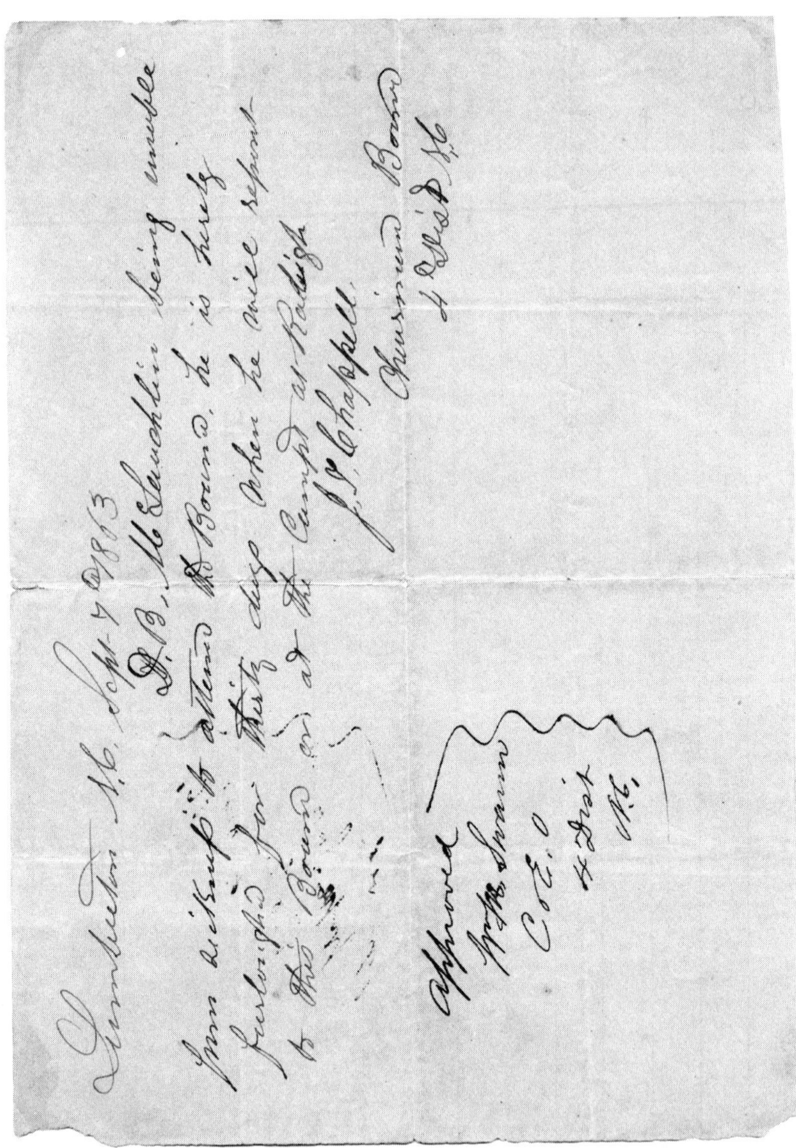

Lumberton N.C. Sept 7 1863
D. B. McLauchlin being unable from sickness to attend the Board he is hereby furloughed for thirty days when he will report to this Board or at the Camp at Raleigh
J. P. Chappell
Chairman Board
4 Dist NC

Approved
Wm. M. Swann
Col E. O.
4 Dist
NC

This document is typical of hand-written furloughs that were used when no printed forms were available. Robeson County resident D. B. McLauchlin was excused from reporting to the enrolling board in Lumberton, North Carolina, for thirty days due to sickness. The furlough was issued by the chairman of the board and approved by 4th Congressional District Enrolling Officer Captain William M. Swann. McLauchlin had already served in the 10th North Carolina Heavy Artillery Battalion from May 1862 until April 16, 1863. He was discharged from that unit for health reasons. By September 1863, when this furlough was issued, the Confederacy was carefully gleaning its male population and reexamining all those who had been discharged for any reason. Records indicate that McLaughlin escaped additional military service. Dimensions: 5 3/4 x 8 inches. Author's collection.

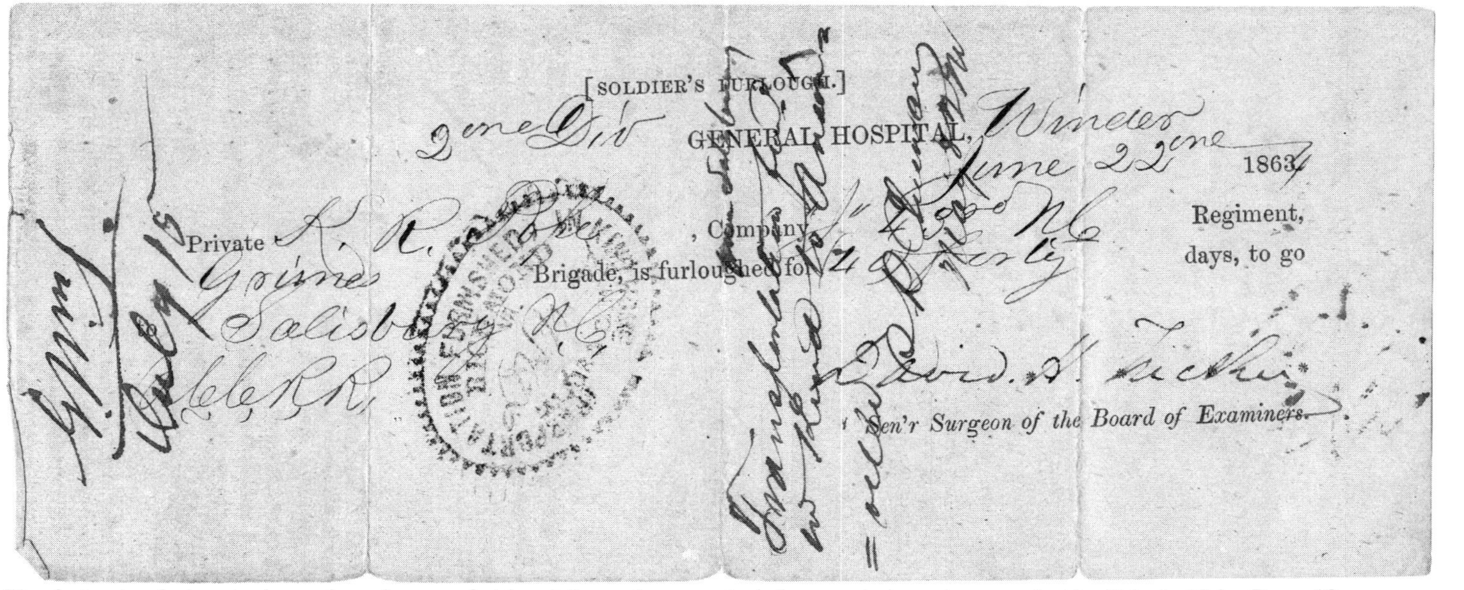

[SOLDIER'S FURLOUGH.]

GENERAL HOSPITAL, Winder June 22nd 1863

Private K. R. Pope, Company Regiment, Grimes Brigade, is furloughed for 40 days, to go to Salisbury N.C.

Sen'r Surgeon of the Board of Examiners.

The forty-day furlough shown here is one of at least three documents (others not shown) generated by Private Kirby Pope (Company I, 43rd North Carolina Troops) after he was shot through the chest at Drewry's Bluff on May 16, 1864. The furlough was issued by the senior surgeon of the medical examining board at Winder General Hospital in Richmond on June 22. Pope was authorized to travel at government expense by train to Salisbury, North Carolina, and then on to Anson County by transportation "in kind." Pope remained in North Carolina until he was ordered back to Virginia. On November 2, he again reported to Winder Hospital, where his furlough was extended for thirty days. He returned to North Carolina. On December 2, his furlough was extended for another thirty days by the 7th Congressional District Examining Board in Wadesboro. The three documents collected a total of twelve signatures and endorsements from doctors, enrolling officers, and officers in the field as Pope traveled back and forth through the Confederate bureaucracy. If called upon to account for his whereabouts during the six month period, Pope would have needed to produce all three documents. Dimensions: 3 1/4 x 8 inches. Author's collection.

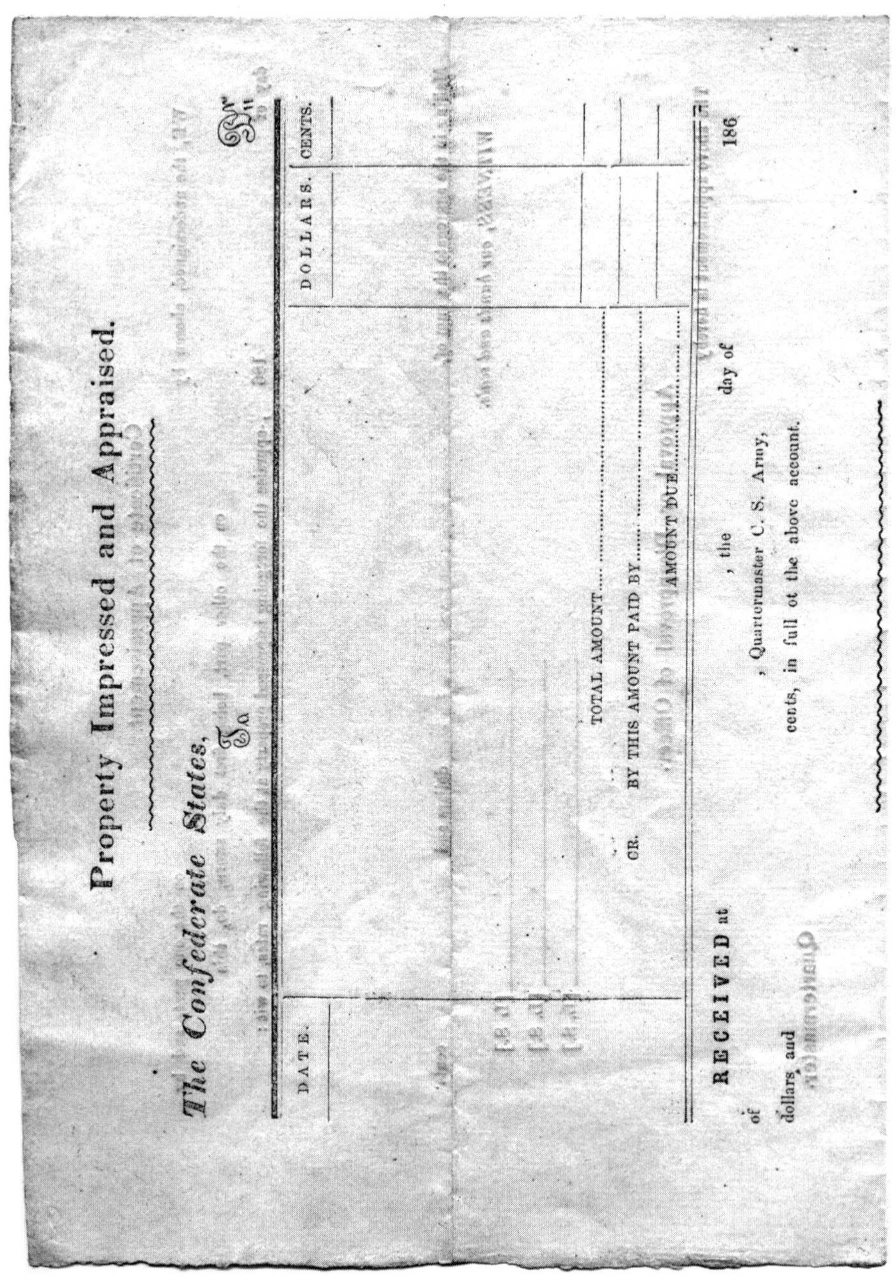

Property Impressed and Appraised.

The Confederate States,

To Dr.

DATE.		DOLLARS.	CENTS.
	TOTAL AMOUNT		
CR.	BY THIS AMOUNT PAID BY		
	AMOUNT DUE		

RECEIVED at , the day of 186

of , Quartermaster C. S. Army,

dollars and cents, in full of the above account.

The seizure of private property by the Confederate government was documented on the two-sided Property Impressed and Appraised and Certificate of Appraisement Form. Listed on the front of the document was the property to be seized, the owner, the impressing agent or quartermaster, and the reimbursement value.

Certificate of Appraisement.

WE, the undersigned, chosen by on the one part, and by on the other part, being first duly sworn, do, this day of 186 , appraise the foregoing impressed property at the following rates, to wit:

Making in the aggregate the sum of dollars and cents.

WITNESS, our hands and seals.

________________[L. S.]

________________[L. S.]

________________[L. S.]

Approval or Disapproval of Officer.

The above appraisement is hereby

Quartermaster.

On the back of the form, the property value was established by a panel of three appraisers. The local army quartermaster was required to approve or disapprove the transaction. Dimensions: 6 x 8 1/4 inches. Author's collection.

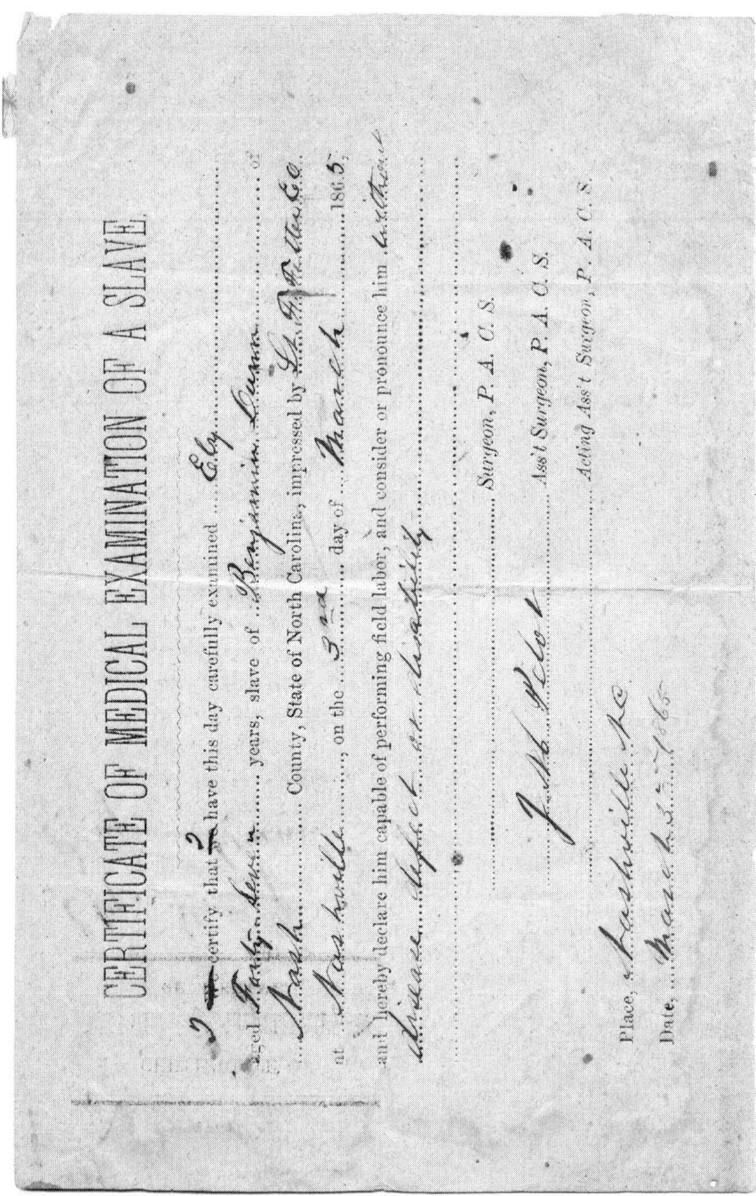

CERTIFICATE OF MEDICAL EXAMINATION OF A SLAVE.

I certify that I have this day carefully examined ... Ely ...
aged Forty Seven ... years, slave of ... Benjamin Dunn ... of
... Nash ... County, State of North Carolina, impressed by Lt. F. A. Fetter E.O.
at ... Nashville ..., on the ... 3rd ... day of ... March ... 1865;
and hereby declare him capable of performing field labor, and consider or pronounce him without
disease, defect or disability ...

.... Surgeon, P. A. C. S.

J. M. Pelot ... Ass't Surgeon, P. A. C. S.

.... Acting Ass't Surgeon, P. A. C. S.

Place, Nashville N.C.

Date, March 3rd 1865

The physical fitness of slaves who were seized from their owners for government work was documented on a form entitled Certificate of Medical Examination of a Slave. In this case, "Ely," a forty-seven-year-old man who was the property of Benjamin Dunn of Nash County, was impressed by the local enrolling officer, Lieutenant F. A. Fetter, on March 3, 1865. Ely was certified by Army Assistant Surgeon J. M. Pelot to be "without disease, defect or disability." His term of government service is not specified. Whether African-American slaves seized by impressment or free white men seized by conscription, in 1865, Southern men faced open-ended servitude in the Confederacy. Dimensions: 8 ½ x 5 ½ inches. Author's collection.

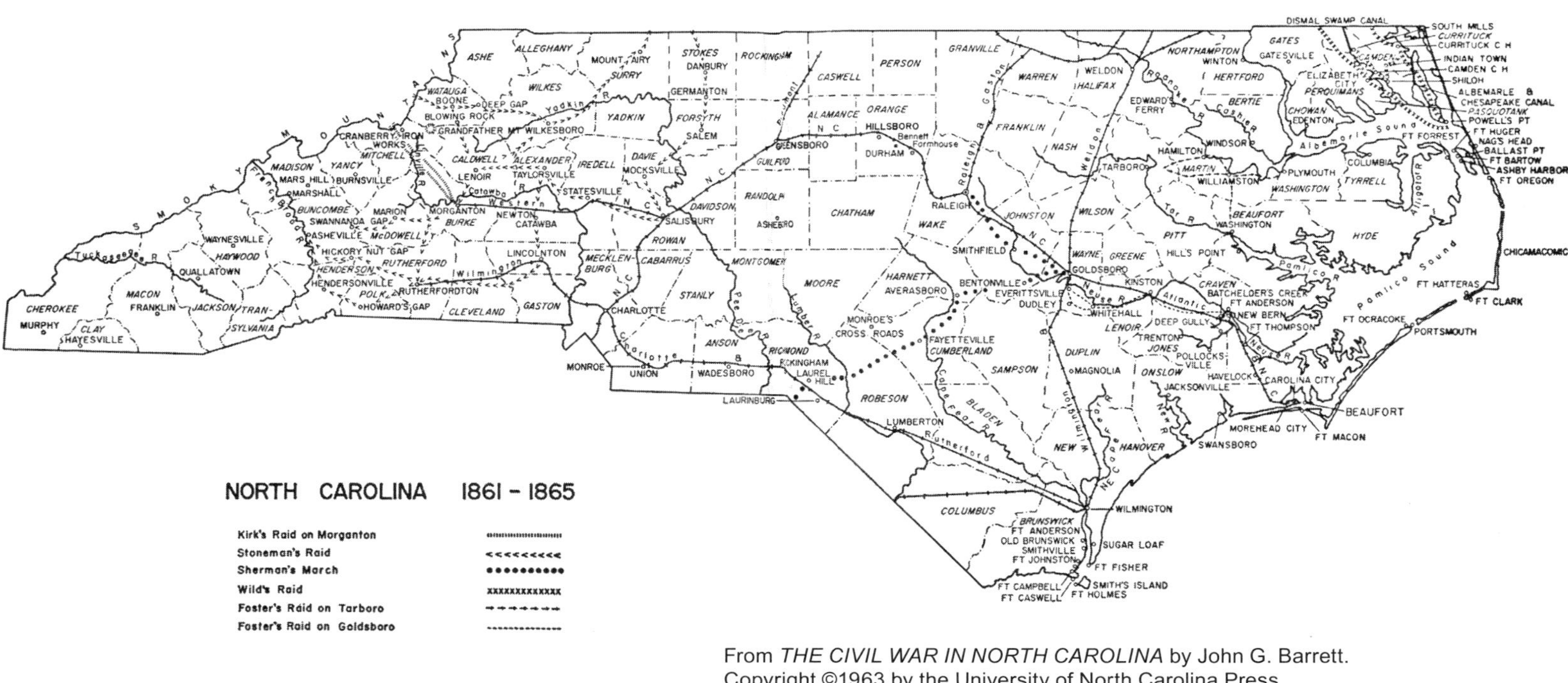
NORTH CAROLINA 1861 - 1865
Kirk's Raid on Morganton
Stoneman's Raid
Sherman's March
Wild's Raid
Foster's Raid on Tarboro
Foster's Raid on Goldsboro
DISMAL SWAMP CANAL
SOUTH MILLS
CURRITUCK
CURRITUCK C H
INDIAN TOWN
CAMDEN C H
SHILOH
ALBEMARLE & CHESAPEAKE CANAL
PASQUOTANK
POWELL'S PT
FT FORREST
FT HUGER
NAG'S HEAD
BALLAST PT
FT BARTOW
ASHBY HARBOR
FT OREGON
CHICAMACOMICO
FT HATTERAS
FT CLARK
FT OCRACOKE
PORTSMOUTH
BEAUFORT
FT MACON
MOREHEAD CITY
SWANSBORO
WILMINGTON
SUGAR LOAF
FT FISHER
SMITH'S ISLAND
FT HOLMES
FT CAMPBELL
FT CASWELL
FT JOHNSTON
SMITHVILLE
OLD BRUNSWICK
FT ANDERSON
BRUNSWICK
COLUMBUS
ASHE
ALLEGHANY
MOUNT AIRY
SURRY
STOKES
DANBURY
ROCKINGHAM
CASWELL
PERSON
GRANVILLE
WARREN
WELDON
HALIFAX
NORTHAMPTON
WINTON
GATES
GATESVILLE
HERTFORD
BERTIE
ELIZABETH CITY
PERQUIMANS
CHOWAN
EDENTON
WINDSOR
HAMILTON
MARTIN
WILLIAMSTON
PLYMOUTH
WASHINGTON
TYRRELL
COLUMBIA
HYDE
BEAUFORT
PITT
HILL'S POINT
TARBORO
EDGECOMBE
NASH
FRANKLIN
WILSON
JOHNSTON
WAYNE
GREENE
GOLDSBORO
KINSTON
CRAVEN
BATCHELDER'S CREEK
NEW BERN
FT THOMPSON
LENOIR
DEEP GULLY
WHITEHALL
JONES
TRENTON
POLLOCKSVILLE
HAVELOCK
CAROLINA CITY
ONSLOW
JACKSONVILLE
DUPLIN
MAGNOLIA
NEW HANOVER
SAMPSON
BLADEN
ROBESON
LUMBERTON
CUMBERLAND
FAYETTEVILLE
HARNETT
AVERASBORO
BENTONVILLE
EVERITTSVILLE
DUDLEY
WAKE
RALEIGH
SMITHFIELD
ORANGE
HILLSBORO
DURHAM
Bennett Farmhouse
ALAMANCE
GUILFORD
GREENSBORO
CHATHAM
RANDOLPH
ASHEBORO
MOORE
MONROE'S CROSS ROADS
RICHMOND
ROCKINGHAM
LAUREL HILL
LAURINBURG
MONTGOMERY
STANLY
ANSON
WADESBORO
UNION
MONROE
CHARLOTTE
MECKLENBURG
CABARRUS
ROWAN
SALISBURY
DAVIDSON
FORSYTH
SALEM
GERMANTON
YADKIN
DAVIE
MOCKSVILLE
IREDELL
STATESVILLE
ALEXANDER
TAYLORSVILLE
WILKES
WILKESBORO
CALDWELL
LENOIR
WATAUGA
BOONE
DEEP GAP
BLOWING ROCK
GRANDFATHER MT
CRANBERRY IRON WORKS
MITCHELL
YANCY
BURNSVILLE
MADISON
MARS HILL
MARSHALL
BUNCOMBE
ASHEVILLE
SWANNANOA GAP
MARION
McDOWELL
BURKE
MORGANTON
CATAWBA
NEWTON
LINCOLNTON
GASTON
CLEVELAND
RUTHERFORD
RUTHERFORDTON
POLK
HOWARD'S GAP
HICKORY NUT GAP
HENDERSON
HENDERSONVILLE
HAYWOOD
WAYNESVILLE
JACKSON
TRANSYLVANIA
QUALLATOWN
MACON
FRANKLIN
CHEROKEE
MURPHY
CLAY
HAYESVILLE
SMOKY MOUNTAINS

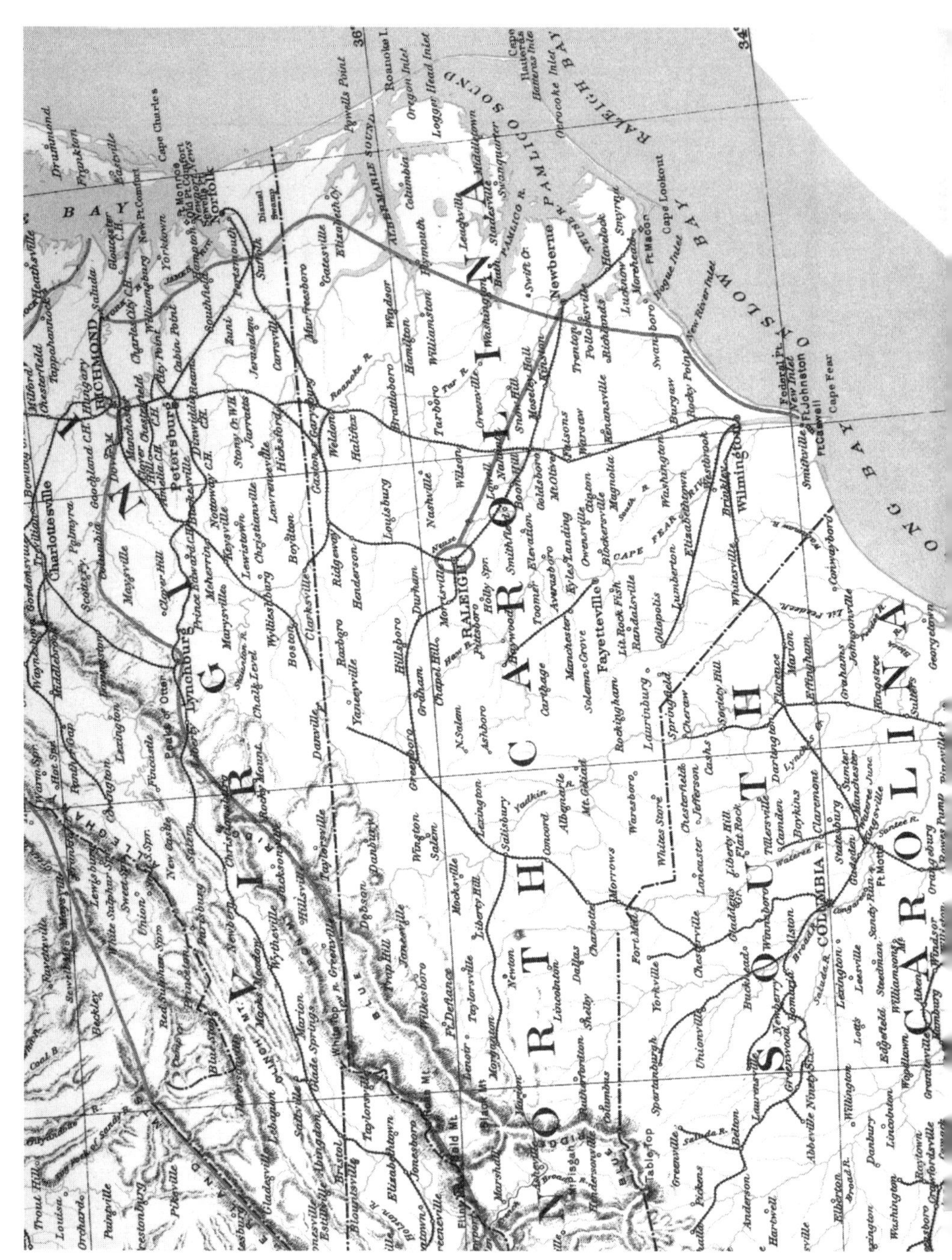

Eastern North Carolina & Virginia map: Official Military Atlas of the Civil War.

Confederate Military Departments
June 30, 1863

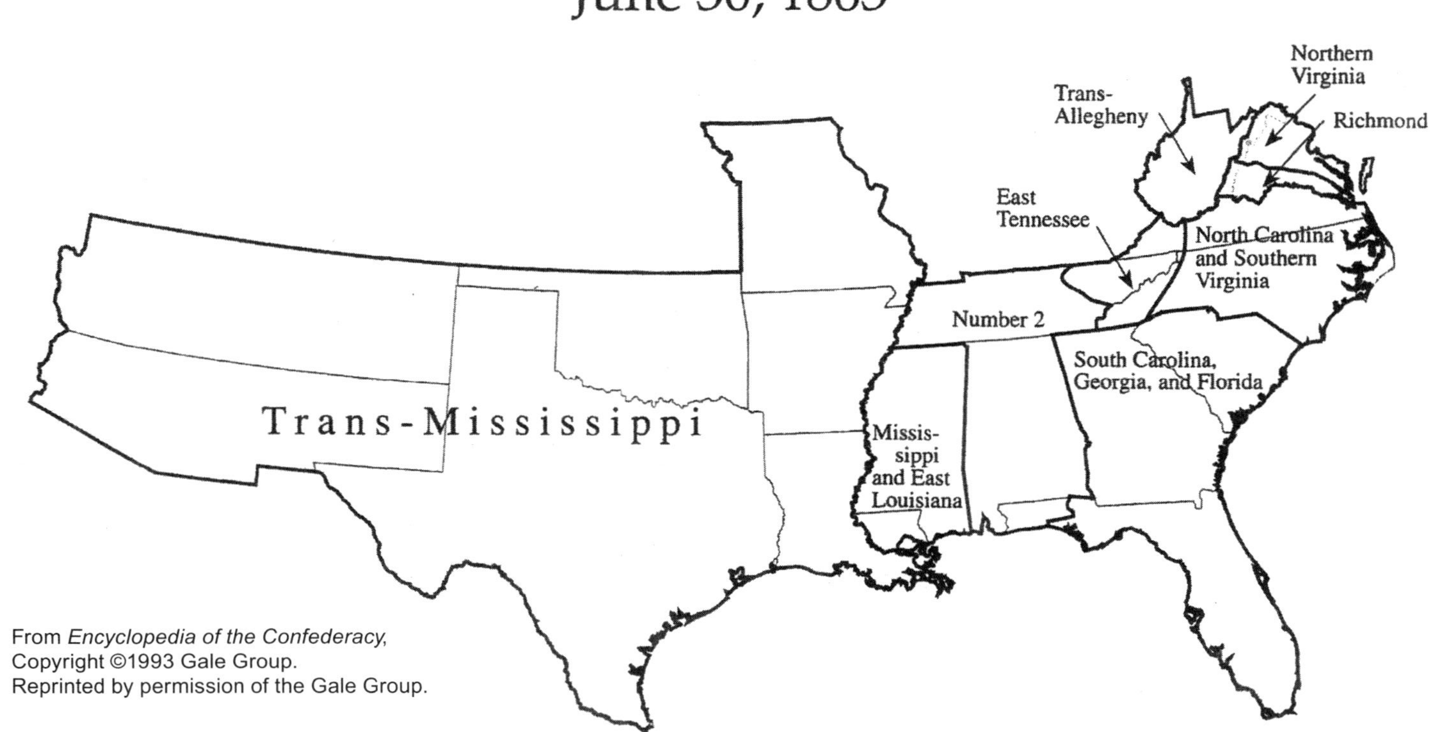

Chapter Six

Mobile Battalions

August 1863 - May 1864

Many western North Carolinians felt little connection with their state government. North Carolina politics were most often dominated by the more densely populated and comparatively affluent eastern half of the state. Issues that drew the east toward war had less influence in the west. The mountain and hill folks had fewer slaves and engaged in significantly less commercial activity than the area east of Raleigh. The state's Quaker Belt region in the northern Piedmont was home to Quakers as well as Moravians, Dunkards, Lutherans, and other anti-slavery, pacifist denominations.[a] Desertions from companies raised in this area were occurring before the conscription laws. The passage of those laws only deepened feelings against the government. As early as September 1862, Colonel Mallett had to send Captain McRae to Wilkes County with a reinforced company of camp guards to arrest deserters "and to quell any outbreak or disloyal proceedings." Members of a secret organization in the Piedmont calling themselves the Heroes of America began working to return North Carolina to the Union. They were likely responsible for numerous acts of violence and sabotage in the western half of the state.[b] Deserters were drawn to the area for these and other reasons.[c]

The mountains of North Carolina were rugged and isolated. There could not have been a better hiding place for the flood of deserters and conscription resisters that arrived in the area during 1863. In July,

---

[a] Counties in the Quaker Belt included Randolph, Davie, Yadkin, Moore, Montgomery, Davidson, Alamance, and Forsyth (Trotter, *Silk Flags And Cold Steel*, p. 145).

[b] The Heroes of America operated in the western half of North Carolina, east Tennessee, and southwest Virginia (Davis, *Look Away!*, p. 276). At the height of their influence, the North Carolina Heros of America may have had as many as ten thousand members. They supported peace candidates and elected some of them to office (Current, *Encyclopedia of the Confederacy*, p. 1154).

[c] The extent to which North Carolinians deserted is still a debated topic. Wartime and many post-war perceptions and studies, admittedly often based on incomplete data, indicate that North Carolina's desertion rate was higher than in other Southern states. More recent analysis indicates that the North Carolina rate was around 12%, not remarkable for the period (McCaslin, *Portraits of Conflict*, p. 42 and *North Carolina Historical Review*, article by Richard Reid, v. 58, p. 234 - 55).

Governor Vance estimated that there were approximately twelve hundred deserters in the mountains. [125] Their motivation for desertion ran all the way from being just plain war-weary, to anti-conscription, to pro-Union. Subjected to increasingly desperate letters from home, most North Carolinians who deserted did so to help their families in times of need. Private Francis Marion Poteet of the 49th North Carolina Troops received a heart-rending letter from his wife. At the time, he had already been arrested for desertion by Mallett's men and was in the guardhouse at Weldon:

> N C McDowell County
>
> My Dear husband   I now seat myself to write you a few lines to let you know that we are not well   the children is sick with bad colds and I haint seen a well day since you left   I have had a very bad head ache ever sins last Sunday but I do hope and pray this will find you in good health   the Raleigh gard never came back no moor   I wish you could have staid with me.... the 1st and 2nd days of this Month was the coldest I ever felt and it aint much warmer yet   I don't believe that we have had but two clear days sins you left.... I don't see how I am to get along with no one to help me   I have to pay the tax on the cows.... O my dear husband you don't know how lonsom I am sins you left   I dread to see night come   O I do hope and pray that the Lord will spar our lives to see each other in peace once moor   O Lord be with my dear husband and bless him for I cant be with him   O Francis it dos seem like it will kill me to be parted from you with no one to protect me and your little helpless children   I pray the lord to save your sole and body fom harm if I never see you no moor   I want you to write soon I am so cold I must quit May the Lord bless and save you is my prayer
>
> Martha A. E. Poteet [a]

Caring family men could hardly be expected to resist this kind of pressure. Newspapers even printed editorials advising soldiers' wives to write cheerful letters to their husbands and not discourage them.

[a] Private Poteet had deserted from his unit on December 1, 1863, most likely due to the illness of his infant son. The child died on December 21. Poteet was arrested on January 27 and returned to his unit after spending four months in the guard house at Weldon, North Carolina (Poteet-Dixon Letters, PC.1825.1, North Carolina Archives. *Roster* v. XII, p. 38).

Desertions tended to rise and fall with the successes and failures of the army. Some soldiers deserted at crop planting or harvesting time, or both, then returned to their units when the work was done. Often leaving the army in groups with their weapons, they were able to bluff or intimidate their way through the countryside. Provost guards at train depots, river fords, and bridges had to be reinforced to turn back bands of armed deserters. Most of them were going home.

Once they arrived, the men lived with or near their families, worked their farms, and hid in the woods when the conscript officers came around. Many of them kept their arms and equipment. As their numbers increased, some formed paramilitary groups to defend against government attempts to return them to the army. The size of these groups varied from several men to several dozen and more. In some areas they dug earthworks, intending to gather and defend themselves against attacks by the Home Guard or Mallett's troops.

While in hiding, the deserters were supported by family and friends or robbed and stole to supply themselves. Those loyal to the Confederacy and the families of conscript bureau soldiers were favorite targets. State and local authorities had been authorized by the Confederate government to apprehend and detain deserters as early as July 1862, but several court decisions and the escalating violence had taken a toll on their willingness to cooperate. Colonel Mallett's conscription bureau with his four hundred man battalion and statewide network of offices came to play a leading role in efforts to combat disloyalty, draft resistance, and desertion.

A soldier's absence from his company triggered the government's response. Desertions from armies in the field were usually first noticed at morning roll call. Notification was made through the chain of command to the regiment, brigade, division, and finally to the war department in Richmond. The war department notified the authorities in the deserter's home state. Scores of notifications were sent each month. In North Carolina, these forms were sent to Colonel Mallett.

Lieutenant Pulaski Cowper received the notices at Mallett's headquarters, logged them in, and assigned each one to the appropriate congressional district. He then mailed the paperwork to the district captain. The captain assigned the case to a county enrolling officer. Upon his receipt of the case, the county lieutenant worked with his own staff, the militia, Home Guard, and sheriff to locate and arrest the soldier. Endorsements consisting of instructions, recommendations, and additional information were added to the documents as they made their way back and forth through the system.[a] Once the deserter was apprehended, he was sent to the camp of instruction and from there back to his unit. If any additional criminal charges were generated during the process, the soldier was held at the camp guardhouse or county jail pending military or civilian court action. Military punishment was usually administered after the soldier returned to his regiment. A thirty dollar reward was paid for each captured deserter by the Confederate government to the individual or agency responsible for the capture. These payments were usually made through Mallett's bureau.

As desertion and draft resistance escalated, the government tried increasingly extreme measures to bring the situation under control. Large sections of the state were subjected to the activities of the Home Guard, Mallett's soldiers, and units sent from the army. These forces scoured the countryside, occasionally searching the homes of entire communities for deserters. They also gathered men who were within the conscription age group but could not produce furlough, detail, or exemption papers. These sweeps were most common in the western half of the state.

While many of the local authorities were loyal to the state and the Confederacy, they often had close ties with deserters and their families. As permanent residents of the communities, the sheriff, militia, and Home Guardsmen were reluctant to enforce conscript laws on their own relatives and neighbors. Frequently, deserters were warned of an enrolling officer's plan to visit a community long before he arrived. Occasionally, notice of the officer's impending visit was published in the local newspaper.[126]

As the public's attitude toward conscription grew more negative, anti-draft violence became commonplace. Deserters who brought weapons home were able to out-gun local men sent against them. Deserters usually had newer rifled weapons. The Home Guards were armed with their own shotguns or other civilian weapons. Deserters were also in better physical shape, had more military training, and had been hardened by their time in the army. They killed a number of conscript and state officers and assaulted dozens more.

Adding to North Carolina's problem was the deteriorating Confederate war effort in Tennessee. Large parts of western

[a] Adjutant and Inspector General Order No. 78 issued October 11, 1864, dictated the proper format for endorsements and threatened courts-marshal for violations (*O.R.*, Series IV, v. 3, p. 720-21).

Tennessee had come under Union control early in the war. During 1863, the Confederacy suffered reversals in the eastern half of the state. Union raiding parties eventually crossed the border at will and operated in the North Carolina mountains. The few Confederate regiments assigned to the area were tied-down guarding the major mountain passes through which any large Union invasion force would have to pass. Small-scale Union raids were conducted through remote approaches with the aid of Unionist civilians on both sides of the border. Anti-conscription and anti-Confederate sentiment aided Union efforts to destabilize the area. Hundreds of pro-Union North Carolinians and Tennesseans volunteered for service in United States Army regiments that were raised in Tennessee. These units conducted operations in both states and South Carolina.

Despite the difficult situation, Colonel Mallett decided to reestablish a strong conscription bureau presence in western North Carolina. He had not had a conscription camp in the area since he closed Statesville's Camp Hill in September 1862. Deserters and conscription resisters were a source of manpower that the South needed to restore to its armies. The city of Morganton appeared to be the best location for a new camp.

Morganton was located on the more secure eastern side of the mountains. The Western North Carolina Railroad line from Salisbury terminated near Morganton and could insure transportation to and from the proposed camp. If necessary, Mallett could quickly reinforce the camp with his own troops from Camp Holmes. Mallett knew that he was not alone in looking at the conditions in western North Carolina. There was growing support in Confederate military circles for additional security in the mountains to counter Union threats from Tennessee. He knew that the problems of the region were more than desertion and would eventually require the attention of Richmond. In the meantime, he could go a long way toward protecting his bureau's interests in the area. He decided to send Captain James McRae with two companies of troops to establish the new camp at Morganton. This was to be only a partial fix for the area's troubles. He also ordered McRae to report on anti-Confederate and pro-Union elements in the population. Mallett intended to add his voice to those calling for reinforcements in the mountains.

Rumors of a move had been circulating at Camp Holmes all summer. The men in Mallett's battalion knew that they could be sent anywhere in the state that was threatened with attack. Weldon and Kinston were always possibilities. As the situation in Tennessee worsened, concern for Asheville's security grew. General Whiting, in command of the military district around Wilmington, expected an attack on that city in July. On that occasion, he advised Governor Vance to "Tell Mallett to have his whole command in readiness to move." [127] Albert Thompson wrote to Cate that same month. He had just returned to camp from a furlough in Rutherford County:

> Camp Holmes Raleigh July the 4 1863
> Well Cate agreeable to promise I will write you a few lines to let you know that I return back to camp safe and sound and found all the mess well and hearty Cowen and Davis had gone out and brought in a half gallon of rasburry and I pitch in and baked them into pies and then you know we eat pies and butter and honey The health of the camp is good at this time they had reported me abson without leaf but I went up and smooth it all off and it is all right I think I had a very nice trip in deed but the thought of leaving my dear ones it did greave me very bad.... the nuse is that we are going west in a short time but I don't know how true it is but I am in hope that we go to Ashville or somers out there Cowen is well and hearty and all the rest of the boys There is some conscript here and some diserters also there is some of the company gone out to hunt up diserters and they just come in and brought some in....

Later that week Thompson was sent to Richmond. He returned with news of the battles at Gettysburg and Vicksburg. While he was gone, "the fever" struck at Camp Holmes:

> Camp Holmes Raleigh N.C. July the 11 1863
> My Dear wife and children.... my mess is all well except N. F. Butler.... we think he has got the fever there is sickness in the camp and some deths.... well Cate I recon you have herd of Visc burg fallen I am very sorry to here of that but Lee has taken 4000 Pr. [prisoners] at GattyBurg and [I] here that they are fighting at Charlestown but I don't know how true it is well Cate I have just returned from Richmond last night I help gard thirty diserters and one yankey prisoner.... we have been in readiness for six or seven days to march Just any where they call on us to go....

Albert Thompson's friend, Private N. F. Butler, died on July 16. On July 29, Thompson's company commander, Lieutenant John McRae, submitted a Form 40 to the Camp Holmes quartermaster, Captain George Baker. The requisition called for twenty tents and tent-flys. The camp rumor mill picked up the information immediately. Obviously Colonel Mallett and Captain McRae had chosen Company B to be part of the redeployment. By August 1, it was common knowledge in the camp that Companies B and D were going "up to the montings in a day or too." [128] Lieutenant McRae provided additional confirmation on August 6 when he requisitioned sixty-six canteens for his company.

Colonel Mallett intended for all concerned to be aware of his plans to begin an aggressive campaign against desertion and draft resistance. He timed the opening of his new camp with action that President Davis had taken. The president called the forty- to forty-five-year-old men to the army. They were to report to camps of instruction on August 20. The president also declared an amnesty for deserters. For a specified time and if not charged with additional crimes, deserters could turn themselves in and have their desertion forgiven. They would be returned to their regiments and, except for a forfeiture of pay while absent, would receive no punishment. Colonel Mallett had the president's amnesty proclamation published in western North Carolina newspapers along with his order that Camp Vance was to be opened on August 10. In the same order, Mallett warned those who were inclined to ignore either the enrollment or the amnesty:

> But it must be distinctly understood that after the expiration of the time set by the President, the most vigorous measures in the power of the government will be instituted for the arrest and punishment of all absent from their commands without leave. None need expect to evade longer the service they justly owe to their country. Let them report at once to their Militia officers to be sent to camp, or come in person without delay.[129]

Captain McRae and Companies B and D arrived at the train station near Morganton during the second week of August and began building their new camp. Camp Vance would need all the same facilities as Camp Holmes.[a] Thompson, who was now only twenty-five miles from home, wrote to Cate as soon as he arrived:

> Camp Vance near Morganton
> August the 13 1863
>
> My Dear wife and children.... We have got with in four miles of Morganton and have raise a camp We have good water... and we have a butiful place for a camp but I think we will have a hard time of it taking up conscript for they say there is a grate many of them round here there was three brought in here to day some of us are going out on a scout to take up diserters.... Cowen has just come in with too chickens and some potatoes and we will have a big dinner tomorrow well Cate I want to see you very bad and all the children....

While some men at the new camp built barracks, officers' quarters, and a guardhouse, the rest searched the nearby countryside. Their efforts were rewarded right away when a makeshift fortress built by local deserters was captured. On August 21, Albert wrote to Cate and told her of the incident:

> well Cate... tell the folk that our boys has taken the Brest works of the diserters and only fired four guns and took some diserters and shot one mans arm off clost to his shoulder and they shot at too more they never got....

Thompson, Cowen, and the others were soon exposed to the misery that war had brought to the mountain people. Even in peace, many small farm families were only one bad crop season away from hard times. In arresting men who were the only source of support for these families, Mallett's men knew they were depriving poor women and children of their best chance to survive a harsh winter. Many of the deserters were loyal Southerners who were brought back home by desperate letters from their wives. Sending their pay back home had not

[a] Mallett likely named the new camp for Governor Vance. Also, the governor's older brother, Robert, was a brigadier general and district commander in the area. The site of Camp Vance is approximately 1/3rd of a mile southwest of the intersection of Zion Road and Settlemyre Road in Morganton (Bumgarner, *Kirk's Raiders*, p. 108).

helped. Confederate soldiers were paid twenty-two dollars every other month. The pay was often five or six months late in money that was made cheap by inflation and rejected by anyone with food for sale.

The harsh realities of the job he was doing took its toll on Thompson. He related an incident to Cate that occurred shortly after he arrived at Morganton. When writing the letter, he had no idea that a similar tragedy would befall his own family:

> I had to guard a diserter to his home and stay with him too days and in the time of it his child did [died] with the bowel complaint.... it lived just two days and there was too more of his children sick and they had nothing to eat.... I could not help shedding tears when the sweet little thing dide....

Thompson and Cowen left Camp Vance for Raleigh on August 22 with a group of conscripts and deserters. The ride between the Morganton train station and Raleigh would become familiar to them and their comrades as they made frequent trips delivering prisoners to Camp Holmes.

When Thompson and Cowen returned from Raleigh, they found that the Camp Vance guardhouse was full of prisoners again. Major John W. Woodfin was organizing a cavalry battalion at Asheville in late August and was conducting small-scale operations in the area.[a] On August 28, he and part of his unit captured a band of thirty-six deserters from the Army of Tennessee. The deserters, most of whom were mounted on stolen horses, were passing through western North Carolina and heading toward Virginia. Major Woodfin and eighteen of his men surrounded and bluffed the deserters into surrendering. Woodfin deposited his prisoners at Camp Vance during the first week of September.[130] The camp was rapidly becoming a factor in the restoration of governmental control in the area.

By the time Albert returned to Camp Vance, his health had deteriorated. During his frequent trips to Raleigh, he could see how war-weary the population was, not only around Morganton, but in

[a] Major Woodfin was an experienced cavalry officer having previously served as a captain in the 1st North Carolina Cavalry and as a major in the 2nd North Carolina Cavalry. In August 1863, he received permission to organize a battalion for service within the state that was to be made up of volunteers who were exempt from conscription (*Roster*, v. II, p. 560).

Salisbury and Greensboro as well. Though ill and frustrated, he remained defiant in regard to the war:

> Camp Vance Nere Morganton
> September the 4 1863
>
> My Dear wife and children... I am not very well at this time My heal is not well and there is some sores on my leg.... Co. D just returned off a scout yesterday they went to Wilkes County and there was so many diserters they had to come back to get reenforcements.... well Cate you wanted me to tell you what I thought of those peace meetings.... I want peace as bad as any one I know and I love my home as well as eny one but I don't love this peace party and Cate you may notice that it is only Abolishnist that want peace in such a way after we have bin fighting for nerly three years and then give it up then never no never til we have a credatibl peace or non.... I would like to be at home with you but I cant be there yet.... tell the children howdy and tell them to be good and smart and learn there books.... Remember me in your prayers....

One of the conscripts brought to Camp Vance that fall was James Burgess Gaither of Iredell County. "Burgess," as he preferred, was chosen to stay with the camp guard and was assigned to Company D with his cousin Sid Summers. Sid's brother, Mel, had been conscripted into Mallett's battalion at Camp Hill in July 1862 and was a sergeant in Company B. Having relatives in the same unit did not help Burgess with his transition to military life. He was miserable at Camp Vance and wanted his father to get him out of the army:

> Dear Father... I am not satisfied in camp life them papers you sent up will do no good and ther is no chance of getting out of the war paw I want you to hire mee a substitute if you can for I would not stay here for all that I ever expect [to] bee worth in this world And I want you to trie to get mee out of this war.... paw if I stay here long I do not expect to liv long for I can not stand camp life.... paw I would give five thousand dollars bee fore I would stay her but I will do the best I can.... your True son untill death J.B.G. [131]

Gaither had reason to be concerned. Skirmishes with deserters were becoming more frequent. Private William Watt of Lieutenant

Robards's Company D wrote that he had occasion to "shoot at a desirter the uther night they likin to run over mee."[132]

Larger groups of Captain McRae's men had to be sent out on patrol because of the more determined resistance they were encountering. Lieutenant Robards's company ran into trouble again on September 9 when they were surrounded by deserters and Union men in Iredell County. Colonel Mallett was in Charlotte when he heard the news. He telegraphed Governor Vance that he would start toward Statesville, but a local militia colonel responded and took charge of the situation. Several days later a Charlotte newspaper recounted the incident:

> IREDELL COUNTY
>
> A company of Mallett's Battalion passed this place a day or two since for Taylor's Spring, a muster ground in the upper part of Iredell, to burst up a Union meeting to be held there. They caught several deserters and shot, or shot at, two others. Fearing the deserters would over power them they sent to Col. Sharpe for the Militia. The Colonel at once, with fine spirit, went to their relief with a number of men. [133]

From the beginning, Captain McRae left many of these missions and the running of Camp Vance to his lieutenants while he attended to the second part of his assignment: evaluating the overall situation in western North Carolina. He examined conditions in the 9th and 10th Congressional districts with regard to desertion, conscription resistance, and pro-Union activity. The desertion problem was obviously beyond the control of the Home Guard and local law enforcement, even when they were inclined to help. Confederate troops assigned to the military district were spread too thinly to mount a reliable defense against Union threats from Tennessee, much less chase deserters for the conscription bureau. A report submitted to McRae by the 10th Congressional District enrolling officer indicated the gravity of the situation:

> Asheville, N.C. August 10, 1863
> Capt. J. C. McRae
> Commanding Conscripts, Morganton, N.C.:
>
> Captain: I am this morning in possession of information that I know to be reliable that the deserters and tories from Tennessee and counties from this State are in force, estimated 300 to 500, and are now in the counties of

Cherokee and Henderson. In the first-named county they are largely in ascendency, and are augmenting their number every day. They are killing stock, disarming the citizens, and the militia, if they were even disposed, I don't think would be sufficient to capture or entirely disperse them. It will be impossible for me to execute the conscription in certain counties without the aid of some military force.... I would most respectfully suggest that a force of cavalry or mounted infantry be stationed somewhere in the district, and be employed for the purpose of arresting deserters....

Very respectfully, your obedient servant,
D. C. Pearson,
Captain and Enrolling Officer Tenth District [134]

Combining Pearson's report with other information and his own observations, McRae advised Mallett of the obvious:

Conscript Office, Camp Vance
Near Morganton, August 13, 1863
Col. Peter Mallett
Commandant of Conscripts, North Carolina:

Colonel: I have the honor to report the state of affairs in the western counties of North Carolina. I enclose also a letter from Captain Pearson, enrolling officer Tenth District, received on yesterday. All the counties on the Tennessee border are infested with deserters, renegade conscripts, and tories, who have collected in the mountains committing depredations upon the peaceful citizens and unprotected wives of soldiers.

The county of Cherokee is 200 miles from Morganton, and the facilities for transporting and subsisting the small body of men under my command are very limited; and as Jackson's brigade of Buckner's division is in Tennessee, about fifty miles from the county seat of Cherokee, I would respectfully suggest that an arrangement be made by which a few companies of cavalry and infantry from his command may be sent to this section to operate until these bands of deserters, etc., are broken up....

Every county in the Ninth and Tenth Districts is infested to a greater or less degree with deserters, etc., and the most rigorous measures are absolutely necessary for the preservation of order and life.

Soldiers wives are constantly robbed by the villains, and great depredations are committed on the citizens.... I have two companies of about 125 men at this camp. There are from 50 to 100 deserters in this county within twenty-five miles, and the same proportion in adjoining counties, while the counties of Wilkes and Yadkin have many more than this proportion.

Though some militia officers are good men, who have aided the officers of conscription materially in the execution of the law, many are entirely unreliable and all are fast losing their influence....

I am, colonel, very respectfully, your obedient servant,
J. C. McRae
Capt., Cmdg. [135]

McRae's recommendations and Mallett's endorsement coincided with other calls for action that had been growing all summer. A number of western North Carolina citizens had expressed their concerns to Governor Vance. He had corresponded at length with the secretary of war.[136]

Perhaps the most compelling analysis of conditions in the region came from Lieutenant Colonel George W. Lay, an inspector for the Bureau of Conscription. Lay had been sent to western North Carolina by Superintendent Preston. He evaluated the 7th and 8th Congressional districts as well as the two districts covered by McRae's report:

OFFICE OF INSPECTOR OF CONSCRIPTION
Salisbury, N.C., September 2, 1863
Col. J. S. Preston,
Superintendent of Conscription:

Sir: When the conscript service was organized the direction that among its duties should be embraced that of collecting and forwarding deserters and skulkers by the use of force was doubtless based on the supposition that such characters would be found lurking about singly, unarmed, acting in no concert, and supported by no local public opinion or party....

The utter inadequacy now of any force that we command without... aid from armies in the field will become apparent when it is realized that desertion has assumed (in some regions, especially the central and western portions of this State) a very different and more

> formidable shape and development than could have been anticipated. It is difficult to arrive at any exact statistics on the subject. The unquestionable facts are these: Deserters now leave the army with arms and ammunition in hand. They act in concert to force by superior numbers a passage against bridge or ferry guards, if such are encountered. Arriving at their selected localities, they organize into bands variously estimated at from fifty up to hundreds at various points....
>
> His Excellency Governor Vance credits official information received by him, that in Cherokee County a large body of deserters (with whom I class also those in resistance to conscription) have assumed a sort of military occupation, taking a town, and that in Wilkes County they are organized, drilling regularly, and intrenched in a camp to the number of 500. Indeed, the whole number of deserters in the latter county is said to be much larger.
>
> The reports of our patrols indicate 300 or 400 organized in Randolph County, and they are said to be in large numbers in Catawba and Yadkin, and not a few in the patriotic county of Iredell. These men are not only determined to kill in avoiding apprehension (having just put to death yet another of our enrolling officers), but their esprit de corps extends to killing in revenge as well as in prevention of the capture of each other.
>
> So far they seem to have had no trouble for subsistence. While the disaffected feed them from sympathy, the loyal do so from fear. The latter class (and the militia) are afraid to aid the conscript service lest they draw revenge on themselves and their property. [137]

Lieutenant Colonel Lay was concerned that the entire western half of the state could be lost. He even warned of "something like civil war" within the state if action was not taken quickly. Lay also indicated that there was public and political support in Raleigh for anti-Confederate activities. This faction had found a champion in William W. Holden. Holden published the *North Carolina Standard* newspaper and was the emerging leader of North Carolina's peace movement. He was an early opponent of conscription and supported the public peace meetings that were being held around the state.

Lay's feelings about Holden and his newspaper were shared by Captain McRae, who had filed a separate and confidential report to Mallett on the peace movement:

CONSCRIPT OFFICE, CAMP VANCE
August 21, 1863
Col. P. Mallett,
Commanding Conscripts, North Carolina

COLONEL: Several peace meetings have been held in the Ninth and Tenth Districts, at which I understand, not officially, that the most treasonable language was uttered, and Union flags raised. Can I have authority to break up any such assemblages, and arrest the ring leaders who are not of conscript age?

I feel it my duty to complain against the publication of the Standard newspaper, which is issued in Raleigh, and extensively circulated throughout this section. From common report, which can be made official intelligence if necessary, I am constrained to believe that most of the trouble in North Carolina, as well as of the desertions from the army, are the direct consequence of the circulation of this incendiary publication.[138]

Like McRae, North Carolinians who remained loyal to the Confederacy regarded Holden's publication as subversive. Soldiers serving in the army, in particular, were enraged by his editorials. Private Charles F. Mills of the 7th North Carolina State Troops with Lee's army in Virginia wrote that "there is a good deal of disaffection among the N.C. troops at this time but I think that things would be wright before long if old Holden's press was stopt, that has done more harm in the army among the soldiers of N. Carolina than every thing else." [139]

Another North Carolina soldier complained bitterly about Holden and blamed the *Standard* for tragic consequences: "There has been a good many N. Carolinians shot in this army for Desertion old traitor Holden is Responsible for most of it.... I think the N.C. Soldiers passing through Raleigh on Furlough ought to stop and hang the old son of a bitch." [140]

The problems of desertion, conscription resistance, and disloyalty to the Confederacy were not unique to North Carolina. In varying degrees, the same conditions existed in most of the Southern states. When General Gideon Pillow resumed his conscription operations in Tennessee, Mississippi, and Alabama in August, he estimated that there were eight to ten thousand "tories" and deserters hiding in northern Alabama.[141] The vast majority of Southern men who were inclined to enter the army without physical resistance had already done so. Pillow realized that the largest part of his conscription responsibilities consisted not of bringing new soldiers into the army, but of capturing deserters and arresting resisters. Peter Mallett had seen the first indications of this trend a year earlier.

Observing the same situation throughout the Confederacy, Superintendent Preston wrote to the secretary of war:

> BUREAU OF CONSCRIPTION,
> Richmond, August 6, 1863
> HON. JAMES A. SEDDON,
> Secretary of War:
>
> SIR: The whole matter of conscription and all other functions hitherto pertaining to the Bureau within the States of Tennessee, Mississippi and Alabama having been transferred to the general commanding Department No. 2, leaves a limited but still important scope for the action of this Bureau. Practically there remains under the control of the Bureau but four States - Georgia, North Carolina, South Carolina and part of Virginia. The number of men liable to conscription in these States is smaller in comparison to their population than in any other portions of the Confederacy. Almost all such are already in the field, and that function of the Bureau almost expires for lack of materiel.... At present, then, by far the gravest portion of its duties consists in its remedial action on the depletion of the Army by straggling, desertion, and other forms of absence....[142]

Bowing to advice from all sides, Seddon began to officially redefine the mission of the conscription bureau. The change had already taken place in the daily operations of units like Mallett's battalion. They were already bringing in considerably fewer first-time conscripts than deserters and draft dodgers. The armed opposition now being offered by these elements threatened conscription enforcement units with outright military defeat in areas like western North Carolina. Seddon decided to raise additional troops in the four states that the conscription bureau controlled at the time. To that end, the Adjutant and Inspector General's office issued Special Orders No. 213 on September 8, 1863:

> The Bureau of Conscription is authorized to raise and equip in each of the states of Georgia, South Carolina,

> North Carolina and Virginia, one battalion of six companies of mounted men who furnish their own horses, and who are not liable to conscription, to be under the orders of the Bureau, for the purpose of conscription, the arrest of deserters, and for local defense, mustered for one year. Companies to elect their officers; the field officer to be assigned from the officers belonging to the enrolling service. Companies not to exceed 100, rank and file.
>
> By command of the Secretary of War:
> Jno. Withers,
> Assistant Adjutant General [143]

Mallett's choice for the officer to organize and command the unit in North Carolina was Captain James McRae. McRae, soon to be breveted to the rank of major, began organizing his battalion at Camp Vance.[a] He intended to establish his headquarters further west, at Asheville, when the unit was close to full strength and could operate independently. The war department had finally recognized the need for mobility in this type of assignment by authorizing these units to be mounted.[b]

While he was organizing the new battalion, McRae was still the ranking conscription officer west of Raleigh. As such, he was responsible for the support of Home Guard units that were enforcing conscription. While many militia and Home Guard officers were not enthusiastic about conscription enforcement, others had remained resolute. Colonel Silas Sharpe of Iredell County's 79th Militia Regiment and 5th Home Guard Regiment was one officer who was not afraid to enforce the law. On occasion, McRae even needed to restrain the colonel in his zeal:

> Conscript Office
> Camp Vance Sept. 30th 1863
> Col. S.A. Sharpe
> Comdg
>
> Colonel I have rec'd today from Lieut. Setzer 16 prisoners. I will release Jesse Parker also the boys under age whom

[a] Although Special Order No. 213 authorized these battalions for one year, congressional action would shorten their service to nine months (*Roster*, v. II, p. 697).

[b] Similar units in the Trans-Mississippi were almost always mounted. General Pillow had used cavalry extensively for conscript enforcement in the central Confederacy. Peter Mallett had requested two cavalry companies in August 1862.

> I cannot hold. I think it would be better for you to take charge of such parties as these and keep them under guard a few days & and give them a good scare instead of sending them here, it is only putting the gov't to expense for nothing. If there is any tangible charge against a person whom you send to me, please have testimony taken in the case upon affidavits and sent with him....
>
> I am colonel Very Respectfully
> Your obdt Srvnt
> J. C. McRae
> Capt Comdg [144]

At Camp Vance, Albert Thompson watched McRae gather men for the new battalion. Duty in the cavalry seemed to be easier than the life of an infantryman. On October 10, he wrote to Cate informing her of the arrival of some unhappy conscripts and mentioned his desire for a transfer:

> well Cate I have tried to get in the calvery but they wont give me up I am determin to go to the Calvery some wher.... the McDowell [county] men has come in this morning and there is severl that I know and they hate it the worst you ever saw.... we had to come in and now they hafto come.

There was no rush of local men wanting to enlist in the new battalion. Colonel Mallett had the war department's authorization for McRae's battalion published in western North Carolina newspapers along with his own call for volunteers.[145] He then provided at least seven company officers for the unit from among his battalion staff and enrolling officers.[146] When the call for volunteers failed to produce the desired results, Mallett allowed McRae to conscript men directly into the unit. McRae was also allowed to supplement his numbers with soldiers from Companies B and D at Camp Vance.[a] In giving McRae his full support, Mallett was making the best of an awkward situation.

[a] A Richmond Conscript Office circular dated July 7, 1863, refers to the war department's approval of using incoming conscripts for this type of duty (*O.R.*, Series IV, v. 2, p. 618). A circular issued by the Bureau of Conscription on Sept. 10, 1863, implied that the assignment of conscripts to these temporary battalions would be allowed even though Special Order No. 213 made no such provision (*O.R.*, Series IV, v. 2, p. 799, para. I). Rosters of McRae's battalion and Companies B and D of Mallett's battalion indicate a considerable sharing of personnel.

For Mallett, McRae's new assignment had a potentially serious disadvantage. The War Department's Special Orders No. 213 directed that McRae's battalion was to act as a "local defense" unit in addition to its conscription duties. Inevitably, this would mean sharing McRae's unit with the military district commander. The district was commanded by Brigadier General Robert B. Vance, the governor's older brother. Vance's forces in the district were not strong enough to prevent the increasingly frequent Union raids. The natural inclination would be for General Vance to utilize McRae's battalion as much as possible.

Although Mallett would rather not have shared the services of the new battalion, his support for McRae's mission was genuine. Anything that strengthened the Confederacy's position in the area also advanced the conscript bureau's goals. The efficient operation of McRae's battalion would protect Camp Vance, support local enrolling officers, and further motivate the Home Guard. Conscripts and deserters could be sent to the army, local subversive elements would be suppressed, and Union cavalry would be less likely to cross the border. On the practical side, Mallett knew that by supplying most of the officers and men to McRae's battalion, he could exercise considerable influence over its activities.

As Captain McRae prepared to move his battalion headquarters to Asheville, construction projects at Camp Vance occupied the soldiers who were not away from the camp chasing deserters. Log cabin duplexes for the officers and barracks for the enlisted men were built, as well as administrative offices, a hospital, stables, and an ice house for the camp surgeons. As busy as life at Camp Vance was, Burgess Gaither still found time to daydream about getting out of the army. By mid-October, he had considered deserting:

> Dear Father... there is so much stiring here at all times there is men comen in here from ever dirrection daly There is 30 or 40 come in to day and theigh keep coming in un tell dark.... paw I find camp life is a hard life for if you don't stand up to your post you will get in the Gard house shure paw I am in liutinant Roberts [Robards's] Company he is a fine man.... If you can get some person to come in my place I think that I will get off that way... for I want to get out of this place but if I cant I will stay as long as any boddy else for it is no use to run away for thiegh would catch you before you could get home Company B went out last week over to Reffiford [Rutherford] County

> and there was a man run from them and theigh shot him dead in his track there was wone shot yesterday afew miles abov here but did not kill him but shot three bullets in him....[147]

The officers at Camp Vance maintained a strict schedule for the men assigned there, as well as for those who were brought in. The camp's perimeter guards were rotated frequently and roll call was held three times each day: dawn, noon, and eight o'clock in the evening. The guardhouse often held fifteen to twenty deserters. If a conscript escaped from the camp, the guards were forced to stand double shifts. Mail, newspapers, food, uniforms, and equipment were delivered to the camp on a regular schedule. The trains then returned to Raleigh carrying deserters, conscripts, and their guards through Statesville, Salisbury, and Greensboro.

Burgess Gaither's luck changed in late October. Along with Thompson's sergeant, Joseph Scoggins, Gaither got a temporary assignment to McRae's unit. The battalion was mustered into service at Morganton in November by General Robert F. Hoke.[148] McRae was never able to reach the authorized strength for his unit, nor were his men able to find enough horses to mount more than three companies. Still, for the next several months, they would spend much of their time between Asheville and the Tennessee border protecting conscript officers, chasing deserters, and watching for enemy cavalry raids. McRae's mounted companies ventured into Tennessee several times during the winter. Burgess Gaither adapted well to his new assignment. He and others were frequently sent back to Camp Vance, escorting captured Union soldiers and Confederate deserters.

In December, Assistant Quartermaster Captain Stephan H. Everett was transferred from the 13th North Carolina Light Artillery and became the quartermaster at Camp Vance. Private Joseph L. Cheely of Lieutenant McRae's company was appointed to be the camp's ordnance sergeant. By then, Camp Vance had become an important stabilizing influence in the area and the hub of conscription activity in the western third of the state. Colonel Silas Sharpe was often in contact with Major McRae and with other officers at the camp. He delivered prisoners, collected deserter bounties, and coordinated his Home Guard activities with operations conducted from the camp.

Even with Camp Vance, McRae's battalion, and General Vance's forces, the Confederate government realized that more would have to be done to protect western North Carolina. Union victories in east

Tennessee promoted anti-Confederate sentiment on both sides of the border. Knoxville fell to the Union army in early September. Disaster struck again at Cumberland Gap, Tennessee, on September 9 when more than seventeen hundred Confederates surrendered, including most of Colonel Love's 62nd North Carolina Troops.[a] Sooner or later, invasion from Tennessee would become a very real possibility.

The secretary of war's comprehensive plan for the region was announced in September with the creation of the Military District of Western North Carolina. At the same time, General James Longstreet and several thousand soldiers were detached from Lee's army and sent to eastern Tennessee. They were to operate in conjunction with General Bragg in regaining control of part the state. Their presence was expected to alleviate conditions on both sides of the North Carolina and Tennessee border by pushing Union forces back west.

In November, a section of Company F of the 13th North Carolina Light Artillery was assigned to McRae's battalion. By then, General Vance and Major McRae were working in coordination with each other. Obviously, the artillery was sent to McRae for use against Union forces as opposed to conscription enforcement. Shortly thereafter, General Vance felt that his force was strong enough to conduct a raid into Tennessee. He disrupted Union communications and returned to North Carolina with "800 hogs and some horses and cattle."[149]

General Vance again raided across the border in early 1864, but this time his efforts met with defeat. He and approximately one-third of his force were captured in Cocke County. Colonel John Palmer, on furlough from command of the 58th North Carolina Troops due to wounds suffered at the battle of Chickamauga, was then assigned to command the district. By that time, the tug-of-war for McRae's battalion had begun.

Inevitably, McRae was drawn more and more deeply into the task of operating directly against Union forces. General Vance had insisted that he could not adequately defend the area without McRae's help. Mallett wanted McRae's activities to remain more closely related to the conscription bureau's mission and tried to distance him from Vance's influence. The effort was unsuccessful and McRae's

[a] When he heard about the capture the 62nd North Carolina Troops, Albert Thompson must have felt fortunate. The conscription bureau's order that removed him from Captain Cowan's company had saved Thompson from a trip to Camp Douglas, Illinois, the prisoner of war camp where thirty-two of his Rutherford County friends would die (*Roster*, v. XV, p. 10).

unit continued to work against Union forces in the region.[a] A disabled officer from the 33rd North Carolina Troops, Captain Thomas H. Gatlin, took temporary command of Camp Vance when McRae moved his battalion headquarters to Asheville.

While the situation in western North Carolina began to improve, anti-Confederate activity in the Piedmont was still on the rise. The presence of pacifist and anti-slavery religious denominations in the area had provided fertile ground for early opposition to secession and the war. Conscription brought the resistance out in the open and publisher William W. Holden's *North Carolina Standard* legitimized the movement. The alarming report filed by Colonel Lay in September had gotten the attention of the secretary of war. Colonel Lay had suggested the use of troops from the Army of Northern Virginia to suppress the pro-Union activity that had developed in the Quaker Belt and surrounding area. Robert E. Lee, while usually reluctant to detach units from his army for such assignments, saw a chance to rebuild his troop strength after the summer's costly fighting at Chancellorsville and Gettysburg. He knew that the area contained hundreds of men who had deserted or who had avoided conscription altogether. Lee chose Robert F. Hoke, a brigadier general from North Carolina, to lead the expedition. Hoke and two regiments, the 21st and 56th North Carolina Troops, were detached from the Army of Northern Virginia and sent to the state. They began their operations on September 8.[150]

Hoke divided his force and conducted sweeps through most of the counties of the 6th, 7th, and 9th Congressional districts. His assignment was twofold: replenish North Carolina regiments in Lee's army and suppress the anti-Confederate activity that had so alarmed Colonel Lay. The presence of Hoke's regiments was also expected to embolden some of the Piedmont's Home Guard units. Governor

[a] It is likely that McRae did little to minimize his participation with General Vance and Colonel Palmer. He was loyal to Mallett, but was known to want a combat assignment. From March to June 1863, he tried to arrange an assignment trade with Captain Rayner Brookfield of the 5th North Carolina State Troops (McRae's old regiment). McRae began corresponding on the matter with several officers during Captain Lucius Johnson's and Colonel August's command at Camp Holmes when it appeared that Mallett might not be able to return to duty. McRae kept Mallett informed about his efforts (J. C. McRae Papers, Manuscripts Department, University of North Carolina at Chapel Hill). When McRae ended up commanding his own battalion in the Department of Western North Carolina, the transfer became a moot point.

Vance intended to support the Confederate efforts in his state and issued orders through Colonel Sharpe to see that it was done:

> Executive Department, North Carolina,
> Adjutant-General's Office,
> Raleigh, Sept 1, 1863.
> Special Order
> No. 5
>
> II. The commanding officer of the Home Guard in Iredell County will call out the Home Guard and arrest every deserter and recusant conscript in the County and deliver them to Capt. J. C. McRae at Morganton. If it be necessary, the deserters can be pursued beyond the county.
>
> Those persons who aid, harbor or maintain deserters will be arrested and bound over to court for trial. Report will be made to this office how this order is being executed
>
> By Order of Gov Vance
> James H. Foote
> A.A.G.
> Col. Sharpe will please deliver to Sr.[senior] Capt who will cooperate with officers from Alex. Union & Caldwell [151]

General Hoke took charge of the entire operation and was issuing orders directly to Home Guard colonels by the end of September.[152]

Better conditions in the western half of the state resulted in an increase in conscripts and deserters arriving at Camp Vance and Camp Holmes. Those gathered at Camp Vance were shipped to Raleigh, there to be assigned guards from the larger camp to escort them to Virginia. Colonel Mallett left the operation of Camp Holmes almost completely to his lieutenants after he had moved his bureau headquarters into Raleigh the previous March. He also finally got the officer he wanted as provost marshal in Raleigh. Captain Samuel Waters's long delayed transfer from duty at the Salisbury prison was approved toward the end of September.

Three days of rioting in Raleigh, beginning on September 9, had left little doubt that the capitol needed extra policing. Georgia soldiers who were passing through town and aware of William W. Holden's anti-government editorials wrecked the offices of the *Standard.* Holden's supporters ransacked the offices of the pro-Confederate *State Journal* the next day. Governor Vance arrived and tried to restore order by personally appealing to the soldiers. On the morning of September 11, Alabama soldiers joined in the unrest and threatened "murder and conflagration," whereupon Vance threatened to recall North Carolina troops from Virginia to maintain peace in the city. President Davis issued strict orders to the army regarding the conduct of troops passing through Raleigh. Order was restored by September 15.[153] Captain Waters was assigned to Mallett eight days later.

Waters was technically transferred to the conscript bureau to become an enrolling officer, but Mallett wanted him to maintain order in Raleigh and keep tabs on military personnel passing through town. Waters had a twenty-one man company of provost guards uniformed and ready for service by October 12. They began assisting local lawmen with disturbances and violations involving soldiers. Soldiers who were away from their regiments were required to produce furlough papers or be arrested. The provost guards also issued passes to military personnel who were in town on official business. Mallett intended to make being a deserter more difficult in Raleigh and wanted the soldiers passing through town to conduct themselves in an orderly manner.

As Mallett's responsibilities increased, he delegated authority to some of his most dependable officers. Two officers in particular gained Mallett's respect and confidence during the second half of 1863. Both were well-educated, and each had been wounded earlier in the war while serving with other units. They had assumed additional responsibilities after Mallett separated his bureau's administrative offices from the camp's headquarters.

Jesse R. McLean was a thirty-three-year-old school teacher when he enlisted on May 13, 1862. He spent two months as a private in the 5th North Carolina Cavalry before being transferred to Camp Holmes as a lieutenant and drill master. He remained at that post until April 1863 when he was transferred to the 8th Congressional District as an enrolling officer. He was promoted to captain the following July and appointed by Mallett to command the district conscript office at Salisbury. While in western North Carolina, McLean gained first-hand knowledge of the dangerous situation there. Mallett ordered him back to Raleigh in December. As 1864 approached, Mallett had plans for McLean that would involve another promotion and additional service in western North Carolina.

When McLean arrived in Raleigh, he joined another teacher-turned-soldier at Camp Holmes. Franz Joseph Carl Johan Hahr had been born in Sweden in 1825. Upon finishing his formal education in 1849, he was rewarded by his father with a trip to America. He spent most of his time in the southern states and decided to stay. He taught school for three years at Limestone Female Academy in South Carolina, and then he took a similar position at Legare's School at Orangeburg. Hahr then moved to North Carolina, where, in Cumberland County, he married Alice Hartman in 1859. Their first child was born the next year. The thirty-six-year-old college professor was one of the first volunteers when war came.

"Frank" Hahr, as he was called in America, enlisted in the Lafayette Light Infantry volunteer company less than a week after Fort Sumter fell. He was promoted to quartermaster sergeant shortly after his company became part of D. H. Hill's 1st North Carolina Volunteers. He was with that unit at the battle at Big Bethel, Virginia. He was later wounded and partially disabled. By the summer of 1862, Hahr had been appointed as a 1st lieutenant and drill master by Colonel Mallett.[154] Like McLean, Lieutenant Hahr impressed Mallett with his leadership and administrative ability. In mid 1863, Mallett designated Lieutenant Hahr as commandant at Camp Holmes. The Richmond authorities would soon require Mallett to make administrative changes affecting both Hahr and McLean.

On November 15, Superintendent of Conscription Preston issued bureau circular No. 55, which changed staff allocations and rank structure for the congressional districts, camps of instruction, and conscription bureau headquarters in the states east of the Mississippi River.[155] Each congressional district was to be supervised by a disabled major or captain. Each county, city, town, district, and parish was to be assigned a first lieutenant. The congressional district and local enrolling offices were also to be staffed with disabled sergeants, corporals, and privates to act as clerks and assistants to the officers.[156]

Circular No. 55 reflected Superintendent Preston's desire to accelerate and expand the changes made in the fall of 1862 concerning the replacement of militia enrolling officers with Confederate army officers. By late 1863, most of Mallett's congressional district offices and approximately one-half of his county offices were supervised by North Carolina captains and lieutenants who were not capable of field service.[157] In the rest of the counties, the Home Guard enforced the conscript laws. Militia colonels were still responsible for gathering non-resisting men and delivering them to Mallett's camps. Preston wanted all conscript offices to be staffed by Confederate army officers and enlisted men.

Circular No. 55 also directed that the commandant of each camp of instruction was to be a major. With McRae on detached service in the western part of the state and unavailable, Mallett wanted Captain McLean and Lieutenant Hahr to have these promotions. The same day he ordered Captain McLean to leave Salisbury and return to Raleigh, Mallett made his recommendation concerning Lieutenant Hahr:

> CONSCRIPT OFFICE
> Raleigh, N.C., December 14th, 1863
> Lt. Col G. W. Lay
> Inspector of Conscription,
> Richmond, Va.
>
> Colonel:
> In order to complete the organization of the Camps of Instruction in this State in accordance with Circular No. 55, I would respectfully recommend the appointment of Frank J. Hahr for the position of Commandant of Camp Holmes with the rank of Major.
> Mr. Hahr now holds a commission as Drill Master with the rank of First Lieutenant, has been discharging the duties of Acting Commandant of the Camp for the past six months, and is fully competent for the position.
>
> Your Obt. Servant
> Peter Mallett Col.
> Commdt. Of Conscription for N.C. [158]

The circular required state commandants to have their recommendations for promotion and other administrative changes accomplished by the first day of January, 1864.[a] In addition, Mallett and

[a] A noteworthy transfer to Mallett's office staff during this period was Graham Daves. Daves had been Governor Ellis's private secretary, but had joined the Confederate army after Ellis died in the summer of 1861. He served as the adjutant of the 22nd North Carolina Troops and was later promoted to captain and assigned as an assistant adjutant general on General S. G. French's staff in Petersburg, Virginia, where he was promoted to major. He was then transferred to General Joseph Johnston's staff in Mississippi. After Vicksburg fell, Major Daves returned to North Carolina and resigned his commission on November 16, 1863. He was then conscripted and sent to Camp Holmes as a private. Mallett became aware of Daves's situation and experience and assigned him to the Raleigh conscript headquarters staff as a clerk. On July 7, 1864, Daves would once again be commissioned as a 1st lieutenant and transferred to General Theophilus Holmes's staff. He would finish the war serving in North Carolina with General Robert Hoke (Ashe, ed., *Biographical History of North Carolina,* v. VI, p. 183).

his staff had to arrange for several dozen unanticipated transfers within the bureau. Richmond had been besieged for months with complaints of inefficiency, favoritism, and outright fraud in the enforcement of conscription in much of the Confederacy. Superintendent Preston decided that a major source of this abuse was the practice of assigning disabled officers to enforce conscription in their hometown communities.[a] In order to lessen the effect of personal ties on the system, Preston ordered the transfer "of each Congressional district and local enrolling officer and each Congressional district medical examining surgeon. Care will be observed not to place an enrolling officer in the district or county of which he is a resident." [159] This was only a partial fix at best. Confederate officers occupied approximately half of North Carolina's county enrolling offices. The militia and Home Guard officers, over whom Mallett had no transfer authority, were even more susceptible to local influence. Also, the transfer of civilian doctors away from their home counties only caused a number of them to resign, forcing Mallett to find replacements.

While dealing with the reorganization of their bureau, Mallett, Hahr, and McLean discussed rumors of a proposed expansion of the conscript laws. They knew that the Confederacy's pool of capable and willing white males between the ages of eighteen and forty-five had been nearly exhausted. The government was looking for ways to conscript additional manpower, better utilize the able-bodied men already in the service, and return more deserters to their regiments. Furthermore, there was a growing perception in civilian and military circles that the conscription process was allowing too many exemptions while not providing enough men for the army. Rumors of changes in the conscription law had been making the rounds for months.

As 1863 drew to a close and conscription officers wondered what the new year would bring, many of the soldiers assigned to Camp Holmes prepared for their second winter in the army. Private James Harwell of Company C, wrote to his wife, Jane, in October:

> camp holmes near raleigh October the 2 Day 1863
>
> Dear wife... i hope these lines find you well.... Jane i want you to make me a shirt A wollen one and i want you to

[a] While there were certainly instances of abuse in North Carolina, the small number of such references in surviving records suggests that Mallett's officers were generally professional in the performance of their duties. It is more likely that militia officers, with closer ties to the local community, were involved in some irregularities.

> die it Blew or red.... frank goodson is in camp hear he is gone to the navy on a gunboat.... Jane i have bin in raleigh to or 3 days garden yankey prisoners.... ther is one hundred and 5 Diserters in the guard house now we have A hard time now we have to Stand gard ever other Day i hope tha will leave hear before long there is 4 hundred conscripts hear now ther ar good menny gettin in this Battalion i hope some of my old friends will come and git in hear too Jane i want to have a good Dinner to day this is my Birth Day i am 38 years old to day i wish i was at home....[160]

Most of the soldiers permanently assigned to Camp Holmes were now in cabins that housed six to eight men. The soldiers were relatively well clothed and equipped. North Carolina's ability to supply her troops had finally dovetailed with their numbers and needs during the previous summer. Mallett's men were issued new uniforms as needed, but the shortage of shoe leather continued. Occasionally, "prepared cloth" shoes (painted and waterproofed canvas uppers with leather soles) were issued when government contractors could not find sufficient leather to produce standard military brogans. There was no shortage of rations at Camp Holmes although the men complained about a lack of variety in their meals.[161]

On November 18, Lieutenant Hahr requisitioned enough uniforms and equipment for three hundred and thirty-six conscripts who were waiting for transportation. With so many of his men away from camp on escorts and two of his companies assigned to Camp Vance, Mallett ordered Lieutenant Hahr to expand the four remaining companies at Camp Holmes to one hundred and twenty-five men each. The need for full company-size, anti-deserter operations away from Camp Holmes had become more frequent during 1863. Mallett wanted to keep enough men at camp to insure security, but he also needed reinforced companies to overpower organized groups of deserters and resisters.

In November, Mallett ordered Company C to Alamance County. They linked up with a thirty-man cavalry unit and established a base of operations called Camp Bethel. Mallett's men harassed deserters' families all over the county, applying pressure to force their men (presumably hiding nearby) back into the army. Private Harwell wrote to his wife and told her of the misery that he and his comrades were causing:

> November the 29 1863
> camp at Bethel alamance county
>
> Dear Sweete wife i take my pen in hand.... we are out hunting up Disurters i expect we will Be out 5 or 6 weeks.... we press [impress] ever thing we eat we take it from Disurters where tha live i don't think it is right....[162]

Harwell never grew accustomed to the unpleasantries of chasing deserters. His attitude was more or less harsh toward their relatives depending on their degree of complicity. On December 11, he told Jane, "i git plenty to eat we go to Disurters hoses and make them cook for us the folks is good round here Jane it makes me sorry for some of the folks...." Harwell and his comrades often relieved captured deserters of valuables, spare clothing, and blankets.

Life at Camp Bethel was tolerable except for the persistent shortage of shoes. Sick soldiers stayed in camp and were cared for by local women. Mail was delivered on Tuesdays and Fridays, so the soldiers got newspapers and had regular contact with their families. Orders from Colonel Mallett were delivered to the company commander, Lieutenant F. A. Fetter, each Friday. Harwell and other soldiers were given brief furloughs during the several months that Company C operated in Alamance County.

Whether stationed at Camp Holmes, Camp Vance, or out hunting conscripts, assignment to a unit that stayed within the state was still an advantage for Mallett's conscripts. Their friends and relatives serving in the Army of Northern Virginia (not to mention the conscripts they escorted to Richmond) were suffering the brunt of the war's violence. Mallett's battalion had been thrown into two fairly large fights during Foster's expedition to Goldsboro, but when compared to active campaigning against the Union army, conscription duty was still less dangerous. Mallett's men felt fortunate in this respect as 1864 began even though the level of conscription resistance had increased during the previous year.

Private Harwell expressed a typical attitude on February 7, 1864 when he wrote to his wife, "Jane i am so glad that i got in my company for i have miss a heap of fights the lord has had pity on me this year...." However, Harwell realized that the advantages of his assignment in Mallett's battalion had diminished appreciably during 1863. In the same letter, he pointed out that "tha are a fighting don at nuburn we have bin looking for orders to go don their...." [a] Harwell had heard false rumors that Mallett intended to keep Company C in Alamance County indefinitely. Another rumor suggested that congress was considering far-reaching changes to the conscription laws. That rumor was true.

The philosophical struggle that had been generated by conscription enforcement methods used by Generals Bragg, Johnston, and Pillow in the central Confederacy had intensified through 1863. The controversy resulted in control of all conscription activities east of the Mississippi River being returned to the Bureau of Conscription at the end of the year. General Pillow was transferred and General Bragg was relieved by General Johnston as commander of the Army of Tennessee. Bragg returned to Richmond and by the end of February had assumed duties as a special military advisor to his friend President Jefferson Davis. Bragg wanted to make profound changes in conscription and regarded his new assignment as an excellent opportunity to do so.

He had watched during 1863 while Richmond-style conscription became more cumbersome and less productive. It seemed that every deserter and draft dodger in the Confederacy had hired a lawyer. Litigation was so common by November 1863 that the secretary of war authorized every congressional district in the nation to retain an attorney to represent the government in conscription cases.[163] Bragg's friendship with the president and his new position would soon allow him to engineer the changes he wanted.

Dissatisfaction with conscription was not confined to military circles. Confederate congressmen had also become suspicious of the amount of resources that were being expended on the process when compared to the number of men actually being assigned to combat units. To have their questions answered, congress requested that President Davis obtain a report from Superintendent Preston showing the number of men employed "in executing the conscript law...."

---

[a] At General Robert E. Lee's suggestion, the Confederacy finally made a serious attempt to recapture New Bern with thirteen thousand men and fourteen navy vessels. The campaign began on February 1. The original plan had been suggested by Brigadier General Robert Hoke, but the expedition was under the command of Major General George Pickett. Pickett's mismanagement of the affair resulted in failure after only a few days. Pickett returned to his headquarters in Virginia, but General Hoke renewed the offensive. His forces captured Plymouth and Washington, North Carolina, in April but were recalled to Virginia the night before they could attack New Bern (Barrett, p. 202-20 and Barefoot, *General Robert F. Hoke,* p. 165).

Preston's report, submitted on the last day of 1863, was technically accurate but only covered the four states of Virginia, North Carolina, South Carolina, and Georgia and tended to minimize the numbers involved. Units like McRae's battalion, Woodfin's battalion, and Captain Waters's Raleigh provost guard were not counted.[a] Similar units existed in other states. The report only hinted that many more resources were dedicated to conscription related activities, such as desertion, furloughs, substitutions, details, and the "general external police of the Army in all its Branches." By narrowly confining his report to the requested information, Preston avoided revealing a great deal of the total expense of conscription.[164]

The year 1863 had been kind neither to the Confederacy nor to North Carolina. Western North Carolina had endured marauding deserters and resisters, violence between pro and anti-Confederate elements within the population, and, perhaps worse, the effect of government efforts to regain control. The Vance-Palmer forces in the Department of Western North Carolina fought against Union incursions from Tennessee. McRae's cavalry battalion chased deserters in the mountains west of Asheville and clashed with Union cavalry along the border. Mallett's two infantry companies at Camp Vance fought skirmishes with deserters and their sympathizers around Morganton. General Hoke's regiments abused the citizenry in a fourteen county area of the Piedmont, and Mallett's Company C was doing much the same in Alamance County. Even militia and Home Guard units engaged in the "wantonness" that Mallett had warned against in November 1862. The actions of government troops hardened many hearts in the population. Still, hundreds of deserters remained at-large between Raleigh and the Tennessee border.

Although driven deeper into hiding, deserters and conscription resisters had become progressively more determined and violent as government troops searched homes, impressed property, and interrogated their family members. Enrolling officers and Home Guardsmen were threatened, assaulted, and murdered. In retaliation, government troops executed deserters and tortured their families. There were more killings in return. Homes, barns, and crops were torched to force men out of hiding. Forest areas were burned off to reveal deserters' camps. While these activities often restored a measure of order and returned hundreds of men to the army, the evil visited upon the population likely outweighed the benefits derived.

[a] Major Woodfin was killed when he and his men were ambushed near Warm Springs, North Carolina, on October 20, 1863 (*Roster*, v. II, p. 560).

Blood feuds in North Carolina and Tennessee that would last for generations began during this period. When General Hoke and his regiments returned to Virginia, he declared the mission to have been successful. Investigations into the conduct of his troops were initiated immediately.[165]

The atmosphere of hatred and revenge, of which Albert Thompson was a part, is revealed in one of his first letters of the new year to Cate:

> January the 14 1864
> Camp Vance Nere Morganton
>
> My Dear wife and children.... well Cate I could have come home or by home if I would have started with the crowd that started to Rutherford yesterday but I dis like the notion of going home to my settlement to take up men for fere they will do me some private injury....

Thompson's company commander was aware that most of his men had been conscripted at Camp Hill and were from the western part of the state. Their participation in conscription activities in their own hometowns could result in retaliation against their families. Lieutenant McRae allowed Private Thompson to stay in camp while other soldiers went to Rutherford county.

Camp Vance got a new commandant in January. Captain Thomas H. Gatlin's resignation from the army due to disability and poor health was accepted on December 22. Colonel Mallett sent Captain Jesse McLean from Raleigh to replace Gatlin, run the camp, and manage conscription operations in western North Carolina. McLean arrived and began to make improvements right away. He emptied the guardhouse by shipping fifty prisoners to Raleigh at one time. He then had the building moved and rebuilt.

In assigning McLean to Camp Vance, Mallett was making preparations for changes that were about to take place. Changes in the conscript laws had been debated in the Confederate Congress and reported in the papers. Even as widely separated as Mallett's companies were, the soldiers knew that their assignments were likely to change. Thompson heard the rumors and read the papers. He broke the news to Cate on February 21:

> Camp Vance Nere Morganton
> My Dear wife and children.... we have some little sickness in camp but no one dangerous bad at this time.... well Cate there is talk of us having to leave and take the field I see the last act that is pass Conscript Camps shall be kept by disable Soldiers and if that be the case we will have to leave here....

It was no surprise to anyone that the government would have to do something. The year 1863 had taught Confederate military men and politicians alike that their nation faced manpower and production problems that would result in defeat in the foreseeable future. The Confederacy's aggressive military campaign of 1863 had not forced the United States to the bargaining table. Chancellorsville was a brilliant victory, but had resulted in twelve thousand Southern casualties, including "Stonewall" Jackson. Gettysburg had been a disappointing strategic gamble that cost the South another thirty-one thousand men. Rather than being grateful to Gettysburg's Union commander, General George Meade, President Lincoln criticized him for failing to pursue and destroy Lee's army. At Gettysburg, Lee and the South learned that the Army of Northern Virginia was not invincible and that Lincoln was not going to settle for anything less than total victory. The military situation was even worse in the central and western Confederacy.

The fall of Vicksburg on the fourth of July had isolated the Trans-Mississippi Department from the rest of the Confederacy and gave control of the entire length of the Mississippi River to the Union. The battle of Chickamauga in northern Georgia in September was a tactical victory for the South, but it had cost another nineteen thousand casualties, men that could not be replaced using current conscription practices. East Tennessee had been lost when General Bragg was maneuvered out of Chattanooga after a disappointing series of battles. From Chattanooga, the Union army could drive toward Atlanta.

Philosophical differences aside, Confederate military and civilian authorities all agreed that the South needed to put more men in the field. In addition to rounding up deserters, there were only three ways to accomplish this: expand the age group of men covered by the conscript laws, reduce the number of job-related deferments, and restrict duty in non-combat assignments to men who were physically incapable of field service. But there was another, more serious problem looming.

As had been the situation two years earlier, the prospect of thousands of soldiers leaving the army when their terms of service expired created a deadline. In 1862, by enacting the first conscription law, congress kept the twelve-month volunteers in service for a total of three years beginning on the date of their original enlistments. That three-year term would expire for most of the 1861 volunteers between May and December of 1864. The large number of coerced "volunteers" from April and May 1862 and the first and largest group of conscripts, those drafted in July and August 1862, would all be eligible to leave the army in the spring and summer of 1865. The Confederate army's ongoing struggle with desertion suggested to lawmakers that many soldiers would not stay beyond their required time. Once again, congress had to keep the army intact and in the field.

In addition to the military manpower shortage, there was the problem of agricultural and industrial production in a nation that was slowly being reduced in size and isolated from the rest of the world. The Union blockade, combined with the loss of the Trans-Mississippi and much of the central Confederacy, was forcing the South to rely almost completely on the few resources and production capabilities that it still had. The Confederacy's ability to wage war was coming to an end. Whatever congress was going to do needed to be done quickly.

This combination of circumstances forced the Confederate Congress to approve an overhaul of conscription on February 17, 1864. The age group of men covered by the law was expanded. Also introduced was the prospect of practically open-ended military service:

> AN ACT to organize forces to serve during the war. *The Congress of the Confederate States of America do enact*, That from and after the passage of this act, all white men, residents of the Confederate States, between the ages of seventeen and fifty, shall be in the military service of the Confederate States for the war.[166]

The wording, "for the war" instead of "three years unless the war shall have been sooner ended" of earlier acts, when combined with an upper age limit of fifty, meant that Confederate soldiers were bound to military service for most of their adult lives unless the war ended. The volunteers who joined the army for twelve months in 1861 and then had their enlistments lengthened to three years in 1862 were now bound to military service until they reached the age of fifty. Men who had been previously discharged from the army for any reason except total disability or religious exemptions were to return to military service, as were those who had hired substitutes.[a] The youngest and oldest men gathered under the new law were to be organized into separate forces, the Junior and Senior Reserves:

> ... all white male residents of the Confederate States between the ages of seventeen and eighteen and forty-five and fifty years shall enroll themselves, at such times and places, and under such regulations as the President may prescribe.... That persons mentioned in this section shall constitute a reserve for State defense and detail duty, and shall not be required to perform service out of the State in which they reside.[167]

The new law controlled the lives of Southern men from the age of seventeen to fifty. All young men were to be conscripted and enter the Junior Reserves when they turned seventeen. Junior Reserve battalions would serve as mobile, on-the-job training units that would eventually be consolidated into regiments. On their eighteenth birthdays, the Juniors would be transferred to a regiment in the field, there to serve until the age of forty-five. They would then be transferred to a Senior Reserve regiment back in their home state and serve there for five more years.[b]

The law directed all able-bodied soldiers to front-line military units and provided for security and defense within the states by using the youngest and oldest soldiers. The number of occupational exemptions was reduced by half. Other measures tightened the government's control over agricultural and industrial production and transportation. More stringent wage and price controls and additional taxes were also enacted. In order to divert able-bodied white soldiers to combat duty, the use of free African-Americans and up to twenty thousand slaves for non-combat military assignments was also approved. Not unexpectedly, the Bureau of Conscription was given responsibility for enrolling this workforce.[168]

---

[a] The allowing of substitutes for military service had been ended by congress on December 28, 1863. The change was announced by Adjutant and Inspector General Order No. 3, issued on Jan. 9, 1864 (*O.R.*, Series IV, v. 3, p. 11).

[b] Had the war continued indefinitely, under the new law a seventeen year old boy faced thirty-three years of military service.

After creating classes of very young and very old soldiers, the law went on to render practically all of the soldiers in Mallett's and McRae's battalions ineligible for continued service within the state:

> ... hereafter the duties of provost and hospital guards and clerks... guards... in the execution of the enrolment acts, and all similar duties, shall be performed by persons who are within the ages of eighteen and forty-five years, and who, by the report of a board of army surgeons, shall be reported as unable to perform active service in the field, but capable of performing some of the above-named duties....

These "light duty" soldiers, as they came to be called, were to replace the camp guards at both of Mallett's camps. Captain Samuel Waters's provost guard company in Raleigh was to be disbanded as well. Perhaps the only good news that Mallett received in February was the notification of Lieutenant Hahr's promotion to major.

The families of men in Mallett's battalion realized that the new law meant that their loved ones would soon be transferred to more dangerous assignments. Like wives all over the South, Cate Thompson had been faced with the grim realities of farm life with no husband at home. Crop management, sick children, and loneliness added more burdens to what was a hard life even in peaceful times. In the first of several letters that she sent to Albert during March 1864, she advised him of the conditions at home. Although she was about to experience a tragedy, she seemed determined to face whatever might come:

> Rutherford NC   March the 1 1864
>
> Mr Thompson my deare one   I again take my seat with pleasure to write you a few lines to let you know that we are all tolerable well except bad colds and coughfs.... We all have the worst colds we ever had   The children looks and coughfs like they had the hooping cough   Doras face is all swelled up   She will cough at night till she almost looses her breath and then she will throw up.... I hardly get any sleep with them   Ocran coughfs and bleeds at the nose.... I have not had a letter since last Sunday was a week ago.... I think I will surely heare from you this week   If I donot I will be bluer than I am.... I have got the gardens fixed up and planted some things   We planted some irish potatoes onions sowed some cabbage mustard and letise...

> but I donot expect you will get to eat any of it I heard this morning that you had to leave Camp Vance I am in hopes that it is not so but am afraid it is If it should be so I hope the Lord be with you preserve and shield you where ever you do have to go I would much rather you stay where you are Mr Thompson if you do think you will have to leave thare I would rather heare it now than after you are gone.... I suppose there is no prospect of peace.... I do wish this ware would stop for I think if it doesnot we will all starve.... The children all sends their love to you.... May the Lord watch over you and shield you and bring you home safe is my dearest desire.... Oh may we meet soon....
>
> M.C. Thompson

Ten days later, Cate and Albert's seven-year-old son, Ocran, died of whooping cough. Camp Vance was close enough for Albert to attend the funeral at Brittain Presbyterian Church, several miles north of Rutherfordton.

During the first months of 1864, McRae's battalion was drawn even further into a combat role along the North Carolina-South Carolina-Tennessee border. In February, one of McRae's Captains, Alexander McMillian, and part of the battalion were close enough to Union raiders to hear their artillery and see smoke rising near Franklin, North Carolina. McMillian advised Colonel Palmer that he would attack the Union force, which was headed into South Carolina, if reinforcements were sent.[169] District commanders in South Carolina, headquartered at Greenville, had also come to rely on McRae's battalion for support in fighting the Union border-raiders.

Colonel Palmer had been responsible for the defense of the District of Western North Carolina since the capture of General Vance. Confederate reversals in east Tennessee continued to weaken Palmer's position. He watched his situation grow steadily worse as spring approached. General Longstreet's forces were returned to Lee's army in April. Palmer could no longer rely on their presence for support. Early that month, he notified Richmond of his situation:

> HDQTRS. District of Western North Carolina
> April 2, 1864
> General S. Cooper, Adjutant and Inspector General:
>
> General: The recent change in position of Lieutenant-General Longstreet's forces exposes the western frontier

> of my district for a distance of nearly 175 miles, and I have been ordered to Richmond by my department commander to report the condition of my district, and to seek to have augmented the forces for its protection. It is now practicable for the enemy to pass directly from East Tennessee to the neighboring sections of North and South Carolina, and an enterprising enemy could without much difficulty reach, by a cavalry raid, our railroad communications through the states referred to.[170]

Palmer also used this communication with the war department to revisit an old disagreement with North Carolina's chief conscription officer. Colonel Mallett had wanted McRae to return to Raleigh the previous November. General Vance, in command of the district at the time, objected to losing McRae's services and asked his brother, the governor, to appeal the matter to Richmond. McRae and his battalion stayed in the mountains. Now, Palmer complained that Mallett had recently ordered the artillery battery that was assigned to McRae's battalion back to Raleigh. Palmer asked Adjutant and Inspector General Cooper to return the artillery and inquired as to why McRae's entire battalion should not be transferred from conscription duty and assigned to him to conduct "general operations in this district." Palmer reasoned correctly that implementation of his suggestion would relieve McRae's battalion of conscription duties and thus comply with the new conscript law.

Palmer's need for reinforcements was real. Not counting McRae's men, Palmer had less than twelve hundred soldiers to defend the area between Asheville and the Tennessee border. His forces were mostly infantry and were tied down guarding the main mountain passes that could be used for an invasion of the state. He could not hope to defend the entire region against smaller cavalry raids. To Palmer, McRae and his battalion seemed to be a partial answer to his manpower problem. To press his point, Colonel Palmer ended his memorandum with a serious warning:

> In closing I desire, with great deference, but with equal earnestness, to state that, in my opinion, unless some additional protection is afforded this country it will before long be overrun with tories and deserters, organized and furnished with arms and ammunition by the Federal authorities, and in all probability, sooner or later, serious and most destructive raids will be made into North and South Carolina.

The disputes and maneuvering between Mallett and Palmer over men and equipment were not borne of pettiness. Each colonel had been given heavy responsibilities and each was doing his best to gather any resources he could. Mallett had supported the formation of McRae's battalion and had donated officers and men to the effort. He realized that McRae would be doing double duty by gathering deserters and conscripts part of the time and fighting Union cavalry on other occasions. Still, he had no intention of losing control of McRae's battalion if he could prevent it. He had built an efficient statewide military organization, but like Palmer, and like military and civilian leaders throughout the Confederacy, Mallett needed more of everything.

In April and May 1864, as February's conscript law changes were being implemented, North Carolina's conscription bureau would reach the height of its influence.[a] The combination of Mallett's leadership and the state's reasonably secure geographic location had provided the stability that was required for conscription to operate efficiently. Mallett commanded or had significant influence over his own six-company infantry battalion and Major McRae's combined infantry and cavalry battalion. Mallett was ultimately responsible for both camps of instruction, the provost guard in Raleigh, the network of city, county and congressional district enrolling offices with their dozens Confederate officers and enlisted staffs, and hundreds of Home Guard and militia officers who were still enforcing the conscript laws.

Mallett's headquarters personnel in Raleigh maintained the medical examining boards attached to each congressional district and filled special requests for mechanics, railroad workers, telegraph operators, and other specialized laborers. They tracked the conscription, detail, or exemption of thousands of North Carolinians, black and white, slave and free, and coordinated the return of thousands of deserters to their commands. Now, as a result of February's conscription law, Mallett was about to be given organizational responsibility and initial authority over entirely new classes of soldiers: the Junior Reserves, Senior Reserves, and light duty men.

[a] With the passage of the new law, one loophole in the conscription process was closed. General Order No. 42, paragraph X, issued on April 14, 1864, finally ended the practice of recruiting for "any particular command." At this late stage in the war, however, the order was little more than a gesture (*O.R.*, Series IV, v. 3, p. 298).

During March and April, Mallett's men kept up with the implementation of the new law. Intermittent camp gossip held out some hope that individual companies might escape being disbanded as long as there were still large groups of deserters. Mallett indicated that this might be a possibility for Company C which was still in Alamance County. Major McRae's men hoped that Colonel Palmer's desire to keep them in western North Carolina might save them from being sent to Virginia or Georgia.

Even so, the determined and violent resistance being offered by many deserters was making duty in Mallett's battalion progressively less attractive. On April 13, James Harwell of Mallett's Company C wrote to his wife:

> Camp Bethel alamance co.
>
> My Dear sweet beloved wife... the diserters ofted [offered to] fight our men the other day ther was 2 of our men come a crouse 2 of them tha told them to give up ther guns tha told them tha wold se them in hell... but ther guns woldnt shoot.... Our men run a little wase and fire ther guns and tha shot one of them but tha didnt git him if we leave hear tha will take the country for tha will fight it will be hard anny place this Sommer i just soon be in the armma [army] as hear for ther is as much danger

Mallett's soldiers awaited their fate as Confederate military authorities began the reorganization. In mid-April, the men at Camp Holmes were told to choose new units in any combat branch of service. The battalion was scheduled to be disbanded in late May or early June. None of the bureau's officers or enlisted men who were fit for active duty would be spared. Both Mallett's and McRae's battalions, more than twelve companies in all, would be affected.

The commandants of conscription were ordered to organize the reserve battalions. In North Carolina, the light duty soldiers and Junior Reserves were to be assembled immediately. The initial plan called for the Senior Reserves to be enrolled at the same time, but Governor Vance prevailed upon the secretary of war, in the case of most of the older men, to postpone enrollment so that they might harvest the season's crops before being taken from their farms.[171]

Mallett issued orders requiring his enrolling officers to gather the men qualified for light duty and the seventeen-year-old boys at the camps of instruction. Congressional district medical boards and newly created advisory boards were immediately swamped with men seeking medical deferments.[a] Including the Senior Reserves, the process would involve inducting approximately ten thousand men into the army and would take the rest of the year. Some of Mallett's sergeants and lieutenants would again be conducting basic training for large groups of recruits. His two camp commandants were in place and ready for the task.

Captain Jesse McLean was promoted to major in April and ordered to remain in command at Camp Vance. Major Hahr was assigned to command Camp Holmes. Their orders were to organize, equip, and train the reserve battalions and to oversee the election of the company and battalion officers. Mallett was responsible for these troops until the process was complete. He was to then transfer them to the control of Lieutenant General Theophilus Holmes, who had returned to the state. Despite a lackluster tenure as a commander in the Trans-Mississippi Department, the elderly Holmes was still popular with Jefferson Davis. His selection as General of the Reserves in North Carolina came as no surprise.[b] Mallett looked forward to working with his old friend again.

As a result of the new conscription law, the secretary of war's authorization for McRae's battalion would end on June 1. Colonel Palmer's hopes of gaining permanent control of McRae's force would end with the month of May. In an effort to keep McRae's battalion together, at least for a while longer, Mallett recommended having the entire unit sent to Richmond.[172] No action was taken on his suggestion. Like the other officers in both battalions, Major McRae would have to find another assignment.

Mallett could foresee trouble. He remembered the first summer of conscription when his camp experienced a mass escape. Now, his companies were to be disbanded within about forty-five days. The replacements authorized by the new law could not be assembled

---

[a] The new conscript law provided for the creation of a three-man advisory board in each county. They were comprised of enrolled men between the ages of forty-five and fifty and were under the supervision of the enrolling officer. The boards investigated the merit of all applications for exemption and detail (*O.R.*, Series IV, v. 3, p. 503).

[b] Lieutenant General Holmes had only reluctantly accepted the Trans-Mississippi command in 1862 at the urging of President Davis. Holmes was almost completely deaf and was keenly aware of his own strengths and weaknesses feeling that he was better at implementing the policies of others than at setting policy himself (Johnston, *Vance*, v. 1, p. 137). He had been blamed for the Confederate defeat at Helena, Arkansas on July 4, 1863 (Castel, "Theophilus Holmes: Pallbearer of the Confederacy," *Civil War Times Illustrated*, July, 1977, p. 16).

and sufficiently prepared for duty within that time. Even deserters in the Camp Holmes guardhouse knew that once Mallett's veterans were transferred, the draft dodgers' lot would improve. One such guardhouse resident, absent without leave from the 45th North Carolina Troops, advised his wife to "tell the rest of the conscripts if they can ceep out 2 weaks longer that the[y] will not be hunted so bad the raley [Raleigh] gard is to be ordered off in the course of one weak to fill up different rigments and the 17 [year old] boys is to take their places."[173] Mallett was right. The lapse in security would cause problems at both of his camps. At Camp Vance, the result would be disastrous.

Mallett's and McRae's men were allowed to transfer to any field unit that was organized before the passage of the first conscription act. Only a few of the officers and men were eligible for light duty assignments, and all were between eighteen and forty-five years of age. Those seeking less dangerous assignments would have to choose carefully. Gone were the days of joining the idle cavalry and artillery units along the coast that General Lee had complained about the previous year. Most of the soldiers accepted their situation and selected North Carolina units serving either in Lee's army around Petersburg or with General Joseph Johnston in Georgia. It was not an attractive choice. Both armies were involved in protracted defensive struggles.

The two battalions were ordered to gather at Camp Holmes in May. Before they left Camp Vance, the men of Companies B and D turned in their stands-of-arms and were issued new uniforms, shoes, and blankets. Thompson, Cowen, and most of Company B were given short furloughs beginning on May 13. Burgess Gaither, the Summers boys, and most of Company D were not so fortunate. They were sent directly to Raleigh, arriving there on May 19. Private Harwell's Company C left Alamance County and arrived at Camp Holmes during the last week of the month.

The North Carolina legislature passed a resolution on May 28 requesting that Mallett's battalion remain intact when transferred. The state's congressional delegation transmitted the request to the House of Representatives where it died in the Military Affairs Committee.

Just as the men were choosing their new regiments, department commander General P. G. T. Beauregard called on Mallett for reinforcements at Weldon. Mallett quickly dispatched Major Hahr with Companies A, D, E, and F to once again protect the railroad bridge. The men in Companies B and C remained at Camp Holmes and prepared for their transfers.

Chapter Seven

Juniors, Seniors, and Light Duty

June 1864 - March 1865

Gathering the two battalions at Raleigh proved to be no simple task. Company D of McRae's battalion was subjected to a series of conflicting orders as they attempted to return to Raleigh. They finally had to detour through Moore and Randolph counties to chase deserters before proceeding to Camp Holmes.[174] Mallett was unable to have Company D of his battalion returned to camp from Weldon until June 7. The other three companies and Major Hahr would have to stay and guard the railroad bridge for the foreseeable future.

For a time, Mallett was caught between the war department's orders to disband his battalion and General Beauregard's refusal to return the companies from Weldon so the order could be carried out. Including cavalry and artillery, there were approximately 1,300 troops occupying fortifications around the Weldon bridge. Hahr's companies comprised almost a third of the infantry force. The Union army was active at Petersburg and along the railroad line leading toward Weldon. General Beauregard was responsible for the bridge and intended to keep as many troops in the vicinity as he could.

Mallett's and McRae's men were given the choice of joining the infantry, cavalry, artillery, or navy. Most of them chose hometown units where they had friends and family and where reprisals for their service in the conscription bureau would be less likely. Others chose North Carolina units in the Army of Tennessee for a similar reason. Mallett's bureau had sent very few conscripts to that army. Major McRae reverted to the rank of captain and joined General Laurence S. Baker's 2nd Military District headquarters at Goldsboro as an assistant adjutant general. Most of McRae's men chose cavalry regiments, most often the 1st North Carolina Cavalry. Counting both battalions and Captain Waters's provost company, more than one thousand officers and men had to be reassigned.

Three of Mallett's companies, B, C, and D were disbanded at Camp Holmes and transferred. The fifty-five members of Lieutenant John McRae's Company B received another uniform and equipment issue on June 3. On June 6, Thompson, Cowen, A. S. Gaddy, and approximately twenty other men from Company B were assigned to the 39th North Carolina Troops. Ten men from Company D went to the 29th North Carolina Troops. These two regiments had originally been raised in western North Carolina and were currently assigned to General Matthew Ector's brigade in General Johnston's Army of Tennessee. Thompson and his friends knew that they would soon be part of Johnston's ongoing effort to resist Sherman's advance on Atlanta. Mallett's Companies A, E, and F never returned to Raleigh, but were disbanded at Weldon.

The majority of Mallett's men went to regiments serving in Virginia or eastern North Carolina. Since so many of his men had been conscripted in western North Carolina, they usually chose companies from that area. The 50th North Carolina Troops was an attractive choice. The regiment was stationed at Washington and Plymouth, contained several western North Carolina companies, and had seen little hard fighting during the war. A number of men chose the 15th and 24th North Carolina regiments, thus reuniting with members of the battalion who had been transferred to those units in March and April 1863.

At least twenty-four men and two officers, including Lieutenant John McRae, chose the 13th North Carolina Artillery. Various companies of Mallett's battalion had served with batteries of this unit at Kinston, Goldsboro, Weldon, and, more recently, at Camp Vance. Lieutenant McRae had received artillery training early in the war.

Approximately one hundred of Mallett's conscripts who wanted less hazardous duty chose to join the navy. They knew of the constant fighting in Georgia and Virginia and reasoned that service in the almost nonexistent Confederate navy was a safer bet. Burgess Gaither and his cousins Mel and Sid Summers agreed. Burgess wrote to his sister, Molly, about the plan:

> Camp Holmes, Near Raleigh
> June the 11 1864
>
> Dear sister
> I seat my self to drop you afew lines to inform you that I am well.... Our battalion is all busted up an is now scatered in the four winds of the earth.... There was 45 left to go to the western army last night.... How hard it was to part with them to see them going to such dangerous place.... I have concluded to go to some place you never thought of me going and I think at this time it is the best... Mollie I am going to Charleston to thee Navy I am not going by my

> self there is 21 going out of our co[mpany].... We have taken this place for the safest place I can not tell how it will turn out.... [175]

Camps Vance and Holmes stayed busy from April through June. Mallett's and McRae's veterans were being reequipped and transferred while hundreds of seventeen-year-old conscripts reported for duty each month.[a] Veteran sergeants of Mallett's battalion spent their last few days at camp Holmes training teenagers to march.[176] For these few months, the camps conducted recruit training as they had been designed to do when conscription was first implemented. The officers and recruits were trained in companies that would remain together for the foreseeable future. Some of the young men were issued the shorter "N.C. rifles" as opposed to standard muskets, "to fit our size," as one recruit put it.[177]

Mallett, now deprived of the services of his veterans, had to put together a new guard for the camp.[b] He managed to retain the services of a few of his less capable older conscripts. Although the conscription of most of the Senior Reserves had been postponed, enough of that age group reported voluntarily along with the light duty men that he was able to staff most of his guard posts. A district supporting force was organized under the command of Captain Jackson Jones.[c] This company was assigned to the 5th Congressional District and remained in the Raleigh area for the next several months.[178]

Mallett's misgivings about having an understaffed, overage, and disabled camp guard were confirmed on June 20. The guardhouse was always full of men who were in better shape than his guards. He

---

[a] Reserve companies were also organized at Goldsboro, Wilmington, and Asheville (*O.R.*, Series IV, v. 3, p. 505-06).

[b] Bureau of Conscription Circular No. 14, issued on April 5, 1864, authorized commandants of conscription "to retain out of the reserve classes a sufficient number to compose their camp guard and supporting force...." (*O.R.*, Series IV, v. 3, p. 270); however, the Junior Reserves were not often used in this capacity.

[c] Captain Jones's company was one of several congressional district supporting force companies authorized by Circular No. 8, Bureau of Conscription on March 18, 1864 (*O.R.,* Series IV, v. 3, p. 223). These companies existed in at least the 4th, 5th, 7th, 8th, 9th, and 10th Congressional districts and contained a number of men who would eventually serve in Senior Reserve regiments (*Company Front*, Nov/Dec. 1990, "North Carolina Land Units in Confederate Service, 1861-1865: An Order of Battle," p. 18-19).

barely managed to conceal his disgust when he reported the incident to Richmond:

> Conscript Office
> Raleigh, N.C. June, 21, 64
> Major C. B. Duffield
> Bureau Of Conscription
>
> Major:
> I have the honor to report that the Guard at this Camp of Instruction, now composed of light duty men, were overpowered on yesterday by fourteen (14) deserters, who, wresting the arms from the Guard, knocked them down indiscriminately & made good their escape. The officers succeeded after some difficulty in capturing eight (8) of the number. Every precaution had been taken by the officer of the day as usual, but it is not a matter of suprise that the deserters should attempt to escape when they know that their Guard is composed of men who cannot "doublequick" fifty (50) yards or offer much resistance.[179]

Mallett also advised his superiors that conscription resistance in various parts of the state had increased since his battalion had been disbanded.

That same month, Lieutenant Colonel Archer Anderson began an inspection tour of the North Carolina Bureau of Conscription. Anderson was ordered to send his reports to Adjutant and Inspector General Cooper through General Braxton Bragg. Mallett knew that Anderson was coming and warned his enrolling officers to be prepared. Anderson filed separate reports on Mallett's Raleigh headquarters, the operation at Camp Holmes, and on several district and county offices.

The report on the Raleigh headquarters, written after Anderson moved on to the conscript office in Salisbury, revealed the amount of administrative support that conscription had grown to require. It also showed the extent to which the Confederate government was exercising control over the nation's wartime economy:

Salisbury, N. C., June 22, 1864
General Braxton Bragg,
Richmond, Va.:

General: I have the honor to report that I reached Raleigh on the 16th instant, and at once entered upon the duty assigned me - the inspection of the conscription service of this State. My attention in that city was particularly directed to the organization of the office of the commandant of conscripts, the amount and dispatch of business passing through it, the organization of the reserve forces recently called out, and the camp of instruction near the town.

Col. Peter Mallett is the commandant for the state. He is immediately assisted... by four officers and nine clerks. Two of the latter are able-bodied conscripts. Lieutenant Parish has charge of the department of applications for detail and the orders consequent thereon. The act of Congress of February 17, by making the Government the custodian and director, to a large extent, of the agricultural and industrial interests of the country, has given immense expansion to this class of business. The applications for detail are almost as numerous as the persons enrolled. For many of these the office at Raleigh is the only channel of communication with the Bureau at Richmond, but it must always be ready to account for any petition. Hence an elaborate system of registration is rendered necessary.

There are over 100 applications for detail or renewal of detail daily. They consist generally of a recital of the claim and circumstances of the party, a report on the case by a board of citizens, and the endorsements of the county and district enrolling officers. It is the duty of Lieutenant Parish to examine each petition carefully and to make such endorsements for Col. Mallett's signature as may be prescribed in cases covered by general rules. In cases in doubt the endorsement is dictated by the commandant.

The papers are then to be recorded. Three clerks find constant employment in this work. One book contains the applications for agricultural details, another those based on the ground of public necessity, and a third those of contractors, Government officers, &c. Three hundred and nine applications of the first class were made in the week ending June 18; 431 of the second class have been made since April 25; thirty of the third class since June 5. I do not think one officer can make these investigations with the patient care which is essential, and yet with the dispatch so necessary to the proper conduct of the office, and I am therefore inclined to agree with Colonel Mallett in the opinion that another should be assigned to have exclusive charge of agricultural details.

Besides investigating such applications going forward, Lieutenant Parish issues all orders, making the details when approved, and supervises the reports of detailed men required by law of railroad companies and all other business related to this class of persons. This officer seems well fitted for his work.

Lieutenant Hardin distributes the mail as it arrives to the proper offices, issues all general instructions to enrolling officers and miscellaneous special orders, and performs the duties of adjutant of the post of Raleigh.... He seems to be kept busy all the time.

Lieutenant Jones writes letters for the commandant, has his desk in the reception office, and disposes of all the verbal communications not requiring the attention of Colonel Mallett. He is also charged with the preparation of the regular returns and reports. There seemed to be sufficient work of this sort to keep him constantly employed.

Captain Cowper has charge of everything relating to the apprehension and return of deserters and other absentees without leave. Each application for the return of an absentee is recorded and then referred to the proper officer. When the paper comes back the final disposition of the man is noted in the record book. Some 7,000 such applications have been returned to commanding officers with the information required.... A clerk has charge of all business relating to the detail or exemption of free negros.

Colonel Mallett's time is occupied with the supervision of these officers, the decision of the more difficult cases, the reception of numerous applicants in person, and the general direction of the conscription service in the State. I passed three days in his office in studying its organization and familiarizing myself with the kind and amount of business transacted. The various duties are judiciously distributed, the necessary records are kept, and the work seems to be faithfully and well done, though without much claim to clerical elegance. I have never seen bureau officers or clerks more steadily engaged....[180]

After completing his inspection of Mallett's headquarters, Lieutenant Colonel Anderson headed for Camp Holmes, where he found a sprawling camp city. Nearby, sutlers did a brisk business selling goods and services to the soldiers. Wagons came and went delivering commissary stores and firewood. Townspeople came out to the camp to watch companies of teenagers drill. Scores of family members were visiting young men who were away from home for the first time. Because the hotels in Raleigh were always full, many of the visitors stayed in makeshift housing nearby.

Anderson met with Major Hahr and was introduced to the camp's staff which included the adjutant, a receiving officer, an assistant quartermaster, an assistant commissary of subsistence, one surgeon, one assistant surgeon, one chaplain, an officer of the guard, and five drill masters.

Anderson's report detailed the process that had put thousands of North Carolinians into the Confederate army:

> As the conscripts come in their names are recorded with a statement of their age, county, the officer by whom enrolled, and other facts entering into a descriptive list. When they leave the camp the assignment made of them is recorded in the same book, which thus presents a complete history of the connection of each conscript passing through this camp with the conscription authorities. Nine thousand and fifty-seven are shown to have been enrolled at Camp Holmes during the year ending June 13, but this figure does not include the whole number enrolled in the State in that period, as many are detailed for various duties without passing through the camp of instruction. The names thus recorded are classified in three other books as follows:
>
> 1. The principals of substitutes-430 so far. 2. Persons exempt prior to the act of February 17 otherwise than by substitution. 3. Those not previously exempt. All conscripts fit for the field are examined by the Medical Board and classified according to their special fitness for artillery, cavalry or infantry service. Besides the above the following books are kept:
>
> 1. A record of the absentees, deserters, &ct., arrested and sent to their commands. Three hundred odd of these arrests were made in May; over 6,000 have been returned through this camp.
>
> 2. Morning report book showing all present in camp.

> 3. Order book. These books preserve a record of all the facts which would seem essential.
>
> There are 136 enlisted men in the camp. Of these, sixty-four disabled conscripts and soldiers constitute the camp guard. The remainder are conscripts whose permanent assignment is delayed for obvious causes....
>
> Staff departments.- The assistant quartermaster, besides discharging the appropriate duties of the camp, pays all the enrolling officers of the State and provides them with stationary. Every conscript is clothed by him before he leaves the camp. Employes: One clerk, one forage-master, one overseer of wood-choppers - all disabled soldiers or conscripts.
>
> The medical officers are the physicians of the camp, and constitute a board for the duties before mentioned. The senior officer has the supervision of all the district medical boards, and is charged with the duty of keeping them filled with proper officers. Every conscript is vaccinated here. A neat hospital with eighteen beds is attached. Employes: one hospital steward, regularly appointed; one clerk, a disabled conscript.

Lieutenant Colonel Anderson took the opportunity of his report to comment on the recently departed conscripts who chose to join the navy:[a]

> It appears that of some 250 conscripts who had been doing duty for two years in Mallett's battalion as a camp guard and supporting force, 100 men without any experience on the water selected the naval service when their temporary organization was disbanded a few weeks since. Thus 100 trained men are lost to the Army when every man is needed. I mention the incident, as it may be thought proper to take measures for their transfer to the Army, or for the alteration of the law at the next session of Congress. With the instructions on this subject (issued by General Rains) it is a matter of surprise that a single conscript goes to the Army.[181]

The majority of Anderson's report on the North Carolina Bureau of Conscription was very favorable. However, he noted that the flow of information and the decision making process between local enrolling

[a] Conscripts were given this option under a circular issued by Brigadier General Rains on March 24, 1863 (*O.R.*, Series IV, v. 2, p. 456).

officers and Richmond authorities was too slow. To illustrate his point, Anderson cited the recent creation of the Junior Reserve battalions. In North Carolina, that process took from February 17 (the date the law was passed) until June 22 when Anderson described the process as "nearly complete." He correctly laid most of the blame on delays that were "inseparable from the system of conscription," implying that the number of bureaucratic levels between the local conscript officer and the Bureau of Conscription in Richmond was the problem. This assessment was exactly what Braxton Bragg wanted to hear.

While Anderson's inspection tour progressed, Mallett attended to the many personnel matters that the break up of his battalion had generated. One of the problems was discontent among his soldiers at having to leave Camp Holmes. Many of the men felt that the government had violated the underlying agreement relating to their service in the conscript bureau. Mallett's men had enforced the most hated law in the Confederacy on fellow North Carolinians in return for having an assignment within the state. Now, after as much as two years of faithful service, most of his soldiers were being transferred to field units where they could expect to live with armed men who despised them. A number of Mallett's soldiers vented their frustration openly. Some expressed their displeasure with the situation in terms that must have sounded treasonous. Mallett dealt with at least one such case:

> Conscript Office
> Raleigh N.C. June 11, 64
> Major Genl. Robert Ransom
> Comdg. Dept. Henrico
> Richmond Va
>
> General:
>
> I have the honor to report that a few days ago Geo. W. McCain, a member of my Camp Guard was sent to Castle Thunder for mutinous language in regard to his assignment to the field.
>
> I take the liberty now of requesting that he may be forwarded to his Regt. 2nd N.C. Troops, Ramseur's Brigade, Rhodes Division, without delay. McCain has heretofore enjoyed a most excellent character having been a Sergt. of my Camp Guard and I feel sure that the punishment

> already inflicted is amply sufficient to prevent a repetition of any misconduct.
>
> I am, General
> Very Respectfully
> Your Obdt. Servant
> Peter Mallett, Col.
> Commdt. Of Conscripts for N.C. [a]

As bitter as some of them were, the rest of Mallett's soldiers managed to report to their assignments in Virginia and Georgia without a stay in the guardhouse.

Toward the end of June, former private, now novice seaman, Burgess Gaither arrived in Charleston. On the same day that his friends Thompson, Cowen, and Gaddy were wounded in the artillery bombardment on Kennesaw Mountain, Burgess wrote to Mollie:

> June the 25 1864
> Charleston, S C
>
> Dear sister
> I seat my self to drop you a few lines.... I have no news to write you at this time I am here at the wreciven ship but I do not know how long I will stay here I can not tell you how I like this place yet for I have not been here long enough to learn yet but I can say to you that I want to get home very bad.... I hope that I will keep my health and get home soon.... Mollie I am in sight of the yankee fleet they shell the town ever day they shell fort sumter ever day there was 30 or 40 shells thrown since I have been here some of them is very large wones I can see them ever day Mollie this is a very hot place....

All that April and May, the gathering of reserves and disbanding of Mallett's and McRae's battalions was being monitored by General John M. Schofield. Schofield, who was responsible for Union army operations in western North Carolina, was headquartered with

[a] Camp Holmes v. 7, p. 142. Castle Thunder in Richmond was a converted tobacco warehouse that was used to incarcerate prisoners other than prisoners of war and common criminals. McCain had served in Company B of Mallett's battalion. Mallett's letter may have helped the situation. McCain was reduced to the rank of private but allowed to report to his regiment. He was seriously wounded and captured in September 1864 but was exchanged and survived the war (*Roster*, v. III, p. 437).

Sherman's army in Georgia. In May, he realized that an opportunity to strike a blow in western North Carolina was approaching. He wanted to destroy Camp Vance, the nearby railroad depot, and, most importantly, the railroad bridge over the Yadkin River near Salisbury. Schofield also hoped to liberate several thousand Union prisoners at the Salisbury prison camp at the same time. Such a raid would require a small, fast moving force of men who knew the area and could gather information and support from the pro-Union element of the local population.

For a successful operation so deep in enemy territory, Schofield knew that conditions would have to be nearly perfect. The attack on Camp Vance, would need to occur after Mallett's two companies and McRae's battalion had departed, but before the Junior Reserves were organized. The telegraph wires at the nearby depot had to be cut before the alarm could be sent to Salisbury. Other than the local Home Guard and militia, the closest source of Confederate reinforcements was the Salisbury prison guard battalion. The Union army's campaign to capture Petersburg and Richmond had recently begun. Schofield knew that any Union activity southwest of Petersburg along the railroad line would cause the Confederates to reinforce Weldon and draw their attention away from western North Carolina.

Schofield chose a reckless young captain named George Kirk to lead the raid. Kirk was a pro-Union native of east Tennessee. He spent the first fifteen months of the war running an "underground railroad" for Confederate deserters and draft resisters who were fleeing from North Carolina. He joined the Union army in August 1862, and by May 1863, he was a captain in the 5th East Tennessee Cavalry (United States). Kirk's talents as an organizer and his knowledge of the Tennessee and North Carolina border made him the perfect choice to gather pro-Union civilians and Confederate deserters for service in the Union army.[182] During late 1863, he recruited and served in the 2nd Regiment North Carolina Mounted Infantry (United States).

By early 1864, Kirk was organizing a similar unit, the 3rd Regiment North Carolina Mounted Infantry (United States), often enticing soldiers from his former units to desert and join this new regiment. By June, he had assembled a force of Native Americans, Confederate deserters, runaway slaves, and veteran Union cavalrymen who were perfect for the Morganton raid.[183] Kirk and his men were hardened survivors of the vicious mountain warfare.

Major Jesse McLean had gathered six companies of Junior Reserves at Camp Vance. On June 24, three of the companies were to leave the camp and report for training at Camp Holmes. One of the enthusiastic young soldiers was D. C. Setser. The night before his company was to depart, Setser wrote to his family:

> Camp Vance June the 23 64
>
> Dear father, I now Seat myself to inform you that I am well and hearty. the object of my writing you this letter is to inform you that we are going to leav her tomorrow morning bright and early fore Raleigh. their we will remain untill further orders. from there we will proceed to Weldon or goldsborough or Kinston. it is uncertain how long we will stay in Raleigh. Sam says we will Stay untill we draw Arms and clothings. the arms we drawed here we return them today and all our Accourtments.... we elected our major this morning.... Our co., that is co. C and Co. A and co. B is a going.... the rest is going to stay.... [184]

Young Setser and the three companies he mentioned left Camp Vance the next morning with their new major. The three remaining companies of Juniors were about to get their first taste of war.

Almost two weeks earlier on June 12, Captain Kirk led about one hundred and thirty hand-picked members of his mounted infantry unit, armed with Spencer repeating rifles, out of Morristown, Tennessee. They traveled only at night and stayed off the main roads. The force made its way into Burke County, North Carolina, just a few miles from Camp Vance. Kirk met with local residents, Davis Ellis and Joseph Franklin, who were connected with the Heroes of America. They made final arrangements for the attack and the raiders departed for Camp Vance.[185]

Major McLean had been granted a furlough and was not at Camp Vance. He left lieutenants Walter Bullock and Edward F. Hanks with instructions to arm and continue organizing the young recruits still at the camp. Lieutenant Bullock had plenty of weapons and equipment on hand, Mallett's two companies having turned in their stands-of-arms prior to leaving for Raleigh. Hanks and Bullock planned to issue the weapons to the Juniors on the morning of June 28.

Dawn broke to the usual sound of Camp Vance musicians playing reveille. As the music faded, a second and unseen band struck up the tune again. These musicians were soldiers in Kirk's raiding-party. Several Union soldiers approached camp headquarters and demanded an immediate surrender. Bullock and Hanks knew Kirk's reputation and assumed that they were outnumbered. They conferred briefly and decided that if they could get good terms, a peaceable surrender was preferable to the alternative. Their unarmed teenagers were no match for Kirk's mountain fighters.

The usual terms were agreed upon: immediate parole for all prisoners and no destruction of their personal property. The deal was struck and the garrison surrendered. Kirk then broke the agreement and placed everyone under arrest and ordered the destruction of the camp. The double-crossed Confederates watched helplessly as Kirk's men set fire to every building except the hospital.

The raiders then headed for the train depot. As they arrived, the telegraph operator managed to send a message to Salisbury to alert troops at the prison. Kirk decided that going any further east was too risky now that Confederate reinforcements were aware of his presence. He ordered the depot, a locomotive, and four railroad cars to be burned. The bridge over the Yadkin River, not to mention the Salisbury prison, would have to wait.

Word of the raid was indeed spreading. Not only was Salisbury sending troops, the Burke County Home Guard was gathering to counterattack. Kirk and his force began their retreat by way of the Piedmont road toward Brown Mountain. The pursuing Confederates attacked them there and again at Winding Stairs Road, but were unable capture the fast-moving force. Other Confederates in the region tried to cut off the raiders' retreat, but Kirk's force escaped into Tennessee with about half of the prisoners. The rest escaped during the chase.

Colonel Mallett reacted to the disaster as quickly as he could, but he had no troops to send until two days after the raid. Captain John S. Hines, formerly of McRae's battalion, arrived in Raleigh with one hundred and sixty-five men. Mallett sent them back to Camp Vance to await further orders. He also notified General Holmes of the raid (because Junior Reserves were involved) and advised him that Kirk's men were being pursued.

Captain Charles N. Allen of the 30th North Carolina Troops was sent to Camp Vance to conduct the initial inquiry.[a] Allen arrived the day after Kirk left. His report provided Mallett with a detailed account of the destruction of Camp Vance:

[a] Captain Allen had been severely wounded in the right arm at Gettysburg and was probably living at his home in Wake County at the time of the Camp Vance raid (*Roster*, v. VIII, p. 352). He was on temporary service with the conscript bureau while he waited for his permanent assignment by the recently established Invalid Corps (*O.R.*,Series IV, v. 3, p. 214).

Camp Vance, N.C., June 29, 1864

Colonel: On my arrival here this morning I found Camp Vance a heap of ruins.... the incendiary's torch was struck to every building except the hospital, which the surgeons by their blarney and ingenious persuasion saved intact.

The officers and men were all taken off under guard, except the surgeons, who were paroled, and about seventy men, whom they managed to get on the sick list and crowd into the hospital. The surgeons succeeded in saving about all of their supplies, all the cooking utensils of the camp, and extinguished the flames in the two double cabins of officer's quarters and one row of privates' cabins. There were 250 bushels of corn burned, about 6,500 pounds of forage, some 100 bushels of rye, and 50 of oats; also some 250 guns and accouterments, a goodly number of which were in bad condition, about 1,500 rounds of ammunition, &c. They burned all the office books and papers and all papers and documents in the quartermaster's and commissary departments. They took off 4 government mules and 4 private horses, leaving the two wagons and one set of harness....

There were some 240 of the Junior Reserves in camp here on the morning of the capitulation besides the officers. The raiding party numbered, so far as I have been able to learn, between 150 and 200 men, being composed of a very few soldiers, some 25 Indians, and the remainder of deserters and tories from Tennessee and Western North Carolina.

All of them were armed magnificently, the most of them with Spencer repeating rifles. They released some of the recusant conscripts and deserters from the guard-house here and armed them immediately. They are retreating and gathering horses and negro men, whom they arm instantly. The home guard and some two companies from the garrison at Salisbury are in pursuit.

I will let you hear from me again soon. The surgeons had sent all the men who were in the hospital home, with orders to report to their respective county enrolling officers. I will have what little they failed to destroy well stored.

I am, colonel, with great respect, your very humble servant,
C. N. Allen,
Captain (retired) [186]

General Schofield submitted his report on the raid to General William T. Sherman in July:[a]

> HEADQUARTERS ARMY OF THE OHIO
> Near Atlanta, Ga., July, 21, 1864
>
> GENERAL: I have the honor to inform you that Capt. G. W. Kirk, Third North Carolina Volunteer Infantry, has returned to Knoxville from the raid I ordered him to make into Western North Carolina. The following is a correct summary of the results of the expedition: He marched with about 130 men from Morristown on the 13th of June, and proceeded via Bull's Gap, Greenville Tenn., and Crab Orchard to Camp Vance, within six miles of Morganton, N.C. At Camp Vance he met the enemy, routing them, with a loss to them of one commissioned officer and 10 men killed; number of wounded unknown. At Camp Vance he destroyed a large quantity of rebel property... besides capturing 277 prisoners, who surrendered with the camp, of which number he succeeded in bringing into Knoxville 132, together with 32 negroes and 48 horses and mules, besides obtaining 40 recruits for his regiment, and perfecting arrangements for others. He did not accomplish the principle of the mission-that is, the destruction of the railroad bridge over the Yadkin River; but made arrangements to do this secretly, it being impossible for him to do it by force. The total casualties for his command were 1 killed, 1 mortally wounded, and 5 slightly, including Captain Kirk himself.
>
> Very respectfully, your obedient servant,
> J. M. Schofield,
> Major-General, Commanding. [187]

[a] Accounts of the raid differ as to whether or not fighting occurred at Camp Vance. Confederate accounts do not mention a fight, although relic hunters have found fired and dropped bullets from muzzle-loading rifles. Fired bullets and cartridge casings from Spencer repeaters have also been found in the vicinity of the camp (Williams, *Burke County's Camp Vance*).

Colonel Palmer heard about the Camp Vance raid the day after it occurred, but was at his headquarters in Asheville and too far away to be of immediate assistance. He vented his frustration directly to Adjutant and Inspector General Cooper:

> HDQRS. DISTRICT OF WESTERN NORTH CAROLINA,
> Asheville, July 4, 1864.
>
> General: On Wednesday evening last a vague rumor reached me to the effect that a band of tories and deserters had on Tuesday at daylight surprised and captured Camp Vance (a rendezvous of conscripts, near Morganton) and a battalion of Junior Reserves recently organized at that place. Camp Vance is not in my district, my command extending only to the Blue Ridge.... If the citizens of Morganton had notified me of Kirk's presence in their vicinity I could have captured his entire band. My forces are still after him, but he will undoubtedly escape.... General Holmes has not only not given me any additional reserves, but has ordered to the eastern part of the State the small battalion of Junior Reserves recently collected and organized at this place. Some cavalry should be sent to me at once, if practicable.[188]

Palmer was understandably bitter. While the protection of Camp Vance was not one of his responsibilities, Kirk's raiders had passed through his district as they traveled to and from the camp. Three months before, Palmer had warned his superiors of the possibility of just such an attack. He had spent most of a year trying to convince Confederate authorities to put additional troops in the area to protect the railroad. True to his prediction, as soon as McRae's battalion and Mallett's two Camp Vance companies were recalled to Raleigh, Union forces struck. Adding insult to injury, Kirk's men burned Colonel Palmer's home during the raid.[189]

Several days after Kirks's attack, the 68th North Carolina Troops, which had been stationed at Weldon since early May, arrived at Camp Vance and began repairing the damage. Zebulon Vance gave a speech at the camp several weeks later during his gubernatorial reelection campaign against William W. Holden.[190] No doubt that Vance's appearance in western North Carolina was partially designed to reassure the pro-Confederate population. Nonetheless, Mallett continued to worry about the camp's exposed location. He knew that eventually his western camp would have to be moved closer to the center of the state.[a]

At Camp Holmes, changes wrought by the new conscription law continued to result in security problems, though not nearly so serious as those at Camp Vance. There was another breakout from the guardhouse in July, this time resulting in a fatality. Major Hahr reported the incident to Mallett:

> Camp of Instruction,
> Camp Holmes, North Carolina,
> July 11, 1864
> Colonel Mallett,
> Commanding Conscripts:
>
> Colonel: I have the honor to enclose descriptive lists of two prisoners, who were shot by the guard at this camp last night, in attempting to escape from the Guard House, and to submit the following particulars, viz: it seems that the prisoners succeeded, between the hours of two and three last night, in unfastening the east door of the guard-house from the inside, without attracting the attention of the guard, but on rushing out, two of them were shot. Wheeler, who seized the gun of the sentinel nearest the door, intending to wrest it from him, was shot in the breast and fell dead after running off a few steps.
>
> Pollard received a severe flesh wound in the thigh while running, which caused him to return and surrender. Other prisoners, intent on following the example of the above, were deterred from carrying out their plan by seeing their comrades fall and the entire guard rush to the rescue. Some confusion arising during this firing and rushing to and from the guard-house, I am pained to say that two men of our guard, while in the zealous performance of

[a] The timing of the Camp Vance raid must certainly have troubled the Confederate military. It appeared that the Union army was able to plan the raid using information provided by local Union sympathizers in western North Carolina coordinated with larger military operations in Virginia and Georgia. That, or the raid benefitted from an extraordinary series of coincidences. When Kirk struck, the camp's commanding officer, Major Jesse McLean, had just left on furlough. Mallett's two infantry companies at Camp Vance had been sent to Raleigh, as had McRae's battalion. Half of the Junior Reserves that had been assembled at the camp had also been sent east. The companies of Junior Reserves that stayed behind were not armed. There was sufficient Union activity along the railroad in Virginia to draw Camp Holmes troops and the 68th North Carolina regiment toward Weldon, and the inevitable Union attack at Kennesaw Mountain was launched the day before the Camp Vance raid.

> their duty, were accidentally wounded by their comrades on post. Their names are as follows: S. M. Wright, of Person County, wounded in the shoulder; Lewis Anderson of Orange County, wounded in the side. The latter is considered by the surgeon as dangerously wounded.
>
> On being waked by the disturbance, I hastened to the scene and found the officer of the guard on the spot with his whole force. The surgeons were immediately called upon and administered relief to the wounded.
>
> B. F. Wheeler, a conscript, had been sent to camp by Lieutenant E. Holt, Randolph [county] stating he tried to pass off for less that forty-five years of age, but that being a notorious character, his word must not be relied upon. He refused also to report to [the] enrolling officer and advised his son twice to run from the militia officer. Being sent here under guard, he was placed in confinement.
>
> F. Pollard, also a conscript, was sent here by Lieutenant Prior, enrolling officer, Eighth Congressional District, and having deserted from here once before in 1862, was also confined to [the] guard-house.
>
> Very respectfully, your obedient servant,
> F. J. Hahr,
> Major, Commanding.[191]

While Colonel Mallett attempted to regain control of his bureau in the wake of changes mandated by the new conscription laws and the damage at Camp Vance, the men who had been transferred out of his battalion were getting used to campaigning with armies in the field. By mid-summer, a number of them had already been wounded in fighting in Virginia and Georgia. Some of those who had joined the navy were not much better off.

Burgess Gaither and the Summers brothers had occasion to reassess their decision that the Confederate navy was the "safest place" to be. On the first day of July, Mel Summers wrote to his father about life in the navy and commented on the news from Camp Vance:

> C.S.N. Ship Charleston
> Harbor S.C.
> July 1, 1864
>
> Dear Farther
> I take thee pleasure of writing you a few lines this

morning.... I havent mutch nuse to write.... we have just came in from drilling and I am very tired we was drilling on little Boats we was runing rases the Boat that I was in beat the Crowd I like drill very well [It is] very hard work [we w]as on picket last night I heard that the yankees had morganton it came in the papers yesterday I was mitty suprised to hear of it I think we might as well give it up I think the enemy is firmly on us.... they are firing on fort pinkney [now] but they don't seem to hurt it any they have damage fort Sumter very mutc it is in half mile of us we can see the flash of the cannons every tim they fire I tell you that it look bad to see them shells flying over our heads [192]

Four days later, Burgess Gaither wrote to Mollie:

James Island July the 5 1864

Dear sister I seat myself to drop you a few lines.... I am here on James Island I hav been here ever since the 1st I do not know how long we will stay here I have been under the fire of the yankee shells now for 4 days I hav not been in any fight yet but I can not tell how soon I might get in wone for the yankees is on thee same island I do not know how many there is some says 8 thousand but I do not now for I have not seen them yet I can see there gun boats theigh are in 2 miles of us.... I think that theigh will take this place if they try for we have not got mutch force up here.... We are camping in the breastworks.... Mollie the most of the yankee force is negroes it looks bad to hav to fight them but I am going to try to do my best on them if theigh come on me....

Wreceiven Ship Charleston S.C. [193]

Gaither's concern over the impending battle was well founded. It began on July 7 with a Confederate attack against Union positions on James Island. Sid Summers wrote home during the three day battle:

Battle field James Island
July the 8 1864

Dear farther
I seat myself this morning.... I and Mel is well and hearty we are in line of Battle yet we havent bin ingaged with Small

> armes yet But I think a few more hours will fetch the fight on the cannons is roing constance and the Shels is liting all around us we have to Save our selfs the Best we Can and that is Bad I am looking to go into a fight every minit and our fors is weak on Johns illand.... they had a fight yesterday they killed 100 and wounded together of our men Our pickets has a fight every day I will be on [picket] to night Times is getting worse sins I comens this letter I never new what hard times was tel now.... you aut to take the Charleston paper and then you could hear from us ofner that we can write we left our napsacks at the Ship and all of our things was in them we have got no paper with us write soon direct your letters to the Ship excuse bad writing and seling So far well Sid Summers [194]

The fighting ended the next day when Union forces were driven from their positions on James Island. They then withdrew from Johns Island and the Stono River area. Union soldiers killed, wounded, and missing during the affair totaled 330 while the Confederates lost 163. The opposing forces settled back into siege warfare. The Union fleet's shelling of Confederate troops in what was left of Fort Sumter resumed.[195]

On July 23, Burgess Gaither wrote to Mollie that he was "not very well at this time." He complained of headaches, weakness, and spoke of death:

> ... oh Mollie why should I be afrighten at death... if I be prepared for death and I hope, and pray that I am Mollie pray for me.... Mollie if I never see you again in this world I hope to met you all in heaven Yours true J B Gaither [196]

With the constant fighting in Virginia and Georgia during the summer of 1864, Southern newspapers were full of death notices. Friends that Burgess Gaither had made while he was in the Confederate service composed his obituary. It appeared in early August:

> Tribute of Respect
>
> *To the memory of J. B. Gaither, of Iredell county, N.C.*
>
> The subject of this memorial died in the hospital in the city of Charleston, S. C. on the 29th of July, 1864, at 11 o'clock, P.M. We having been associated for many months by the strongest ties of friendship, [this] is a task that makes the hand and heart tremble with sorrowful emotions; every word that we pen reminds us we are paying the last tribute

> of respect to the memory of one whose hand we shall never grasp again, whose voice we shall never hear, and whom we shall meet no more on earth. Such are our feelings as we record the death of our Friend.
>
> He was a good soldier. He was at his post at all times and always did his duty without a murmur and was beloved by all who knew him, especially by his comrades in the Army. He leaves a father and mother and two sisters and one brother to mourn his death. May the ashes of this noble young man repose in peace. His memory will long be cherished by his family and friends, and will ceased to be cherished only when one by one they pass away. [197]

While the stalemate continued at Charleston and western North Carolina recovered from the shock of Kirk's attack, Mallett's organization of the Junior Reserves progressed. Several companies had been organized at Camps Vance and Holmes by early August. The young soldiers, after being uniformed and schooled in drill maneuvers, elected their company officers. The company officers then elected majors to command the battalions. Once the battalions were turned over to General Holmes, Mallett's authority over them ended.

Mallett took advantage of the lull between the organization of the Junior Reserves and the arrival of the forty-five to fifty age group to close Camp Vance.[a] Union activity from Tennessee showed no signs of diminishing, and he no longer had six companies of veterans to rush to trouble spots. Captain McRae had been transferred. Major Hahr had been ordered to Wilmington with two companies of light duty soldiers (see Appendix B). Mallett could not hope to protect two widely separated camps with only two or three companies of guards.

Mallett decided to move his Camp Vance operations to Camp Stokes at Greensboro. Greensboro and Raleigh were connected by the railroad and close enough to each other to insure mutual support in an emergency.[b] Major McLean, who had managed to keep his conscript bureau assignment, established the new camp in October and took command of two small light duty companies that were ordered to assemble there. [198]

[a] *Asheville News*, Oct. 27, 1864. Camp Vance continued to operate as a militia and Home Guard center (Bradley, *North Militia and Home Guard Records*, v. 3, item 1254-580).

[b] The site of Camp Stokes is in Greensboro at the intersection of Green Valley Road and Westover Road near the railroad tracks. A North Carolina historic marker is on the site.

Mallett's bureau had been considerably reduced since the previous spring. A September 1864 report showed that in addition to the 5th Congressional District supporting force company, Mallett's battalion consisted of a sixty-five man guard at Camp Holmes and the two companies at Camp Stokes.[a]

Mallett's network of local enrolling offices throughout the state had not been changed by the February conscription law. Approximately ninety officers, their staffs, and thirty surgeons remained in their assignments (see Appendix A). All soldiers on furlough were still required to report to them on a regular schedule. The enrolling officers were still responsible for the apprehension of deserters and resisters in their counties.

The new law caused an increase in the number of men seeking to be detailed to civilian jobs rather than being sent to the army. The medical examining boards were nearly overwhelmed. Soon after the Junior Reserves were organized, men liable for duty in the Senior Reserves began reporting. Because of their age, hundreds of them sought medical deferments, and a large number was granted. Several thousand African-American men were also examined for service in the non-combat assignments that the February law had authorized. The Confederate adjutant and inspector general was still requiring medical boards to reexamine all furloughed wounded men on a regular schedule.

During the late summer and fall of 1864, the few remaining able-bodied officers still assigned to conscript service were transferred to the field. The Invalid Corps replaced them with permanently disabled officers. The organization of the Senior Reserves was largely complete by December. The few conscripts that were being gleaned from the population, along with the larger number of deserters and resisters, were kept at the camps only briefly until they could be escorted to Virginia or Georgia. Mallett's conscript camps now housed more prisoners than conscripts.

The mobilization of the reserves, light duty men, and African-American laborers was the last significant gathering of manpower that the Confederacy was able to complete. While the new law put thousands of additional names on rosters in North Carolina and other

[a] *O.R.*, Series IV, v. 3, p. 634. While Mallett exercised initial control over the new congressional district supporting forces, Conscript Office Circular No. 1, dated January 11, 1865, indicates that congressional district inspectors were later given command of these companies (*O.R. Supplement* - Part II, Record of Events - v. 49, p. 531-32).

Confederate states, the measure did little to alleviate the manpower crisis in the Army of Northern Virginia or the Army of Tennessee. The law stated that the reserves could only serve within their respective states, replacing able bodied eighteen- to forty-five-year-old soldiers so that they could be sent to the armies.[a] But the vast majority of able-bodied soldiers between eighteen and forty-five had already been sent to the front. The men that had been left behind in Mallett's battalion, McRae's battalion, and similar units in the other states were too few to have any real impact on the South's war effort when they were transferred. In the case of the free African-Americans and slaves approved for non-combat service in the army, thousands of African-Americans had served in this capacity since the beginning of the war. Many of the African-Americans enrolled under the new conscript law were detailed within their home states. Like the reserves, they were not concentrated in the South's major armies.

Thousands of civilian workers who had been more or less permanently detailed to essential wartime industrial production were the last large group of men to be organized into military units. In North Carolina, three regiments of such men were established in late fall. These regiments were only to be called upon in local emergencies and had no impact on the Confederacy's shortage of combat troops.

By the end of 1864, the South had exhausted its resource of physically fit white men who were willing to submit to military service without serious resistance.[b] In December, General Holmes implemented conscription bureau orders that mobilized the only untapped source of soldiers left in the state. Soldiers already disabled by wounds or illness, but not yet given full time assignments, were ordered to report for duty:

> HEADQUARTERS, RESERVE, NORTH CAROLINA,
> RALEIGH,
> December 13, 1864
> GENERAL ORDERS,
> NO. 20.
>
> In pursuance of Circular No. 33, Bureau of Conscription, current series, all light duty men not assigned in a staff

[a] Several North Carolina Reserve units saw limited service in Virginia, South Carolina, and Georgia (Clark's *Histories*, v. 4, p. 2).

[b] Even as early as November 1863, the adjutant general of North Carolina lamented that there were not enough men left in one particular militia district to hold an election (Bradley, *North Carolina Confederate Militia and Home Guard Records*, v. 1, item 1317-509).

> department, all men of the Invalid Corps fit for guard duty and all soldiers temporarily disabled for field service, in the State of North Carolina, (except of Franz J. Hahr's Battalion, and those at the posts of Charlotte, Salisbury, Greensboro, and Raleigh, in regard to whom specific instructions have been given) will report in person at one of the camps of instruction, for examination by select medical examining boards. Those found unable for field service, but fit for guard duty, will, under directions of the commandant of camp, be organized into companies of not less than sixty men, "for continuous local service," or will be assigned to companies already organized. They will be mustered in for the war, and duplicate muster rolls forwarded to this office to be transmitted to the Secretary of War, for the assignment of proper officers.
>
> By command of,
> Lieutenant-General Holmes
> John W. Hinsdale,
> Assistant Adjutant-General.[199]

Similar orders were issued in other states. With the Confederacy's white male population depleted by the Bureau of Conscription as it functioned under Preston, another approach to gathering recruits was revisited.

In summer and early fall 1864, Braxton Bragg intensified his campaign to reorganize the conscription process for the entire nation. Though removed as a field commander early in the year, Jefferson Davis brought him back to Richmond as a military advisor. Immediately, Bragg began working to reintroduce methods that he and Generals Johnston and Pillow had used in parts of the central Confederacy during 1863.

Bragg's approach to conscription law enforcement was to deny jurisdiction to all authority except the military: civil rights did not apply. Even though these methods supplied thousands of soldiers to the army, the legal and bureaucratic controversies that were generated eventually resulted in Richmond authorities forcing General Pillow to dismantle his operation. Still, a number of generals and several governors felt that Pillow's methods were effective. General Bragg blamed his own defeat in Tennessee on manpower problems that Richmond had prevented Pillow from solving.

Bragg embarked on a campaign to discredit the conscription bureau to such an extent that Davis would allow him to reshape the entire process. During the spring of 1864, he ordered inspections to be made of conscription bureaus in several Deep South states. These inspections were neither authorized by nor coordinated with Superintendent Preston. The resulting reports said just what Bragg wanted them to say: Conscription in Georgia, Mississippi, and Alabama was "in a startling state of affairs.... " and the conscription bureau needed "a complete renovation.... "[200] Bragg also circulated a memo that was highly critical of Preston's office staff and his administration of the bureau.[201]

Bragg's tactics angered Preston, who responded with a salvo of countermemos during the next two months.[a] He pointed out that the conscription bureau was ultimately responsible for mobilizing the military, industrial, and agricultural resources of the entire Confederacy. He argued that the civil rights reviews, as applied by the courts and his bureau, were necessary and worthy components of the process and should continue. Preston believed that in the states where conscription had been properly administered and enforced, the system was an efficient supplier of soldiers for the armies and workers for production.[b] He also charged that Bragg's reports were "defective" and that the inspections had been conducted by Bragg's operatives acting "rather as detectives than military inspectors." Using statistics from Gideon Pillow's conscription programs of 1863, Preston estimated that implementing Bragg's methods throughout the Confederacy would require six thousand officers and thirty-six thousand enlisted men "to do the work of conscription."[202]

In writing to a South Carolina congressman on the debate, Preston grappled with the issues of a republic trying to maintain its integrity while waging total war:

> But war is not confined to merely the military business to organize, discipline, and movement. War embraces the legislative action and civil process necessary to the creation of armies; it embraces the Treasury, the Department of Justice, the civil and social institutions, the industries and productions, the support and protection

[a] At one point during the controversy, Preston submitted his resignation (*O.R.*, Series IV, v. 3, p. 641). President Davis did not accept it.

[b] In an April 30, 1864 memo to Secretary of War Seddon, Preston said that conscription had been "eminently successful" in Virginia, North Carolina, and South Carolina. "All the complaints of the evils and failures of conscription," he said, came from Georgia, Alabama, Mississippi, and Florida (*O.R.*, Series IV, v. 3, p. 357).

> of the people. The military condition is a necessary, but merely incidental and partial, element of a state of war, and to be controlled always by the capacity of the country to maintain it.... Undertake to make or maintain armies by the means of the armies themselves and you establish military despotism.... No wise government has ever permitted the experiment.

In the same letter, Preston stated the basic question that distinguished him from Bragg:

> The true issue is, whether the law of Congress is that conscription is to be determined by pure military authority and administered by military force, and on the principles of mere military regulation, or whether it is a law covering and protecting civil and personal rights, and at the same time providing that the wants of the Government are to be supplied by a process which, after adjudication, may be enforced by military power. [203]

Preston was not blind to problems that existed in the system he defended. He recognized that conscription needed change, but remained steadfast in his belief that civilian control should temper military necessity.[a]

In a Confederacy that was winning the war, where supposedly sovereign states had not already given up most of their power to the central government, and where the conscription system controlled by civilian authority was supplying enough troops to win, Preston's philosophy might have had a chance. But such was not the Confederacy of late 1864. By then, the South had been losing the war in the central Confederacy and Trans-Mississippi for three years. General John Bell Hood was bleeding the Army of Tennessee to death in Georgia and Tennessee. Sherman had occupied Atlanta in September, then burned a sixty-mile wide path through Georgia to Savannah, arriving there in time for Christmas. The eastern Confederacy had been effectively reduced to South Carolina, North Carolina, and Virginia. Lee's army was practically under siege by Grant at Petersburg. Confederates

[a] Preston wanted President Davis to take a firm hand by promoting a simplified system of deferments and exemptions that did not remove entire categories of individuals from military service. A functional Confederate supreme court could have helped settle the controversy. The absence of such a court (not a surprising circumstance given the Confederacy's foundation in state's rights) made a final and binding decision of the Preston versus Bragg conflict impossible.

were heavily outnumbered by Union forces on all fronts and that disparity was growing each day. Confederate authorities estimated that one hundred thousand Southern men had deserted from the army, with many thousands more refusing to report for duty. Thousands of additional men were fraudulently manipulating the detail and exemption system and clogging the courts and conscription bureau with endless appeals. The South desperately needed those men. Braxton Bragg intended to put them in the army.

Bragg worked behind the scenes to gather support for his ideas. He used his friendship with President Davis, congressional contacts, self-serving inspection reports, and Preston's own admission that *something* needed to be done. Adjutant and Inspector General Cooper favored many of Bragg's proposals, as did Major General James L. Kemper who commanded the Virginia conscription bureau and reserves.

Even as memos flew back and forth in Richmond, Bragg's plan was succeeding. General Order No. 73 abolished the position of congressional district enrolling officer and, more importantly, put the reserve generals in charge of "conscription and enrollment in their respective States...."[204] This move was Bragg's use of the incremental approach to get his way. Abolishing the position of congressional district enrolling officer did not release any officers for field service (they were all disabled), nor was that the intention. General Bragg wanted to remove that entire level of the conscription bureau's hierarchy from the decision making and appeals process.[a]

Putting the reserve generals in charge of conscription and enrollment was designed to open the door for Bragg's ultimate goal of having large forces available in each state to hunt deserters and resisters. Conscription and enrollment activities had dwindled to the smallest part of the conscription bureau's activities. The major part of the work had become deserter and resister apprehension. Bragg was preparing to utilize thousands of Senior Reserves to enforce *all* conscription-related laws.[b]

---

[a] The same order allowed reserve generals to appoint an "inspector of conscription" for each congressional district. This provision utilized the former congressional district captains as quality control personnel while keeping them out of the decision-making process.

[b] North Carolina Home Guard and militia officers were still rounding up a respectable number of deserters. Between August 24 and November 19, four hundred and twenty-one "deserters and recusant Conscripts" were arrested by state officers and eight hundred and sixty-eight more surrendered under a clemency proclamation issued by Governor Vance *(O.R. Supplement*, pt. 3, v. 3, p. 703).

Most of all, Bragg wanted to end civilian judges' interference with conscription and to further reduce the number of conscription bureau appeals that stood between an individual's enrollment and his assignment to the army. Bragg argued that these two factors constituted the greatest obstacle to an efficient conscription system. He might have used an entirely routine incident involving Major McLean and his staff at Camp Stokes to prove his point.

Major McLean had assembled his staff, completed the organization of his two camp guard companies of light duty men, and by November, had the Greensboro camp of instruction up and running. Among the officers on McLean's staff were Captain Charles N. Allen, who had filed the initial report on the destruction of Camp Vance, and another disabled officer, Captain John J. Drake.

A tedious and all too common episode (as far as Braxton Bragg was concerned) involving McLean, Allen, Drake, and local court officials reveals the legal and bureaucratic entanglements that plagued the conscription system. At issue was the case of James T. Carson, a conscript who claimed to be a citizen of Maryland. Carson contended that he was not liable for conscription because Maryland was not in the Confederacy.[a] Major McLean apparently considered Carson to be an escape risk.

From his cell in the guardhouse at Camp Stokes, Mr. Carson retained the services of Scott and Scott, Attorneys at Law. Messrs. Scott filed the inevitable petition for a writ of Habeas Corpus on November 5, 1864:

> State of North Carolina
>
> To the Honorable R. S. French, one of the judges of its Superior Court of Law and Equity for the state aforesaid: James T. Carson, by his petition respectfully shows to Your Honor, that he is a citizen of the state of Maryland and consequently, under the laws of the Confederate States of America, he is not liable to be conscripted and cannot be compelled to do service in the Armies of the Confederacy; that he hath both been improperly and illegally enrolled by the County Enrolling Officer for Guilford and is now wrongfully and illegally imprisoned and restrained of his

[a] Scores of men from several states, when about to be conscripted, suddenly decided that they were citizens of Maryland. This particular draft dodge was so common that the Bureau of Conscription issued Circular No. 19 in April 1864 to advise commandants of the ploy (*O.R.*, Series IV, v. 3, p. 311).

personal liberty by Capt. C. N. Allen, Commandant of Conscripts at Camp Stokes:
Your petitioner, therefore, most respectfully prays your Honor to grant unto him a writ of Habeas Corpus to be directed to the said Capt. C. N. Allen, Commandant as aforesaid, commanding him to have the body of your petitioner together with the cause of his arrest and detention before your Honor, to this end and that the matters may be gone into and relief granted to your petitioner and as in duty bound he will ever forego.

Scott and Scott
Attorneys

The petitioner reattests oaths that the facts set forth in his petition are true and correct.

James T. Carson
Sworn to and subscribed
Before me this 5th day
Of Nov. 1864. Witness
My hand & official seal
Lyndon Swain, Clerk
Of Guilford County Court

Judge French granted the petition and issued a writ of Habeas Corpus the next day:

State of North Carolina

To Captain C. N. Allen
Comdt. Conscripts, Camp Stokes, No. Ca.

We command you that the body of James T. Carson in your custody detained as alleged, together with the day and cause of his capture and detention, you have before me, R. S. French, one of the judges of the Superior Court of Law and Equity in and for the state aforesaid at the residence of Thomas Settle, Esquire, of Rockingham County, on Friday next, the 11th day of the present month, then and there to do and receive what shall be considered in his behalf.

Witness R. S. French, Judge of the
Superior Court of Law & Equity

In and for the State aforesaid
November 6th, 1864
R. S. French
Judge

On November 8, Captain Allen sent his acknowledgment of the writ to Judge French and took the opportunity to notify the court of his position on the matter:

> Camp Stokes, N.C.
> Nov 8th 1864
> Hon. R. S. French
> Judge Superior Court, N.C.
>
> I hereby acknowledge the service of a writ of Habeas Corpus in the case of J. T. Carson and in obedience to its suit will have the body of said J. T. Carson before your Honor together with the cause of his arrest and detention in camp on Friday the 11th inst. I beg leave to reply that said J. T. Carson was ordered to camp and detained on the grounds that he owes service to the Confederate Govt. by virtue of the conscript act, he being a citizen of the Confederate States between the ages of eighteen (18) and forty-five (45) years.
>
> C. N. Allen
> Capt. & Act. Comdt.

Rather than have all of the parties appear at a hearing in Rockingham County, Judge French allowed each side to give sworn testimony and submit affidavits for his consideration. The affidavits were taken and forwarded to the judge, who rendered his decision on November 11:

> This matter is heard upon the petition, return and affidavit pled and upon consideration it is ordered and adjudged that the petitioner be remanded to the custody of Captain C. N. Allen. The costs of this proceeding to be taxed to the Clerk of the Superior Court of Guilford to be paid by the petitioner.
>
> R. S. French
> Rockingham County Judge S C L & E
> November 11, 1864

Thus, the local court case should have ended. Mr. Carson had been ordered by Judge French to become Private Carson. However, the next day, attorney William L. Scott filed a complaint with Major McLean in regard to the manner in which Captain Allen had taken the sworn testimony that was submitted to the court. He requested that Carson be kept at Camp Stokes until the matter was resolved:

> Greensboro, Nov 12th, 1864
> Maj. McLean
> My Dear Sir:
>
> In the case of Carson, a Marylander, we obtained a writ of Habeas Corpus from Judge French. As soon as it was served on Capt. Allen, he came in to see us and we agreed to take affidavits in the case together. Capt. Allen, remarked in the presence of Sheriff Bower that he desired to take the testimony of Col. John Sloan and of Sheriff Bower. I remarked to him that we desired to take the testimony of Col. Sloan ourselves. He then sent Mr. Drake over and the testimony was taken in our room, Levin doing the writing, and we cross-examining.
>
> The petitioner considered the affidavits as much his as that of the prosecution. Of course we did not, nor was it necessary, to take another affidavit setting forth identically the same thing. This would have been, to say the least, a work of superior agitation. We expected to be dealt with fairly in the matter, but our client tells us that the affidavits of Col. Sloan and Sheriff Bower were not sent up. We were astounded to learn that we had been so treated. Whoever left them out certainly acted wrong. We desire that you hold Carson until this thing can be investigated before Judge French and justice be done the petitioner. Sheriff Bower will tell you that Capt. Allen agreed that the testimony should be taken together. We are not prepared to receive such treatment at the hand of Capt. Allen. We feel assured that when you know the true state of the case that you will not permit Carson to be sent off.
>
> Very Truly & Sincerely,
> Will. L. Scott

That same day, a clerk at Camp Stokes received Mr. Scott's complaint, added a synopsis of the incident, and passed the documents on to Major McLean. McLean immediately sent them on to Captain Allen for an explanation:

Camp Stokes, N.C.
Nov. 12th, 1864

Respy. Referred to Capt. C. N. Allen for his remarks. The Messrs. Scott complain that they have not been fairly dealt with in this, that it was the understanding between yourself and them that the affidavits were to be taken together and sent up but that two of them were suppressed without their knowledge or consent. It is also proper to say that Capt. Drake's recollection accords with the statement of the Atty.

J. R. McLean, Maj

McLean had already asked Captain Drake about the incident and was tactfully advising Captain Allen that Drake would not lie about the incident even if Allen chose to do so.

Carson's simple draft dodging case had involved local attorneys, the sheriff, retired Colonel Sloan of the 27th North Carolina Troops, the clerk of court, and a superior court judge. Now, Major McLean and his staff were embroiled in an internal investigation to answer the lawyers' allegation of misconduct on the part of the one-armed Captain Allen.

Captain Allen finally admitted to withholding statements from the court, but he arrogantly implied that Captain Drake had agreed to the joint taking of affidavits without permission:

Camp Stokes
Nov 12th 1864

I did not send Capt. Drake, my deputy, to take evidence for the Messrs. Scotts, but for the Govt, hence I felt that I have a perfect right to suppress any evidence that I had taken if it did not suit me.

C. N. Allen
Capt.

Now, the much vexed Major McLean needed to have Captain Drake record his recollection of the incident on the thoroughly handled documents:

> Camp Stokes
> Nov 14th /64
>
> Respty. referred to Capt Drake, who will please say wether it was the agreement, according to his understanding of it that the affidavits of Messrs. Sloan and Bower should go up to the judge.
>
> J. R. McLean
> Maj. Comdg.

Captain Drake settled the internal investigation of Carson's case by confirming the lawyer's allegations against Captain Allen:

> Camp Stokes
> Nov 14th, 1864
>
> Respty retturned to Maj McLean, Comdg Camp Stokes. I was under the impression that the affidavits were taken to be sent up.
>
> J. J. Drake
> Capt. [205]

This kind of endless legal and bureaucratic wrangling was occurring throughout the Confederacy. It was delaying the military service of thousands of potential soldiers and was just what Braxton Bragg intended to stop.[a] While Superintendent Preston argued that the protection of civil rights was an appropriate part of conscription, General Braxton Bragg was developing a way to systematically deny such protection.

The internal conflict over conscription escalated through the fall of 1864 and intensified the crisis atmosphere that already existed within the Confederate government.[b] Unfortunately for Colonel Mallett, a series of clerical errors made by his office staff surfaced during the same period. The episode damaged Mallett's reputation as an efficient administrator and reinforced Richmond's perception that

[a] Presumably, Carson appealed to higher courts. There is no record of his ever having served in the Confederate army.

[b] The conscription controversy became so bitter that on one occasion, Adjutant and Inspector General Cooper endorsed a memo containing an exchange between Preston and Major General J. L. Kemper, general of the Virginia Reserves (and Bragg supporter), by saying, "I scarcely know what remarks to make on the subject of this unpleasant controversy...." (*O.R.*, Series IV, v. 3, p. 856).

Governor Vance was withholding manpower from the Confederate army.

Governor Vance's refusal to allow the conscription of his militia and Home Guard officers was well known in Richmond. He had received substantial criticism even though his use of those same officers had made North Carolina a leading provider of troops to the Confederacy. Mallett's routine monthly reports to the war department showed that Governor Vance was indeed withholding approximately fifty-five hundred militia and Home Guard officers from the Confederate military. Unfortunately, during September, October, and November 1864, Mallett's office staff erroneously compounded the monthly totals and reported 14,675 exempted state officers in North Carolina, approximately three times the actual number and more than ten times that of any other state.[a] The same miscalculation occurred in the reporting of men exempted from military service by reason of physical disability, resulting in 35,032 such exemptions being reported as opposed to the actual figure of approximately "10,000 or 11,000." [206]

Before Mallett discovered the error and could send an amended report to Richmond, Superintendent Preston submitted the figures to the secretary of war, who in turn sent them on to President Davis, who promptly rejected them.[207] Mallett corrected and explained the error as best he could, but the damage was done. The superintendent and secretary of war were greatly embarrassed by the episode, which could not have occurred at a worse time. Bragg found the incident useful in his crusade against Preston and the conscription bureau. Mallett, who had enjoyed an excellent reputation up to this point, received a particularly harsh reprimand from Preston.[208] War Department Circular No. 34 was generated by the incident, and on November 29, Preston wrote that he had ordered a special investigation concerning the faulty reports.[b] He also threatened to have Mallett removed "from the conscription service." [209]

[a] Particularly in Georgia and North Carolina it is likely that some exemptions other than those for the militia were included is this report (*O.R.*, Series IV, v. 3, p. 850-51). Georgia's statistics fluctuated wildly from 1,012 exempt state officers in November 1864 to 8,229 in February 1865 (*O.R.*, Series IV, v. 3, p. 1102). A November 19, 1864, report from North Carolina's Adjutant General Richard C. Gatlin lists "2,650 militia officers, and 1,312 Home Guard officers" (*O.R. Supplement*, v. 3, ser. 95, p. 704).

[b] This report was filed on December 27 and shows 5,153 "State officers" and 7,885 "Physical Disability" exemptions (McKinney, *The Papers of Zebulon Vance*, microfilm). Further confusing these statistics was the Union army's occupation of several North Carolina counties. Additionally, a number of state officers held commissions in both the militia and the Home Guard.

Chapter Eight

Braxton Bragg's Way

January - May 1865

General Bragg continued his reformation of the Bureau of Conscription into the new year. More evidence of his success came from the adjutant and inspector general's office in February:

> ADJT. AND INSP. GENERAL'S OFFICE
> GENERAL ORDERS
> No. 8
>
> I. Generals of the reserves will immediately place upon active duty every man belonging to that class who is not specifically detailed, or who has not been turned over to generals commanding armies, departments or districts. They will organize them into convenient bodies, and will employ them vigorously in arresting and returning to the army all deserters and absentees.
>
> II. This service will, for the present, constitute the primary duty of officers of the reserve forces, and they will enter actively upon it.

While the order went on to allow generals to retain the reserves that were "indispensably necessary in the field," General Holmes and reserve generals in the other states were now responsible for enforcing the conscript laws pertaining to soldiers illegally absent from the army.[210] The order greatly increased the number of soldiers assigned primarily to conscription-related duties. The first part of Bragg's plan was accomplished. The enforcement arm of conscription in what was left of the Confederacy now closely resembled Gideon Pillow's system as it had operated in 1863. Bragg's next goal was the elimination of the conscription bureau itself.

Preston never acted on his threat to transfer Colonel Mallett. Still, Mallett watched for months as his bureau grew smaller and lost influence. He knew that Bragg's behind-the-scenes maneuvering was intended to remove most of the bureaucratic levels between county conscript officers and the secretary of war. Mallett also knew that *his* job was one of those bureaucratic levels. Newspaper reports and rumors circulating during the first week of March indicated that he and the other state commandants of conscription might soon be put out of their assignments.[211] When another general order was issued toward the end of the month, it contained the most sweeping changes of all.

General Order No. 17 abolished the Bureau of Conscription and the camps of instruction and restructured the medical evaluation process for conscripts. Reserve generals were given complete responsibility for all conscription enforcement within their respective states. They were to report to the secretary of war through an "Officer of Conscription" in Richmond, who was attached to Adjutant and Inspector General Cooper's office. State commandants and county enrolling officers were ordered to report to their reserve generals for assignment.[212]

The new procedure required enrollees to be examined by army medical boards *after* their assignment to the field. Only those too sick or feeble to report for duty, as certified by a "respectable physician or... army surgeon," could be temporarily excused from the process. These cases would be reviewed by congressional district medical boards that were to consist of one civilian surgeon and two army surgeons. The district medical boards would review all medical furloughs every month. Non-medical appeals were to be decided by reserve generals. Their decisions could only be appealed to the secretary of war. Conscripts who were waiting for the secretary's decision were to serve with their units in the field and perform their duties. During this time, they were subject to military law. Bragg's transformation of Confederate conscription was complete.

Bragg's system was designed to keep Southern men beyond the reach of state courts, sympathetic civilian doctors, and accommodating conscription officers. State commandants like Mallett were reduced to serving as focal points for the reams of paperwork generated by local enrolling officers and their advisory boards. They had no real decision-making authority except on purely administrative matters. As bad as it was, Mallett was pleased that he would not be transferred away from his family and that he would continue working for General Holmes.[a]

[a] General Holmes had spent more than a year and a half in the western Confederacy as a department and district commander. He knew firsthand the problems of conscription enforcement. As early as December 1862, he had complained to President Davis about "the growing disaffection to the war among the people" and recommended marshal law as a remedy (Arkansas Historical Quarterly, v. 52, p. 225).

Under the reorganization, Camps Holmes and Stokes were little more than storage depots and jails. Camp commanders issued equipment to conscripts as they passed through the camps and acted as wardens for those who had to stay. The county enrolling officer continued to be the Confederate government's most visible local representative.[a] He was still responsible for monitoring furloughed soldiers, draft-exempt men, and detailed civilian workers. He was also the local regulator for the increasing involvement of African-Americans in the Confederate war effort.

The Confederacy would not last long enough to perfect Bragg's overhaul of its compulsory military service system. By early 1865, defeat was inevitable. Ulysses S. Grant intensified operations around Petersburg after months of siege warfare. Petersburg was an important transportation and distribution center twenty-five miles south of Richmond where several railroad lines and plank roadways converged. Most of the troops and war material from North Carolina that sustained Lee's army in the defense of the Confederate capitol passed through Petersburg. Richmond could not be defended if Petersburg fell.

General George Meade's Army of the Potomac was following Ulysses S. Grant's orders to pursue Lee wherever he went. Grant's primary objective was the destruction of Lee's army, and he knew that Lee had to save Petersburg. Lee warned Richmond that either his army would have to be substantially strengthened or he would eventually be forced to abandon Petersburg to avoid being surrounded. The loss of Petersburg and Richmond was generally recognized as the end of hope for Confederate independence.

Fort Fisher, guardian of the Confederacy's last major port of Wilmington, was captured on January 15 after an unprecedented naval bombardment and land battle. On February 22, Union forces occupied Wilmington as the Confederates withdrew. Major Hahr's light duty battalion was assigned to Colonel George Jackson's brigade at Wilmington during this period.[213] Meanwhile, on February 17, Confederates evacuated Charleston, South Carolina. Sherman's army entered Columbia that same day. Retreating Confederates burned military property and cotton to keep it from falling into Union hands. Other fires were set by Sherman's men as they destroyed railroad facilities, government buildings, warehouses, and private property.

---

[a] Some militia and Home Guard officers remained in their positions as local enrolling officers until the end of the war.

High winds pushed flames through the city. The fires and destruction lasted through February 19, when the Union army began heading toward North Carolina.

In late February, with Sherman moving out of Columbia, prisoner exchange officers were looking for a safe place to parole hundreds of Union soldiers who had been held in South Carolina. The Northerners were transported to Charlotte and then to Wilmington. Wilmington was being shelled when they arrived and the parole could not be completed. The prisoners were transported to Raleigh, where they spent several days at Camp Holmes, which one Union prisoner described as an "old conscript camp."[214]

On February 22, General Joseph Johnston was again assigned to command the Army of Tennessee. He spent the end of February and the beginning of March sending troops to reinforce Braxton Bragg, who had been sent by President Davis to North Carolina. When Johnston arrived, he took command of all Confederate forces in the state. General Holmes and Colonel Mallett were rounding up any troops they could find and sending them to Bragg. Communications were beginning to fail, but Mallett was able to contact some enrolling officers by telegraph and couriers during the second week of March. He ordered them to gather any exchanged soldiers who had not yet reported to their commands and send them to the army. Bragg and Johnston needed enough troops to give Sherman a decent fight when he arrived. They wanted to buy enough time to link up with Lee's army. The Confederacy's last hope was for a combined army led by Lee to defeat the Union armies as they converged.[a]

Part of Bragg's force, under the command of General Robert F. Hoke, fought a three-day battle at Wise's Forks near Kinston in early March. They attacked General Schofield's army as it advanced from New Bern. The Confederate offensive ran out of momentum and Hoke withdrew toward Goldsboro. On March 15, after consolidating the wide-ranging elements of his army around Fayetteville, Sherman headed toward Goldsboro. The next day, he attacked a force under General William Hardee near Averasboro. Hardee withdrew his

---

[a] During the last weeks of the war, General Johnston clung to the idea of uniting all Confederate forces somewhere in North Carolina in order to defeat Grant's forces and Sherman's army before they could combine. General Lee had been ambivalent about the plan, wanting instead to stay closer to Petersburg and Richmond, although a consolidation of Confederate forces would have been likely had Lee managed to escape and move south. Johnston operated on the assumption that the forces would eventually unite (Thomas, *The Confederate Nation: 1861 - 1865*, p. 282-83, 300).

outnumbered Confederates that night after the fighting stopped. As the Confederates worked to muster all the strength they could, Sherman was trying to coordinate his movements with those of General Schofield, who was now approaching from Kinston, and General Terry, who was coming inland from Wilmington. There were now approximately one hundred thousand Union soldiers in North Carolina.

On March 19 near Bentonville, Johnston attacked two corps of the Union army under the command of General Slocum. The opposing forces were evenly matched on the first day with about sixteen thousand men each. Repeated attacks failed to break the Union line. Johnston repositioned his army, but by the afternoon of March 20, he realized that his line of retreat was threatened by a Union flanking movement and that Sherman's army was approaching. On March 21, the Confederates fought to hold their position during the day, but withdrew that night. Major Hahr had been previously transferred and was serving with General Kirkland's brigade at Bentonville. Several North Carolina Reserve regiments took part in the fighting as well. Confederate losses at Bentonville totaled approximately twenty-six hundred. Peter Mallett's younger brother, Lieutenant Colonel Edward Mallett of the 61st North Carolina Troops, was among those killed. The two Camp Holmes guard companies had been sent to the area but stayed at Smithfield guarding the railroad.

While Bragg and Johnston tried to stall the separate armies of Sherman, Schofield, and Terry, General George Stoneman and four thousand Union cavalrymen began a sweeping, month-long raid through the western part of the state. They struck at Wilkesboro and moved on to Boone on March 28.

Lee's forces at Petersburg tried to break Grant's stranglehold on March 25. The Fort Stedman attack was a failure and resulted in the loss of approximately four thousand Confederates, most taken prisoner. The South's top field commander was out of options. He gave orders to begin the retreat from Petersburg and Richmond. On April 1, Lee's army lost another five thousand men at the battle of Five Forks. The participation of fifteen thousand African-American Union soldiers in the year-long siege of Petersburg helped resolve a controversy that had reemerged in the Confederate government. [215]

Even as the Confederacy was collapsing, congress tried to squeeze its last resource out of the civilian population and into combat. Thousands of slaves and free African-Americans had served the Confederacy in a variety of roles during the war, willingly and unwillingly. Still, the South had not authorized the use of slaves as combatants. In 1863, when the South's manpower shortage first became a serious threat, discussions surfaced on the use of slaves as soldiers. In January 1864, General Patrick Cleburne, an Army of Tennessee division commander, unveiled his recommendation to train and arm African-American men. He offered to personally command such a division. The suggestion stirred a great deal of debate in senior military and political circles. Cleburne's proposal was so controversial that President Davis had it suppressed.[216]

In late 1864, the idea surfaced again, this time with some political support. The governors of Mississippi, Georgia, South Carolina, and North Carolina endorsed changing military policies concerning slaves. Henry Allen, governor of Louisiana, supported the conscription of slaves as combatants and advocated rewarding them with freedom. By this time, President Davis was convinced that the Confederacy was running out of options. On November 7, he told congress, "should the alternative ever be presented of subordination or of the employment of the slaves as soldiers, there seems to be no reason to doubt what should be our decision." [217]

In January 1865, the most respected man in the Confederacy went on record in support of enrolling the qualified male slave population as soldiers. Robert E. Lee knew that African-American soldiers were rendering dependable service in the Union army. Lee's corps commanders had already assured him that there would be no serious resistance from their soldiers if African-American's entered the army in large numbers. In February, Lee wrote, "In my opinion, the negroes... will make efficient soldiers.... I think those who are employed should be freed." General Lee did not stop with the idea of rewarding only those slaves who entered the army. In correspondence with Virginia legislator, Andrew Hunter, Lee advocated the gradual emancipation of all slaves as part of any plan to employ African-American men as soldiers.[218]

Given the Confederacy's desperate situation and Lee's support, the issue was settled. On March 9, 1865, the Confederate Congress approved the use of slaves as soldiers. Signed by President Davis four days later, the law required that these new "troops shall receive the same rations, clothing, and compensation as are allowed to other troops in the same branch of the service." The law, as passed by congress, left the reward of emancipation for faithful service to the individual state legislatures.[219] However, the adjutant and inspector general's orders that implemented the law stated that "No slave will be accepted as a recruit unless with his own consent and with the approbation of his master by a written instrument conferring, as far as he may, the rights of a freedman...."[220] Instead of being conscripted, African-American men were to be volunteers.

Driven to this defining moment, the Confederate Congress again rose to meet the crisis just as it had in April 1862 with the passage of the first conscription law. Congress, President Davis, and the nation's top military commanders chose to abandon the South's fundamental socioeconomic feature, slavery, in a last chance bid for independence.[a] Letters began "pouring into the [war] department from men of military skill and character, asking authority to raise companies, battalions, and regiments of negro troops."[221] Colonel Mallett was one of the early applicants.[b] Requests for African-American soldiers to fill the ranks of Lee's decimated regiments began to arrive at his headquarters within forty-eight hours of the law's passage. During the last days of March, African-American Confederate soldiers were seen marching in the streets of Richmond.[222]

It was too little, too late. On April 2, the Confederate army evacuated Richmond. Part of Lee's army was caught and badly mauled by pursuing Union troops at Sayler's Creek on April 6. Almost eight thousand Confederates surrendered as the battle ended. Lee's army began to disintegrate. Each day, scores of his men gave up and surrendered to Union pickets and skirmishers. Any hope of linking up with General Johnston's forces in North Carolina ended when Lee found that he was surrounded and out of food near Appomattox Courthouse. He surrendered what was left of his army, less than thirty thousand men, on April 9. The next several days were occupied with issuing paroles to the Confederates so they could travel home when their regiments were dismissed for the last time. The Union army's commissary department issued thousands of rations to the once proud Army of Northern Virginia to keep Lee's men from starving. Ironically, most of the rations had been recently seized from a captured Confederate supply train.

---

[a] John B. Jones, a clerk in the office of the secretary of war, exclaimed in his diary, "There is a strong indication that Gen. Lee is an emancipationist. From all the signs slavery is doomed!" (Miers, *A Rebel War Clerk's Diary,* p. 501).

[b] Colonel Mallett was aware that the use of African-Americans as combat troops was imminent. On March 8, he submitted a request to the secretary of war for authority "to raise a negro brigade." His request was obviously coordinated with a recommendation by North Carolina Confederate congressman, W. N. H. Smith, for Mallett's promotion to brigadier general (National Archives, Record Group 109, Chapter 1, v. 158, p. 381, entry 56 and Chapter 1, v. 151, p. 8, entry 53).

With Lee's surrender and Johnston in retreat, North Carolinians could see that the war would end in their state. The Confederacy had been shipping war material to Salisbury for weeks. Tons of supplies had been removed from Columbia and Richmond as Union forces advanced on both fronts. The Salisbury Union prisoner of war camp, evacuated weeks earlier, was now an immense storage depot. Local warehouses were also stacked high with military stores. The Confederacy was building this huge stockpile to supply the combined armies of Lee and Johnston that had been expected to consolidate in North Carolina.[223]

General Stoneman's cavalry arrived near Salisbury on the morning of April 12 and clashed with approximately thirty-seven hundred Confederates commanded by General William Gardner. Gardner's force included armed citizens, Home Guards, the Lenoir reserves, four hundred detailed factory workers, three hundred former Union prisoners who had joined the Confederate army, some Virginia soldiers who were passing through town, and fourteen pieces of artillery. The Confederates fought a delaying action, trying to buy time so that several heavily laden freight trains could leave before Stoneman arrived. General Gardner's men retreated toward town, where the hard fighting ended with the surrender of most of the Confederate troops and all of their artillery.[224]

There was some house-to-house skirmishing while part of the Union force, with the captured artillery, headed for the bridge across the Yadkin River several miles away. Stoneman wanted to destroy the bridge that Kirk's raiders had failed to reach the previous June. From earthworks on the far side of the river, twelve hundred Confederates commanded by Colonel Zebulon York kept up a spirited fight until nightfall when the Union force withdrew, leaving the bridge intact.[225]

Stoneman allowed the townspeople to take what they wanted from the commissary stores and non-military stockpile. Everything else was burned. An immense amount of government property went up in flames, including $100,000 worth of medical supplies, ten thousand stands-of-arms, six thousand pounds of gunpowder, tons of artillery ammunition, one million rounds of small arms ammunition, seventy-five thousand uniforms, two-hundred fifty thousand blankets, and twenty thousand pounds of leather. Commissary stores that were destroyed included one hundred thousand pounds of salt, fifty thousand bushels of wheat, twenty-seven thousand pounds of rice, twenty thousand pounds of sugar, and ten thousand bushels of corn. The prison buildings were burned as were the Carolina and

Western Railroad offices, two freight depots, a large machine shop, and railroad car sheds. That night, flames and explosions were visible for miles around the town.[226]

The quick capture of Salisbury by Union troops and Stoneman's orders forbidding destruction of private property prevented the chaos that swept Greensboro during the last weeks of the war. The permanent residents of Greensboro who were still in the area surely thought that their world was coming to an end. Normally a town of under two thousand inhabitants, the population of Greensboro and surrounding area had grown to more than ninety thousand by the end of April. Eastern North Carolinians had been arriving since early in the war, as had people from the mountains. As the Confederacy collapsed around central North Carolina, thousands of frightened, hungry refugees crowded into the town. When the residents of Mecklenburg County heard that Stoneman's cavalry might attack, many of them headed toward Greensboro as well. Hundreds of wounded soldiers from the battles of Wise's Forks, Averasboro, and Bentonville arrived along with hundreds more from Virginia. On March 25, Mallett closed his Raleigh offices and moved to Greensboro. His enrolling officers were advised to mail all reports and correspondence to Camp Stokes "until further orders." [227]

By April 17, on the heels of Lee's surrender, word of President Lincoln's assassination was spreading. Deserters and, later, parolees from Lee's army descended on the town. As rumors circulated that Generals Johnston and Sherman were negotiating a surrender, several thousand of Johnston's soldiers crowded into town looking for food while they waited to be sent home. Inevitably, military and civilian order collapsed as desperation and fear spread.[228]

Mobs of soldiers and civilians roamed streets in ankle-deep mud, stealing food, merchandise, horses, mules, and anything else that was not guarded. Warehouses, shops, and private homes were invaded. Looting, mob violence, and property damage continued for several days. Individual officers with small groups of soldiers tried to regain control of the situation and fought several skirmishes with rioters. A number of people were wounded and killed in the streets. One overwrought Confederate officer, when confronting a group of female looters, threatened to have his men fire into the crowd.[229]

On April 18, at the James Bennitt farm house near Durham Station, Sherman and Johnston signed a surrender document that was intended to end fighting all over the South. The United States government rejected the agreement as being too broad and generous.

Under the threat of renewed fighting, Johnston signed a document on April 26 that was more consistent with the Appomattox surrender. The last major Confederate army had capitulated. United States Army provost troops began administering oaths and issuing paroles to approximately thirty-seven thousand Confederates.[a] The Union army gave the Confederates ten day's rations so that they would be well away from Greensboro when they ran out of food.

Two days after the surrender, Governor Vance issued a proclamation acknowledging that the war was lost and that incidents of civil unrest were occurring throughout the state. He called upon all law abiding citizens and soldiers to remain at their homes "and to exert themselves in preserving order." He also asked that, should it become necessary,

> ... good and true soldiers of North Carolina, whether they have been surrendered and paroled or otherwise, to unite themselves together in sufficient numbers in the various counties of the State, under the superintendence of the civil magistrates thereof, to arrest or slay any bodies of lawless and unauthorized men who may be committing depredations upon the persons or property of peaceable citizens.[230]

Several of the reserve regiments that Mallett had organized stacked their arms for the last time at Greensboro. A number of young soldiers identifying themselves as "Mallett's Junior Reserves" surrendered with Johnston's army. The two companies of Camp Holmes guards surrendered. Major McLean's Camp Stokes guards were paroled on May 18.

As the war ground to a halt, the men of Mallett's original battalion who had not been killed or captured since their transfer the previous June, surrendered at various locations throughout the South. Those who had chosen North Carolina regiments serving in Virginia were paroled with Lee's army at Appomattox or with their units elsewhere in that state. Those who had joined the 29th and 39th North Carolina regiments on Kennesaw Mountain were paroled at Meridian Mississippi on May 8. Survivors of the one hundred men who had so piqued Colonel Archer Anderson by joining the Confederate

[a] Another four thousand Confederates did not wait for parole papers and simply left (Kent McCoury, assistant manager, Bennett Place State Historic Site, Durham, North Carolina)

navy surrendered along the coast or further inland where they had retreated. Union officers arrived at wayside hospitals and issued paroles to surgeons, hospital stewards, and convalescent soldiers. The names of Mallett's veterans often appeared on hospital rosters.

At North Carolina conscript offices, Confederate soldiers, Home Guardsmen, and militiamen turned themselves over to the first Union officer that appeared. Deserters, upon hearing that the fighting had ended, came out of hiding.

It was over. Thousands of men who were forced into the war by Peter Mallett's bureau, those who had served in his battalion, and those who had fled beyond his reach could finally go home.

Epilogue

Peter Mallett: post-war photograph
Image courtesy of Mr. Mike Mallett, Laurel, Mississippi

With North Carolina overrun by Union forces, Colonel Mallett was assigned to escort President Davis and his party through the state. He was with Davis in Charlotte on April 19 when news of Lincoln's death reached that city. Later that month, Mallett was seen in Fayetteville with General Holmes. For several years after the war, he lived with his wife and children in Wilmington. In 1868, observing that he had "done all the harm I could down South...." he returned to New York City and resumed his career as a businessman. He was active in the New York United Confederate Veterans Camp. His wife, Annabella, died, but he remarried later in life. Peter Mallett died in 1907 at his daughter's home in Wilmington at the age of eighty-four. He is buried in Wilmington's Oakdale Cemetery.

James Cameron McRae: post-war photograph
North Carolina Collection,
University of North Carolina Library at Chapel Hill

Captain McRae was promoted to the permanent rank of major after he was transferred out of Mallett's battalion. On April 20, 1865, while assigned to General Laurence Baker's staff in North Carolina, Major McRae issued the final orders that would disband Baker's brigade. McRae signed his oath and was paroled on May 6. After the war, he married, resumed his law practice, and became active in the Episcopal Church and Masonic Order. He was instrumental in reopening the University of North Carolina, which had closed in 1868, and was the presiding officer at a temperance convention in Raleigh in 1881. He served as a superior court judge and was an Associate North Carolina Supreme Court Justice from 1892 until 1894. In 1899, he was appointed Dean of the University of North Carolina Law School. Under his leadership, the school's physical facilities, library, and student body doubled in size. On October 17, 1906, McRae died in Chapel Hill at the age of seventy-one. He is buried in the Cross Creek Cemetery in Fayetteville.

Albert Gallatin Thompson:
post-war photograph

After having his foot amputated at Kennesaw Mountain, Albert Thompson returned to North Carolina and spent the rest of his life in Rutherford County. His application for a prosthesis was approved by North Carolina's Artificial Limb Department in 1867. When he received his Jewett's Patent artificial left foot on May 31 of that year, he attested that the appendage "appears to work well." He and Cate built a fine new home on the banks of Cane Creek, where they farmed and operated their country store. They had three more children. Albert served two terms in county government and was an incorporator of the Spartanburg and North Carolina Railroad in the 1880s. He walked on crutches most of the time because the artificial foot made his leg hurt. He only wore it on Sundays when the family attended church. Albert died in 1899. Cate died in 1905. They are buried at Brittain Presbyterian Church near Rutherfordton.

Stonewall Confederate Cemetery, Griffin, Georgia
Courtesy of Ms. Alice Pounds
James S. Boynton Chapter No. 222,
United Daughters of the Confederacy

Alfred C. Cowen

No photograph of Albert Thompson's best friend is known to exist. Thompson's letter of June 26, 1864, stating that Cowen had been wounded "but was not hurt bad enough to leave his post" is the last known eyewitness information about him. A letter written by Sgt. Joseph Scoggins in late September 1864, indicates that Cowen was killed near Atlanta. His grave has not been located. Rutherford County court documents show that a guardian was appointed for his son in 1866. Alfred's widow, Nancy, remarried in 1867.

Appendices

Appendix A

Below is a roster of officers, enlisted men, and army surgeons who were assigned to conscription duty in North Carolina. The list has been compiled from John Moore's *Roster of North Carolina Troops In the War Between the States*, Clark's *Histories*, the North Carolina Archives's *North Carolina Troops: A Roster,* Broadfoot's *Confederate State Roster*, University of North Carolina's Southern Historical Collection, and other sources. The list does not include scores of civilian surgeons and disabled enlisted men who were assigned to conscription duty for varying periods of time. Also not included are the enlisted men of Mallett's battalion, McRae's battalion, Hahr's battalion, McLean's battalion, Captain Waters's provost company, or the several thousand militia and Home Guardsmen who assisted North Carolina's conscription bureau.

Complete rosters of Mallett's and McLean's battalions, approximately one thousand names, are available in Broadfoot's *Confederate State Roster* for North Carolina, Volume III. Major James C. McRae's battalion roster is contained in *North Carolina Troops: A Roster*, Volume II.

Most of these men were wounded and disabled while serving in prior assignments. Once transferred to the conscription bureau, many of the officers had various assignments but are generally listed here only once. The officers who served at Camp Hill and Camp Vance are listed in their permanent assignments.

North Carolina Conscription Bureau Headquarters, Raleigh, N.C.

Col. Peter Mallett, Commandant of Conscripts
Capt. George B. Baker, Chief Quartermaster
Sgt. James Calvin Marcom, Assistant Quartermaster
Capt. John M. Walker, Chief Commissary
1st Lt. Pulaski Cowper, Deserter and Registration Department
1st Lt. Josiah Jones, Assistant, Deserter and Registration Dept.
1st Lt. S. M. Parish, Detail Department
Pvt. A. B. Smith, Clerk, Detail Department
Pvt. C. W. Clay, Clerk, Detail Department
Pvt. Ellington , Clerk, Detail Department
Pvt. Paylor, Clerk, Detail Department

Pvt. L. S. Perry, Clerk, letter files
Pvt. R. M. Oldridge, Clerk, endorsements, instruction book, personnel orders
Pvt. J. H. Bryan, Jr., Free Negro Department
Pvt. Graham Daves, Clerk
2nd Lt. E. J. Hardin, Adjutant at headquarters
Pvt. J. C. Bellamy, Clerk, letter copy books
Capt. Samuel B. Waters, Raleigh Provost Guard

Camp Holmes, Camp of Instruction No. 1

Capt. James C. McRae, commander, Camp Guard Battalion
1st Lt. Frans J. Hahr, commandant of Camp Holmes
1st Lt. Wright Huske, Clerk and Receiving Officer
1st Lt. E. N. Mann, Adjutant
2nd Lt. Charles H. Wright, Adjutant
Lt. L. L. Prather, Adjutant
Lt. Robert K. Williams, Camp Guard Battalion, Company A
2nd Lt. J. J. Reid, Camp Guard Battalion, Company A
1st Lt. John McRae, Camp Guard Battalion, Company B
2nd Lt. Milus M. Bailey, Camp Guard Battalion, Company B
2nd Lt. Henry Fetter, Camp Guard Battalion, Company B
2nd Lt. John G. Rencher, Camp Guard Battalion, Company B
2nd Lt. W. H. Jones, Camp Guard Battalion, Company B
1st Lt. James J. Speller, Camp Guard Battalion
1st Lt. Joseph A. Hill, Camp Guard Battalion, Company C
2nd Lt. F. A. Fetter, Camp Guard Battalion, Company C
1st Lt. Robert S. Robards, Camp Guard Battalion, Company D
2nd Lt. James McKee, Camp Guard Battalion, Company D
2nd Lt. H. S. Whittaker, Camp Guard Battalion
2nd Lt. E. F. Royal, Camp Guard Battalion
2nd Lt. George F. Skirven, Camp Guard Battalion
2nd Lt. Philow Peter Hoke, Camp Guard Battalion
1st Lt. E. B. Goelet, Camp Guard Battalion
2nd Lt. John S. Hines, Drill Master
2nd Lt. Arthur Collins, Camp Guard Battalion, Company F
2nd Lt. James C. Sutherland, Camp Guard Battalion

1st and 2nd Congressional Districts

Union forces occupied and raided much of this region. As a result, the two districts were often administered as one. Conscription officers were active, but they usually confined themselves to the area west of the Chowan River.

First Congressional District: Martin, Hertford, Perquimans, Gates, Chowan, Pasquotank, Camden, Currituck, Northampton, Tyrrell, Bertie, and Washington County.

Second Congressional District counties: Halifax, Edgecombe, Beaufort, Wilson, Pitt, Greene, Lenoir, and Hyde.

Surgeon:
John C. Merrell

Assistant Surgeons:
W. R. Wood
H. C. Herndon
R. F. Baker
W. F. Harlee

Inspector for both districts:
Captain David Barrow

Enrolling Officers:
2nd Lt. J. W. Payne
2nd Lt. R. B. Gilliam
2nd Lt. William White
Capt. P. M. Charles
1st Lt. James Tiddy
1st Lt. Kenneth Thigpen
2nd Lt. J. M. Little
Capt. Thomas M. Jordan
Capt. A. J. Moore
1st Lt. J. A. Summers
Lt. Colonel H. A. Rogers
Private John W. Sheets

3rd and 4th Congressional District Enrolling Officers

The 3rd Congressional District: Carteret, Craven, Jones, Onslow, Duplin, Wayne, Sampson, and Johnston County. The Union army was also active in parts of this area. The district medical officers were Surgeon A. M. Doyle and assistant surgeons L. T. Smith and A. F. Mallett.

The 4th Congressional District consisted of New Hanover, Brunswick, Columbus, Bladen, Robeson, Cumberland, Harnett and Richmond County. The medical officers were assistant surgeons J. H. Faison and W. L. Ledbetter.

Inspector for both districts:
Captain J. A. Barnett

County Enrolling Officers for both districts:
2nd Lt. R. J. Pearsall
2nd Lt. C. T. Stevens
2nd Lt. Walter Bullock
2nd Lt. Gabriel Holmes
2nd Lt. T. J. Wilson
2nd Lt. J. B. Buchanan

2nd Lt. Hardy B. Willis
2nd Lt. Robert Tait
1st Lt. S. W. Bennette
Capt. Augustus Landis, Jr.
2nd Lt. W. C. Rencher
Capt. A. H. Tolar
1st Lt. A. McCallum
Capt. A. F. Mallett

5th Congressional District

Counties: Warren, Franklin, Granville, Wake, Orange, and Nash

Surgeons & Assistant Surgeons:
R. B. Baker
George E. Redwood
J. M. Pelot
H. W. Caffey
E. S. Pendleton

District Inspector:
Captain W. M. Swann

Enrolling Officers:
Capt. E. Porter
2nd Lt. Frederick J. Hill
2nd Lt. J. C. Warren
1st Lt. W. G. Meachum
2nd Lt. Frederick A. Fetter
1st Lt. John T. Price

6th Congressional District

Counties: Alamance, Person, Caswell, Rockingham, Guilford, Stokes, and Forsyth.

Surgeons & Assistant Surgeons:
R. S. Lewis
W. J. Gilbert
A. H. Harris
W. H. Hodnett
H. K. Cochran
E. M. Rivers

District Inspector:
Lieutenant James C. Dobbs

County Enrolling Officers:
2nd Lt. W. M. R. Johns
2nd Lt. Joseph A. Haywood
2nd Lt. H. C. Willis
1st Lt. F. B. Ward
2nd Lt. W. A. Albright,
2nd Lt. John C. Baker,
Capt. A. H. Moore
Capt. James A. Barnett

When Camp Stokes was established in 6th Congressional District near Greensboro, Major Jesse R. McLean was appointed camp commandant. Officers assigned to the camp included Captain C. N. Allen, Captain S. H. Everett, Captain Thomas H. Long, and 2nd Lieutenant Arthur Collins, acting commissary. Captain J. J. Drake commanded the camp guard. Lieutenants P. H. Williamson, J. C. Morrison, George F. Robb, and Milus M. Bailey supervised the two companies of camp guards.

7th Congressional District

Unlike most congressional districts, extensive files from the 7th Congressional District remain in tact. Approximately twelve hundred documents pertaining to the 7th district are held in the Manuscripts Department of the University of North Carolina. Counties in the district: Randolph, Davidson, Chatham, Moore, Montgomery, Stanley, and Anson.

Surgeons:
A. H. Scott
H. Killey
A. D. Lindsey

District Inspector:
1st Lieutenant John M. Little

County Enrolling Officers:
1st Lt. J. A Thompson
2nd Lt. E. R. Holt
2nd Lt. J. Tysor
Capt. W. L. Thornburg
Capt. Van Brown
2nd Lt. George H. Haigh
1st Lt. B. G. Coone
Lt. W. T. Smith
2nd Lt. W. G. Meachum

Enlisted men on Conscription Duty:
Color Sergeant J. O. Mansfield
1st Sgt. W. J. Ross
Pvt. Eli Bradfford
Pvt. J. D. Dorsett
Pvt. W. C. McMackin
Pvt. John Louis
Sgt. L. B. Bynum
Pvt. James P. Deaton
Pvt. W. M. Harpin
Pvt. Jackson M. Hathcock
Militiaman J. J. Nobbs

7th Congressional District Supporting Force:
(organized: June 22, 1864)

John Kemp	Dillard P. Webster	B. M. Land
Noah Haw	George Cole	Daniel McBain
J. J. Fox	Emsley Scott	C. Stone
J. C. Howard	Lorenzo Goodwin	Thomas Crop
J. A. Gilmore	Haywood Bobbitt	Green Hathcock

8th Congressional District

Counties: Rowan, Cabarrus, Mecklenburg, Gaston, Lincoln, Catawba, Cleveland and Union County.

Medical Examining Board Chairman:
J. B. Alexander

Surgeon:
N. H. Payne

Assistant Surgeons:
N. Hunt
J. L. Rucker

District Inspector:
Major John M. Prior

County Enrolling Officers:

1st Lt. O. M. Pike	2nd Lt. John K. Hoyt
2nd Lt. C. W. Alexander	2nd Lt. A. W. Wells
2nd Lt. R. H. Maxwell	2nd Lt. D. C. Waddell
2nd Lt. F. Nixon	Corporal Caleb F. Smith

9th Congressional District

Counties of Ashe, Alleghany, Wilkes, Caldwell, Alexander, Yadkin, Surrey, Davie, Iredell, and Burke.

Surgeon:
J. T. S. Baird

Assistant Surgeons:

H. N. Young	W. T. Finley

District Inspector:
Lt. Joseph K. Burke

Enrolling Officers:
Capt. W. D. Manning
Capt. T. S. Bouchelle
Capt. J. H. Jones
2nd Lt. D. H. Ray
2nd Lt. F. D. Carlton
2nd Lt. W. H. Partick
Capt. A. A. Hill
2nd Lt. David Edwards
1st Lt. W. A. Luckey
2nd Lt. J. H. Welborn

10th Congressional District

Counties: Clay, Cherokee, Macon, Jackson, Madison, Buncombe, Transylvania, Henderson, Polk, Yancey, McDowell, Rutherford, Mitchell, Haywood, and Watauga

Surgeons:
W. J. Davids
A. Hicks

District Inspector:
Captain D. C. Pearson

County Enrolling Officers:
1st Lt. Thomas S. Robards
1st Lt. L. H. Rabb
2nd Lt. J. H. Webb
Capt. John H. Anderson
2nd Lt. John H. Fletcher
Capt. H. W. Abernathey
1st Lt. David T. Millard

Assistant Enrolling Officer:
Lt. Col. C. L. Harris, 69th Battalion NC Home Guard

Appendix B

Major Hahr's Battalion

In October 1864, two companies of light duty men under the command of Major Frank Hahr were sent to Wilmington, North Carolina. They remained in the Wilmington area during both attacks on Fort Fisher. A roster for Company B of this battalion was discovered in the Percy P. Turner Collection in the North Carolina State Archives (*Guide to Private Manuscripts*, item 1409). For several years this roster has been mislabeled as "Maj. Hoke's Batt. L. D. Men."

This company was one of the early light duty units raised by Peter Mallett's conscription bureau. While some of these men were veterans of Mallett's battalion, it is likely that service in Hahr's battalion by many of them has been unknown until now.

Officers:
Captain W. H. Jones
1st Lt. J. S. Bryan
2nd Lt. Adams

Sergeants:

1st Sgt. J. T. Turner	3rd Sgt. A. Vincannon
2nd Sgt. J. E. Robitzsck	4th Sgt. W. H. Dobbs

Corporals:

1st Cpl. A. Coble	3rd Cpl. P. E. Hutson
2nd Cpl. W. G. Morgan	4th Cpl. E. H. Sego

Privates:

S. Arnold	I. McPhail	Atkin
T. M. McSwain	L. Atkinson	A. Mills
S. Barnes	J. Paul	J. L. Bennett
P. W. Phelan	George Black	S. Pierce
T. V. Brooks	A. Pritchet	W. B. Byrum
N. Ridge	S. J. Cass	William Roach
H. R. Cherry	W. A. Roach	J. Chilton
B. Rose	J. M. Conner	W. J. Rouse
B. F. Cox	I. L. Routh	William Edwards
S. K. Rush	D. Grant	W. Shaw

Privates (continued):

B. F. Grear	G. R. Shook	O. C. Gupton
N. Snipes	A. N. Hamlet	J. P. Stout
N. M. Hamrick	C. Swain	J. M. Harry
B. H. Swinson	B. Hill	B. Thompson
Hosey	A. Tiner	William Jones
Tolar	H. S. Lamb	J. S. Trogdon
J. Lambert	Jno. Ward	J. S. Linsey
Jno. Warren	C. Long	M. H. Wells
Martin	J. H. Wheeler	N. McClamb
Geo. Williams	McColum	G. Williams
W. A. McGrady	W. J. Wilson	S. McPeters
T. J. Wren		

Soldiers listed as "Deserted:"

H. S. Lamb	J. P. Stout	W. A. Roach
B. F. Cox	H. Huneycutt	J. M. Allred
B. Cox	J. L. Britt	

Soldiers listed as the "Camp Guard:"
(only last names listed)

London	McCrakan
Wilkerson	Fonville
Robins	

Listed as "Cooks:"

McGuffie	Routh
Edwards	Bowen
Dillinger	

Listed as "Discharged:"
J. T. Leach

Bibliography

Primary Sources

Chapel Hill, North Carolina:
Southern Historical Collection, University of North Carolina
Peter Mallett Papers
Gaither Papers
Sharpe Papers
Durham, North Carolina:
Duke Manuscript Collection, Duke University
Eutawville, South Carolina:
Walter C. Hilderman III Collection
Albert and Cate Thompson letters

Period Newspapers

Carolina Watchman (Salisbury, N.C.)
Daily Bulletin (Raleigh, N.C.)
Fayetteville Observer
National Tribune (Washington, D.C.)
New York Herald
North Carolina Argus (Wadesborough, N.C.)
Raleigh Journal
Raleigh Progress
Semi-Weekly Raleigh Register
State Journal (Raleigh)
Weekly Raleigh Register
Western Democrat (Charlotte, N.C.)

Published Primary Sources

Howe, W.W., *Kinston, Whitehall and Goldsboro (North Carolina) Expedition, December, 1862*, New York, W.W. Howe, 1890).

Secondary Sources

Arnett, Ethel Stephens, *Confederate Guns Were Stacked at Greensboro, North Carolina*; (Greensboro, N.C., Piedmont Press, 1965).

Ashe, Samuel A., ed., *Biographical History of North Carolina* (Greensboro, N.C., Charles L. Van Noppen, 1907).

Barden, John R., *Letters to the Home Circle* (Raleigh, N.C., North Carolina Department of Cultural Resources, Division of Archives and History, 1998).

Barefoot, Daniel W., *General Robert F. Hoke* (Winston-Salem, N.C., John F. Blair, 1996).

Barrett, John G., *The Civil War in North Carolina* (Chapel Hill, University of North Carolina Press, 1963).

Boatner, Mark M. III, ed., *The Civil War Dictionary* (New York, Vintage Books, 1991).

Bradley, Stephen E., Jr., *North Carolina Confederate Militia and Home Guard Records*, 3 vols. (Wilmington, N.C., Broadfoot Publishing, 1995).

Bridges, Hal, *Lee's Maverick General Daniel Harvey Hill* (New York, McGraw-Hill, 1961).

Bumgarner, Matthew, *Kirk's Raiders* (Hickory, N.C., Piedmont Press, 2000).

Carbone, John S., *The Civil War in Coastal North Carolina* (Raleigh, N.C., North Carolina Department of Cultural Resources, Division of Archives and History, 2001).

Caren, Eric C., ed., *Civil War Extra*, vols. 1 and 2 (Edison, N.J., Castle Books, 1999).

Casstevens, Francis H., *The Civil War in Yadkin County, North Carolina* (Jefferson, N.C., McFarland & Company, 1997).

Clark, Walter, ed., *Histories of the Several Regiments and Battalions from North Carolina in the Great War, 1861-'65.* 5 vols. (Raleigh, E. M. Uzell, 1901; reprinted by Broadfoot Publishing Company, Wilmington, 1996).

Connelly, Thomas Lawrence, *Autumn of Glory* (Baton Rouge, Louisiana State Press, 1971).

Cook, Gerald Wilson, ed., *The Last Tarheel Militia 1861-1865* (Winston- Salem, N.C., privately published, 1987).

Current, Richard N., ed., *Encyclopedia of the Confederacy* (New York, Simon & Schuster, 1993).

Davis, Charles, *Clark's Regiments: An Extended Index* (Gretna, Louisiana, Pelican Publishing Company, 2001).

Davis, George B. et al., *Official Military Atlas of the Civil War* (New York, Fairfax Press, 1983 ed.).

Davis, William C., *Look Away!* (New York, The Free Press, 2002).

Dowdey, Clifford and Louis H. Manarin, eds., *The Wartime Papers of Robert E. Lee* (New York, Bramhall House, 1961).

Durden, Robert F., *The Black and the Gray* (Baton Rouge, Louisiana State University Press, 1972).

Evans, Beverly D, IV, Jason H. Silverman, and Samuel N. Thomas, Jr., *Shanks* (Cambridge, Perseus Books group, 2002).

Escott, Paul D., ed., *North Carolina Yeoman: The Diary of Basil Armstrong Thomasson, 1853-1862* (Athens, University of Georgia Press, 1996).

French, Samuel G., *Two Wars* (Nashville, Confederate Veteran, 1901. New edition: Huntington, W.Va., Blue Acorn Press, 1999).

Groom, Winston, *Shrouds of Glory* (New York, Atlantic Monthly Press, 1995).

Hahn, George W., *The Catawba Soldier of the Civil War* (Hickory, N.C., Clay Printing 1911, 1987 printing, ed. Mrs. Robert S. Brown).

Hardee, William J., *Rifle and Light Infantry Tactics* (Memphis, Tenn., Hutton & Freligh, 1861; reprint, Glendale, N.Y., Benchmark Publishing, 1970).

Hardy, Michael C., *The Thirty-Seventh North Carolina Troops* (Jefferson, North Carolina, McFarland & Company, 2003).

Harris, William C., ed., *In the Country of the Enemy* (University Press of Florida, 1999).

Hewett, Janet B. and Joyce Lawrence, eds. *The Confederate Roster, North Carolina Confederate Soldiers 1861-1865,* 3 vols. (Wilmington, N.C., Broadfoot Publishing, 1999).

Holoman, Charles R. and Talmadge C. Johnson, *The Story of Kinston and Lenoir County,* (Raleigh, Edwards & Broughton, 1954).

Hill Jr., D. H., *Confederate Military History,* (New York, Thomas Yoseloff, 1962).

Hughes, Nathaniel C., *Bentonville: The Last Battle of Sherman and Johnston* (Chapel Hill, The University of North Carolina Press, 1996).

Hughes, Nathaniel C., Jr. and Roy P. Stonesifer, Jr., *The Life and Wars of Gideon Pillow,* (Chapel Hill, University of North Carolina Press, 1993).

Inscoe, John C. and Gordon B. McKinney, *The Heart of Confederate Appalachia* (Chapel Hill, University of North Carolina Press, 2000).

Johnston, Frontis W., ed., *The Papers of Zebulon Baird Vance,* vol. 1 (Raleigh, State Department of Archives and History, 1963).

Jones, Archer, *Confederate Strategy from Shiloh to Vicksburg* (Baton Rouge, Louisiana State University Press, 1961).

Jordan, Weymouth T., and Louis H. Manarin, eds. *North Carolina Troops, 1861-1865: A Roster*, 15 vols. to date (Raleigh, Division of Archives and History, North Carolina Department of Cultural Resources, 1966 to present).

Key, William, *The Battle of Atlanta and the Georgia Campaign* (Atlanta, Peachtree Publishers Limited, 1981).

King, H. T., *Sketches of Pitt County: A Brief History of the County, 1704-1910* (Raleigh, Edwards & Broughton, 1911).

Knox, Dudley W., ed., *Official Records of the Union and Confederate Navies in the War of the Rebellion* (Washington, D.C., United States Government Printing Office, 1927).

Lefler, Hugh Talmage and Albert Ray Newsome, *North Carolina* (Chapel Hill, University of North Carolina Press, 1954).

Livermore, Thomas Leonard, *Number and Losses in the Civil War in America 1861-1865*, (Bloomington, Indiana University Press, 1957).

Long, A. L. and Marcus J. Wright, eds., *Memoirs of Robert E. Lee* (Secacus, N.J., The Blue and Gray Press, 1983).

Long, E. B., *The Civil War Day By Day* (Garden City, N.Y., Doubleday & Company, 1971).

Manarin, Louis H., *A Guide to Military Organizations and Installations North Carolina 1861-1865* (Raleigh, North Carolina Confederate Centennial Commission, 1961).

Mast, Greg, *State Troops and Volunteers*, v.1 (Raleigh, North Carolina Department of Cultural Resources, Division of Archives and History, 1995).

McCaslin, Richard B., *Portraits of Conflict* (Fayetteville, University of Alabama Press, 1997).

McKinney, Gordon and Richard McMurray, *The Papers of Zebulon Vance,* microfilm (Frederick, Maryland, University Publications of America, 1987).

Miers, Earl Schenck, *A Rebel War Clerk's Diary*, by John B. Jones (New York, Sagamore Press, Inc., 1958).

Miles, Jim, *Fields of Glory* (Nashville, Rutledge Hill Press, 1989).

Mitchell, Memory F., *Legal Aspects of Conscription and Exemption in North Carolina 1861-1865* (Chapel Hill, University of North Carolina Press, 1965).

Mobley, Joe A., ed., *The Papers of Zebulon Baird Vance,* vol. 2 (Raleigh, Division of Archives and History, North Carolina Department of Cultural Resources, 1995).

Moore, Albert Burton, Ph.D., *Conscription and Conflict in the Confederacy* (New York, Hillary House Publishers, 1963).

Moore, John W., *Roster of North Carolina Troops in the War Between the States* (Raleigh, Ashe & Gatlin, 1882).

Murray, Elizabeth R., *Wake: Capitol County of North Carolina,* (Raleigh, Capitol Publishing Company, 1983).

Palm, Ronn, et al., eds., *The Bloody 85th: The Letters of Milton McJunkin, a Western Pennsylvania Soldier in the Civil War* (Daleville, Virginia, Schroeder Publications, 2000).

Powell, William S., ed., *Dictionary of North Carolina Biography* (Chapel Hill, N.C., University of North Carolina Press, 1991).

Price, William H., *Civil War Handbook* (Arlington, Virginia, Prince Lithograph, 1961).

Rhea, Gordon C., *The Battle of the Wilderness* (Baton Rouge, University of Louisiana Press, 1994).

Rogers, Edward H., *Reminisces of the Military Service in the Forty-Third Regiment, Massachusetts Infantry, During the Great Civil War, 1862-1863* (Boston, Franklin Press, 1883).

Root, Elihu, et al, *The War of the Rebellion: A Compilation of the Official Records of the Union and Confederate Records* (Washington, D.C., Government Printing Office, 1900).

Shiman, Philip, *Fort Branch And The Defenses of the Roanoke Valley 1862-1865* (Hamilton, N.C., Fort Branch Battlefield Commission, 1990).

Silverman, J.H., and S.N. Thomas, Jr., *A Rising Star of Promise* (Campbell, California, Savas Company, 1998).

Stone, DeWitt Boyd, Jr., ed., *Wandering to Glory* (Columbia, University of South Carolina Press, 2002).

Swanson, Mark, *Atlas of the Civil War, Month by Month* (Athens, University of Georgia Press, 2004).

Thomas, Emory M., *The Confederate Nation: 1861-1865* (New York, Harper & Row, 1979).

Trotter, William R., *Silk Flags and Cold Steel* (Greensboro, Signet Research, 1988).

Warner, Ezra J., *Generals in Gray: Lives of the Confederate Commanders* (Baton Rouge: Louisiana State University Press, 1959).

Watt, W.N., *Iredell County Soldiers in the Civil War* (privately published, 1995).

Wegner, Ansley Herring, *Phantom Pain* (Raleigh, Office of Archives and History, North Carolina Department of Cultural Resources, 2004).

Williams, Dewey E., *A Civil War Camp in North Carolina, Burke County's Camp Vance*, (Morganton, N.C., privately published, 1977).

Yates, Richard E., *The Confederacy and Zeb Vance*, (Tuscaloosa, Confederate Publishing Company, 1958).

Yoseloff, Thomas, *Confederate Military History*, v. 4 (New York, Thomas Yoseloff, 1962).

Articles

Bardolph, Richard, "Inconsistent Rebels: Desertion of North Carolina Troops in the Civil War." *North Carolina Historical Review*, v. 41.

Bogue, Hardy Z., "Confederate Manpower Mobilization." *Confederate Veteran* July-August, 1989, p. 6-10.

Brooks, R. P., "Conscription in the Confederate States of America 1862-1865." *The Military Historian and Economist*, v. 1, No. 4 (October, 1916), p. 419-43.

Calkins, Chris, "Petersburg-The Wearing Down of Lee's Army." *Hallowed Ground*, v. 4, No. 1 (Spring, 2003) p. 26-32.

Cashion, Jerry C., ed., "Let This Be the Last Resort." *Tar Heel Junior Historian*, v. 26, No. 2 (Spring, 1987).

Castel, Albert, "Theophilus Holmes: Pallbearer of the Confederacy." *Civil War Times Illustrated*, v. 16 (1977).

Elkins, William Franklin, "In the Junior Reserves" *Confederate Veteran*, v. 40 (May, 1932), p. 171.

Harrison, Lowell H., "Conscription in the Confederacy." *Civil War Times Illustrated*, July, 1970, p. 11-19.

Lewellen, Faye, "Salisbury's Fate in the Final Days." *Confederate Veteran*, 2003, v. 3, p. 12-17.

Mast, Greg, ed. "Setser Letters." *Company Front: Magazine of the Society for the Historical Preservation of the 26th North Carolina Troops*, August-September, 1989, p. 14-15.

Mast, Greg, "North Carolina Land Units In Confederate Service, 1861-1865: An Order of Battle." *Company Front: Magazine of the Society for the Historical Preservation of the 26th North Carolina Troops*, November/December, 1990.

Moneyhon, Carl H., "Disloyalty and Class Consciousness in Southwest Arkansas, 1862-1865." *Arkansas Historical Quarterly*, v. 52 (Autumn, 1993), p. 223-43.

Norris, David A., "Foster's March to the Sea (Almost)." *Civil War Times Illustrated*, August, 2002.

Pollitt, Phoebe and Reese, Camille N., "War Between the States, Nursing In North Carolina." *Confederate Veteran*, v. 2, 2002.

Scovill, A. L., "Rebellion Record for December" (1862) *Farmers' and Mechanics' Almanac for 1864.*

Smith, David P., "Conscription and Conflict on the Texas Frontier: 1863-1865" *Civil War History*, VI (September, 1990), p. 250-61.

Unpublished Typescripts

Durham, J. Lloyd, "The Grand Review: North Carolina Militia and Volunteers, 1784-1860."

Wiles, Abraham, "*Of Warp and Weft*," Western Carolina University senior thesis, (1990).

Government Records

Confederate Adjutant and Inspector General's Office Special Orders 1861 - 1864, four volumes, War Department, Washington, D.C. (not dated), National Archives, Washington, D.C.

Civil War Collection, Military Collection, Archives, Division of Archives and History, Department of Cultural Resources, Raleigh, N.C.

Compiled Service Records of Confederate Soldiers Who Served during the Civil War, Record Group 109, National Archives, Washington, D.C.

Endnotes

[1] Private Albert G. Thompson to his wife Mary Catherine Andrews Thompson (herein referred to as Albert to Cate).

[2] 1st Sergeant A. J. Price to his wife, June 26, 1864. North Carolina Archives, Private Manuscript Collections, item 1364: A. J. Price file.

[3] Perry Summers to Mollie Gaither, Gaither Papers (No. 3517), Southern Historical Collection, University of North Carolina Library, Chapel Hill, N.C. (herein referred to as Gaither Papers).

[4] W. H. Price, *The Civil War Centennial Handbook,* p. 5.

[5] *War of the Rebellion: A Compilation of the Official Records of the Union and Confederate Armies*, (herein referred to as *O.R.*) Series III, v. 1, p. 68-69.

[6] *O.R.*, Series III, v. 1. p. 72.

[7] Tar Heel Junior Historian, Spring 1987, v. 26, number 2, p. 3.

[8] Greg Mast, *State Troops and Volunteers,* Vol. I, p. 7. In September 1861 the state militia was reorganized into twenty-eight brigades containing 116 regiments.

[9] H. T. King, *Sketches of Pitt County: A Brief History of the County, 1704-1910*, p. 123-24.

[10] Walter Clark, ed., *Histories of the Several Regiments and Battalions from North Carolina in the Great War 1861-1865* (herein referred to as Clark's *Histories*), v. I, p.7. General Martin's ten State Troops regiments were authorized by the May 8, 1861, act of the legislature and were to be enlisted for a period of three years or the war, whichever was shorter. General Hoke organized the early volunteer regiments (Manarian, *A Guide to Military Organizations and Installations North Carolina 1861-1865,* p.1).

[11] Clark's *Histories*, v. I, p. 7 and D. H. Hill, Jr., *Confederate Military History, Vol. 4, North Carolina.,* p. 17. Other estimates of North Carolina soldiers supplied up to this time reach 45,000.

[12] *Daily Bulletin*, Charlotte, N.C., April 14, 1862. Abraham Wiles, *Of Warp and Weft.*

[13] John G. Barrett, *The Civil War in North Carolina* (herein referred to as Barrett), p. 47.

[14] Barrett, p. 36.

[15] Barrett, p. 33 & 37.

[16] Barrett, p. 45.

[17] Barrett, p. 68.

[18] *Ibid.*

[19] Albert M. Moore, *Conscription and Conflict in the Confederacy* (herein referred to as Moore), p. 6-7.

[20] Paul D. Escott, ed., *North Carolina Yeoman: The Diary of Basil Armstrong Thomasson, 1853-1862,* p. 322. *Daily Bulletin,* Charlotte, N.C., February 1, 1862, and April 1, 1862.

[21] Moore, p. 3.

[22] *O.R.*, Series IV, v. 2, p. 43.

[23] *O.R.*, Series IV, v. 1, p. 1095.

[24] *Ibid.*

[25] Frontis Johnston, ed., *The Papers of Zebulon Baird Vance* (herein referred to as *Vance Papers*), v.1, p. 135.

[26] *O.R.*, Series IV, v. 1, p. 1097-098.

[27] *National Magazine*, March 1892, "The Southern Society." *Vance Papers*, v. 1, p. 175.

[28] Louis H. Manarin, Weymouth T. Jordan, et al, *North Carolina Troops 1861-1865: A Roster* (herein referred to as *Roster*), v. III, p. 511.

[29] *Vance Papers*, v. 1, p. 137. One or two of the volunteer camps, including Camp Mangum near Raleigh, operated until August 1.

[30] *O.R.*, Series IV, v. 2, p. 67-69. Governor Clark's successor, Z. B. Vance, would issue much stronger orders to militia officers, requiring them to assist Mallett. *Vance Papers,* v. 1, p. 176.

[31] *O.R.*, Series IV, v. 1, p. 1097.

[32] Peter Mallett Papers, Camp Holmes letter copy book, v. 6 (herein referred to as Camp Holmes, v. 6), p. 25. Southern Historical Collection.

[33] *O.R.*, Series IV, v. 1, p. 1148.

[34] *O.R.*, Series IV, v. 1, p. 1152.

[35] Memory F. Mitchell, *Legal Aspects of Conscription and Exemption in North Carolina, 1861-1865*, p. 17.

[36] *O.R.*, Series IV, v. 2, p. 5.

[37] North Carolina Adjutant General's letter copy book, North Carolina Archives, A.G. 45, p. 228.

[38] Camp Holmes, v. 6, p. 15.

[39] Camp Holmes, v. 6, p. 17.

[40] Camp Holmes, v. 6, p. 7.

[41] Camp Holmes, v. 6, p. 26.
[42] *Vance Papers*, v. 1, p. 186 (Gen. Ord. No. 2, Sept. 9, 1862).
[43] *Roster*, v. VI, p. 10.
[44] Camp Holmes, v. 6, p. 27.
[45] *O.R.*, Series IV, v. 1, p. 1098.
[46] Camp Holmes, v. 6, p. 54.
[47] *O.R.*, Series IV, v. 2, p. 68.
[48] *Ibid.*
[49] *Ibid.*
[50] Camp Holmes, v. 6, p. 28.
[51] Camp Holmes, v. 6, p. 62.
[52] *Dailey Bulletin,* April 21, 1862, in quoting a *North Carolina Standard* article.
[53] *Vance Papers*, v. 1, p. 191.
[54] *Semi-Weekly Raleigh Register,* April 19, 1862.
[55] *Semi-Weekly Raleigh Register*, August 6, 1862.
[56] Albert to Cate, April 19, 1863.
[57] *Vance Papers*, v. 1, p. 281.
[58] *O.R.*, Series IV, v. 2, p. 161-68.
[59] Camp Holmes, v. 6, p. 133.
[60] *North Carolina Argus*, November 20, 1862.
[61] N. N. Patterson letter, November 15, 1862. Private Patterson's letter is reproduced here with the kind permission of Mrs. Mildred Miller of Stoney Point, N.C.
[62] *O.R.*, Series IV, v. 2, p. 164-65.
[63] *O.R. Supplement* - Part III, Correspondence - Vol. 2 (Series 94), p. 746.
[64] Camp Holmes, v. 6, p. 183.
[65] *Roster,* v. IX, p. 272 and Albert to Cate, November 20, 1862.
[66] Barrett, p. 110-11.
[67] Barrett, p. 121-22.
[68] Barrett, p. 129.
[69] William C. Harris, *In the Country of the Enemy*, p. 76 and 136.
[70] Pvt. Henry Guy, 43rd Massachusetts Infantry. Letter to "Josephine," Dec. 23, 1862 (herein referred to as Pvt. Guy). Author's collection.
[71] W. W. Howe, *Kinston, Whitehall and Goldsboro (North Carolina) Expedition, December, 1862* (herein referred to as Howe), p. 12.
[72] Howe, p. 9-10.

[73] Ordinance Day Book, No. A.G. 27, p. 308, North Carolina Archives. The "N.C. Rifles" listed in the day book were most likely two band Fayetteville Rifles that were manufactured in North Carolina. Rifles, as opposed to muskets, were usually issued to the flank companies in a battalion or regiment.

[74] DeWitt Boyd Stone, Jr., *Wandering To Glory*, p. 89.

[75] *O.R.* Series I, v. 18, p. 115.

[76] J. H. Silverman and S. N. Thomas, Jr., *"A Rising Star of Promise,"* p. 62.

[77] *O.R.*, Series I, v. 18, p. 115.

[78] National Archives Microfilm, M836: Civil War Confederate States Army Casualties, "List of Officers and Men captured at Kinston N.C. and other points December 14th, 15th, and 16th, 1862, and paroled at that place. December 1862." All but a few of the prisoners reported on these lists were taken at Kinston on December 14. Mallett's own figure for his men captured that day was one hundred seventy-five (*O.R.*, Series I, v. 18, p. 116). Curiously, Mallett identified himself as "Peter Mallett Col. 68th NC Troops." The 68th North Carolina Troops was not organized until after July 1863.

[79] Pvt. Guy.

[80] Clark's *Histories*, v. I, p. 516.

[81] Pvt. Guy.

[82] A. L. Schovill & Co.'s *Farmers' & Mechanics' Almanac for 1864*, "Rebellion Record for December" (1862). Author's collection.

[83] Howe, p. 24.

[84] *Roster,* v. XIV, p. 601.

[85] Barrett, p. 147-48. *O.R.*, Series I, v. 18, p. 60.

[86] *O.R.*, Series I, v. 18, p. 53.

[87] Holoman and Johnson, *The Story of Kinston and Lenoir County*, p. 104-05.

[88] *O.R.*, Series IV, v. 2, p. 378-79

[89] *Roster*, v. V, p. 163.

[90] Camp Holmes, v. 6, p. 295.

[91] Camp Holmes, v. 6, p. 314.

[92] Camp Holmes, v. 6, p. 320.

[93] Camp Holmes, v. 6, p. 320.

[94] Camp Holmes, v. 6, p. 338.

[95] Camp Holmes, v. 6, p. 347.

[96] *Western Democrat*, Jan. 20, 1863.

[97] James C. Miller to his wife, January 31, 1863. Pvt. Miller died of disease at a Raleigh hospital in April 1863. The letter and information on Private Miller are used with the kind permission of Mrs. Mildred Miller of Stoney Point, N.C.

[98] Captain Baker to Col. Mallett, Southern Historical Collection, No. 480, Peter Mallett file.

[99] Joe A. Mobley, ed., *The Papers of Zebulon Baird Vance*, v. 2. (herein referred to as *Vance Papers*, v. 2), p. 26-27.

[100] *O.R.*, Series IV, v. 2, p. 305.

[101] *Vance Papers*, v. 2, p. 54.

[102] *O.R.*, Series IV, v. 2, p. 389.

[103] *O.R.*, Series IV, v. 2, p. 725.

[104] *Vance Papers*, v. 2, p. 127.

[105] *Western Democrat*, Oct. 6, 1863.

[106] *O.R.*, Series I, v. 33, p. 1087.

[107] *O.R.*, Series I, v. 33, p. 1085.

[108] *O.R.*, Series IV, v. 2, p. 163.

[109] *Vance Papers*, v. 2, p. 98. Vance's irritation with this practice is understandable. He had already complained in September of 1862 to then Secretary of War George W. Randolph about this same problem. On that occasion, General Kirby Smith was enlisting North Carolinians for service in the Department of East Tennessee. Those enlistments were not being counted toward meeting North Carolina's required troop quota *(Vance Papers*, v. 1, p. 177).

[110] Nathaniel Cheairs Hughes, Jr., and Roy P. Stonesifer, Jr., *The Life and Wars of Gideon Pillow* (herein referred to as *Gideon Pillow*), p. 271.

[111] Hal Bridges, *Lee's Maverick General Daniel Harvey Hill,* p. 163 and 168. *Vance Papers*, v. 2, p. 77.

[112] Robert F. Hoke letter, April 13, 1863, Southern Historical Collection, No. 480, Peter Mallett Papers.

[113] *Vance Papers*, v. 2, p. 78.

[114] *Vance Papers,* v. 2, p. 205.

[115] *Vance Papers*, v. 2, p. 112.

[116] *Vance Papers*, v. 2, p. 100.

[117] *Vance Papers*, v. 2, p. 97.

[118] *O.R.*, Series IV, v. 2, p. 913.

[119] Albert to Cate, September 4, 1863.

[120] *Vance Papers*, v. 2, Introduction, p. xvi.

[121] *O.R.*, Series I, v. 25, pt. 2, p. 746-747.

[122] *Vance Papers*, v. 2, Introduction, p. xvi.
[123] Albert to Cate, March 25, 1863.
[124] *O.R.*, Series I, v. 18, p. 752.
[125] *Vance Papers*, v. 2, p. 224.
[126] *Carolina Watchman*, May 2, 1864.
[127] *O.R.*, Series I, v. 27, pt. 3, p. 951.
[128] Private James Harwell letter, August 1, 1863, James Harwell Papers, P.C., 1858 (herein referred to as Harwell Papers), North Carolina Archives, Raleigh, N.C.
[129] *Daily Bulletin*, August 10, 1863.
[130] *Western Democrat*, September 29, 1863.
[131] Gaither Papers, Burgess to his sister and father, 1863.
[132] W. N. Watt, *Iredell County Soldiers in the Civil War*, p. 133, W. T. Watt to W. L. W. Ellis
[133] *Western Democrat,* Sept. 15, 1863.
[134] *O.R.,* Series IV, v. 2, p. 734.
[135] *O.R.*, Series IV, v. 2, p. 732.
[136] *Vance Papers,* v. 2, p. 179, L. S. Gash to Vance June 1, 1863; p. 224, Vance to Seddon, July 25, 1863; p. 255, Vance to Seddon, Aug. 26, 1863.
[137] *O.R.*, Series IV, v. 2, p. 783-85.
[138] *O.R.*, Series I, v. 29, pt. 2, p. 660.
[139] *North Carolina Historical Review,* v. 41, p. 184. C. F. Mills to H. Mills, Sept. 6, 1863, Amanda Mills Papers, Duke Manuscript Collection, Duke University.
[140] *North Carolina Historical Review*, v. 41, p. 184. J.W. Bell to Ike Bell, March 14, 1864. A.W. Bell Papers, Duke Manuscript Collection, Duke University.
[141] *Gideon Pillow,* p. 268.
[142] *O.R.*, Series IV, v. 2, p. 694.
[143] *O.R.*, Series IV, v. 2, p. 796.
[144] Sharpe Papers, No. 3592, Southern Historical Collection.
[145] *Western Democrat*, Oct. 20, 1863.
[146] *Roster*, v. 2, McRae's Battalion.
[147] Gaither Papers, October 18, 1863.
[148] Clark's *Histories*, v. IV, p. 379.
[149] *O.R.*, Series I, v. 29, pt. 2, p. 836.
[150] Daniel W. Barefoot, *General Robert F. Hoke, Lee's Modest Warrior*, p. 97.
[151] Sharpe Papers, Southern Historical Collections.

152 General Hoke to Colonel Sharpe, September 20, 1863, Sharpe Papers.

153 Barrett, p. 195-196.

154 *Roster*, v. III, p. 3 and p. 32.

155 *O.R.*, Series IV, v. 2, p. 966. In the *O.R.* this circular is not numbered, but it is dated four days before Circular No. 56. It is apparently the circular to which Mallett refers as No. 55.

156 *O.R.*, Series IV, v. 2, p. 966.

157 *O.R.*, Series IV, v. 2, p. 1071.

158 National Archives, Compiled Service Records of Confederate Soldiers, F. J. Hahr file.

159 *O.R.*, Series IV, v. 3, p. 57.

160 Harwell Papers.

161 Harwell Papers, October 2 and 17, 1863.

162 Harwell Papers, November 29, 1863.

163 *O.R.*, Series IV, v. 2, p. 967.

164 *O.R.*, Series IV, v. 2 p. 1070.

165 Daniel W. Barefoot, *General Robert F. Hoke, Lee's Modest Warrior*, p. 103.

166 *O.R.*, Series IV, v. 3, p. 178.

167 *Ibid.*

168 *O.R.*, Series IV, v. 3, p. 209 and p. 897.

169 *O.R.*, Series I, v. 35, pt. 1, p. 575-76.

170 *O.R.*, Series I, v. 32, pt. 3, p. 741.

171 *O.R.*, Series IV, v. 3, p. 307.

172 "Camp Holmes Letter Book No. 7, 1864," Southern Historical Collection, Peter Mallett Papers, University of North Carolina, Chapel Hill, N.C. (herein referred to as Camp Holmes, v. 7), p. 7.

173 Letter: Nathan Frazier to his wife, May 6, 1864, Nathan Frazier Papers (Coll. No. 390.1), Special Collections Department, J. Y. Joyner Library, East Carolina University, Greenville, N.C.

174 Camp Holmes, v. 7, p. 13.

175 Gaither Papers.

176 Sgt. Perry M. Summers to his father, July 1, 1864. Author's collection.

177 *Confederate Veteran*, v. 40, p. 171 (May 1932).

178 *O.R. Supplement*, pt. II, v. 49, p. 531.

179 Camp Holmes, v. 7, p. 184.

180 *O.R.*, Series IV, v. 3, p. 504-07.

181 *O.R.*, Series IV, v. 3, p. 490.

[182] Matthew Bumgarner, *Kirk's Raiders*, p. 26, and *O.R.*, Series I, v. 39, pt. 1, p. 237.

[183] Bumgarner, *Kirk's Raiders*, p. 35.

[184] Greg Mast, ed., *Company Front* (August-September 1989) p. 14-15.

[185] Bumgarner, *Kirk's Raiders*, p. 36.

[186] *O.R.*, Series I, v. 39, pt. 1, p. 236.

[187] *O.R.*, Series I, v. 39, pt. 1, p. 232.

[188] *O.R.*, Series I, v. 39, pt. 1, p. 235.

[189] Bumgarner, *Kirk's Raiders*, p. 44.

[190] Clark's *Histories,* v. III, p. 718.

[191] *O.R. Supplement*, pt. III, v. 3, p. 568.

[192] Author's collection.

[193] Gaither Papers.

[194] Author's collection.

[195] E. B. Long, *The Civil War Day By Day*, p. 534.

[196] Gaither Papers.

[197] Gaither Papers, clipped newspaper obituary, no date.

[198] Bumgarner, *Kirk's Raiders*, p. 109.

[199] *O.R. Supplement*, pt. 3, v. 3 p. 726.

[200] *O.R.*, Series IV, v. 3, p. 624.

[201] *O.R.*, Series IV, v. 3, p. 609.

[202] *O.R.*, Series IV, v. 3, p. 641.

[203] *O.R.*, Series IV, v. 3, p. 883.

[204] *O.R.*, Series IV, v. 3, p. 675.

[205] Documents in author's collection.

[206] *O.R.*, Series IV, v. 3, p. 868.

[207] *O.R.*, Series IV, v. 3, p. 866.

[208] *O.R.*, Series IV, v. 3, p. 894.

[209] *O.R.*, Series IV, v. 3, p. 866-67.

[210] *O.R.*, Series IV, v. 3, p. 1113.

[211] *Western Democrat*, March 7, 1865.

[212] *O.R.*, Series IV, v. 3, p. 1176.

[213] *O.R.*, Series I, v. 46, pt. 2, p. 1187.

[214] Letter to the *National Tribune* by James B. Kirk, formerly of the 101st Pa. Infantry, November 3, 1904.

[215] *This Hallowed Ground*, v. 4, no. 1, p. 32. "Petersburg - The Wearing Down of Lee's Army," by Chris Calkins.

[216] *Civil War Times Illustrated*, July, 1970. Lowell H. Harrison, "Conscription in the Confederacy" (herein referred to as Harrison), p. 17.

[217] Harrison, p. 17.

[218] Harrison, p. 19.

[219] *O.R.*, Series IV, v. 3, p. 1161.

[220] *Ibid.*

[221] *A Rebel War Clerk's Diary*, p. 518-19.

[222] Harrison, p. 18.

[223] *Confederate Veteran*, v. 3, 2002. Faye Lewellen, "Salisbury's Fate in the Final Days" (herein referred to as Lewellen), p. 14.

[224] Lewellen, p. 15-16.

[225] *Ibid.*

[226] *O.R.*, Series I, v. 49, pt. 1, p. 334.

[227] *Western Democrat*, April 4, 1865.

[228] Ethel Stephens Arnett, *Confederate Guns Were Stacked At Greensboro* (herein referred to as Arnett), p. 77.

[229] Arnett, p. 80-81.

[230] Arnett, p. 105-06.

Index

A

B

C

D

E

F

G

H

I

J

K

L

M

N

O

P

Q

R

S

T

U

V

W

Y